FREE

Free Study Tips DVD

In addition to the tips and content in this guide, we have created a FREE DVD with helpful study tips to further assist your exam preparation. **This FREE Study Tips DVD provides you with top-notch tips to conquer your exam and reach your goals.**

Our simple request in exchange for the strategy-packed DVD is that you email us your feedback about our study guide. We would love to hear what you thought about the guide, and we welcome any and all feedback—positive, negative, or neutral. It is our #1 goal to provide you with top-quality products and customer service.

To receive your **FREE Study Tips DVD**, email freedvd@apexprep.com. Please put "FREE DVD" in the subject line and put the following in the email:

    a. The name of the study guide you purchased.

    b. Your rating of the study guide on a scale of 1-5, with 5 being the highest score.

    c. Any thoughts or feedback about your study guide.

    d. Your first and last name and your mailing address, so we know where to send your free DVD!

Thank you!

PHR Study Guide 2019-2020

PHR Certification Prep 2019 & 2020 and Practice Test Questions for the Professional in Human Resources Exam (Updated for NEW Official Outline)

APEX Test Prep

Table of Contents

Test Taking Strategies

1. Reading the Whole Question

A popular assumption in Western culture is the idea that we don't have enough time for anything. We speed while driving to work, we want to read an assignment for class as quickly as possible, or we want the line in the supermarket to dwindle faster. However, speeding through such events robs us from being able to thoroughly appreciate and understand what's happening around us. While taking a timed test, the feeling one might have while reading a question is to find the correct answer as quickly as possible. Although pace is important, don't let it deter you from reading the whole question. Test writers know how to subtly change a test question toward the end in various ways, such as adding a negative or changing focus. If the question has a passage, carefully read the whole passage as well before moving on to the questions. This will help you process the information in the passage rather than worrying about the questions you've just read and where to find them. A thorough understanding of the passage or question is an important way for test takers to be able to succeed on an exam.

2. Examining Every Answer Choice

Let's say we're at the market buying apples. The first apple we see on top of the heap may *look* like the best apple, but if we turn it over we can see bruising on the skin. We must examine several apples before deciding which apple is the best. Finding the correct answer choice is like finding the best apple. Although it's tempting to choose an answer that seems correct at first without reading the others, it's important to read each answer choice thoroughly before making a final decision on the answer. The aim of a test writer might be to get as close as possible to the correct answer, so watch out for subtle words that may indicate an answer is incorrect. Once the correct answer choice is selected, read the question again and the answer in response to make sure all your bases are covered.

3. Eliminating Wrong Answer Choices

Sometimes we become paralyzed when we are confronted with too many choices. Which frozen yogurt flavor is the tastiest? Which pair of shoes look the best with this outfit? What type of car will fill my needs as a consumer? If you are unsure of which answer would be the best to choose, it may help to use process of elimination. We use "filtering" all the time on sites such as eBay® or Craigslist® to eliminate the ads that are not right for us. We can do the same thing on an exam. Process of elimination is crossing out the answer choices we know for sure are wrong and leaving the ones that might be correct. It may help to cover up the incorrect answer choice. Covering incorrect choices is a psychological act that alleviates stress due to the brain being exposed to a smaller amount of information. Choosing between two answer choices is much easier than choosing between all of them, and you have a better chance of selecting the correct answer if you have less to focus on.

4. Sticking to the World of the Question

When we are attempting to answer questions, our minds will often wander away from the question and what it is asking. We begin to see answer choices that are true in the real world instead of true in the world of the question. It may be helpful to think of each test question as its own little world. This world may be different from ours. This world may know as a truth that the chicken came before the egg or may assert that two plus two equals five. Remember that, no matter what hypothetical nonsense may be in the question, assume it to be true. If the question states that the chicken came before the egg, then choose your answer based on that truth. Sticking to the world of the question means placing all of our biases and assumptions aside and relying on the question to guide us to the correct answer. If we are simply looking for answers that are correct based on our own judgment, then we may choose incorrectly. Remember an answer that is true does not necessarily answer the question.

5. Key Words

If you come across a complex test question that you have to read over and over again, try pulling out some key words from the question in order to understand what exactly it is asking. Key words may be words that surround the question, such as *main idea, analogous, parallel, resembles, structured,* or *defines*. The question may be asking for the main idea, or it may be asking you to define something. Deconstructing the sentence may also be helpful in making the question simpler before trying to answer it. This means taking the sentence apart and obtaining meaning in pieces, or separating the question from the foundation of the question. For example, let's look at this question:

> Given the author's description of the content of paleontology in the first paragraph, which of the following is most parallel to what it taught?

The question asks which one of the answers most *parallels* the following information: The *description* of paleontology in the first paragraph. The first step would be to see *how* paleontology is described in the first paragraph. Then, we would find an answer choice that parallels that description. The question seems complex at first, but after we deconstruct it, the answer becomes much more attainable.

6. Subtle Negatives

Negative words in question stems will be words such as *not, but, neither,* or *except*. Test writers often use these words in order to trick unsuspecting test takers into selecting the wrong answer—or, at least, to test their reading comprehension of the question. Many exams will feature the negative words in all caps (*which of the following is NOT an example*), but some questions will add the negative word seamlessly into the sentence. The following is an example of a subtle negative used in a question stem:

> According to the passage, which of the following is *not* considered to be an example of paleontology?

If we rush through the exam, we might skip that tiny word, *not,* inside the question, and choose an answer that is opposite of the correct choice. Again, it's important to read the question fully, and double check for any words that may negate the statement in any way.

7. Spotting the Hedges

The word "hedging" refers to language that remains vague or avoids absolute terminology. Absolute terminology consists of words like *always, never, all, every, just, only, none,* and *must*. Hedging refers to words like *seem, tend, might, most, some, sometimes, perhaps, possibly, probability,* and *often*. In some cases, we want to choose answer choices that use hedging and avoid answer choices that use absolute terminology. It's important to pay attention to what subject you are on and adjust your response accordingly.

8. Restating to Understand

Every now and then we come across questions that we don't understand. The language may be too complex, or the question is structured in a way that is meant to confuse the test taker. When you come across a question like this, it may be worth your time to rewrite or restate the question in your own words in order to understand it better. For example, let's look at the following complicated question:

> Which of the following words, if substituted for the word *parochial* in the first paragraph, would LEAST change the meaning of the sentence?

Let's restate the question in order to understand it better. We know that they want the word *parochial* replaced. We also know that this new word would "least" or "not" change the meaning of the sentence. Now let's try the sentence again:

> Which word could we replace with *parochial*, and it would not change the meaning?

Restating it this way, we see that the question is asking for a synonym. Now, let's restate the question so we can answer it better:

> Which word is a synonym for the word *parochial*?

Before we even look at the answer choices, we have a simpler, restated version of a complicated question.

9. Predicting the Answer

After you read the question, try predicting the answer *before* reading the answer choices. By formulating an answer in your mind, you will be less likely to be distracted by any wrong answer choices. Using predictions will also help you feel more confident in the answer choice you select. Once you've chosen your answer, go back and reread the question and answer choices to make sure you have the best fit. If you have no idea what the answer may be for a particular question, forego using this strategy.

10. Avoiding Patterns

One popular myth in grade school relating to standardized testing is that test writers will often put multiple-choice answers in patterns. A runoff example of this kind of thinking is that the most common answer choice is "C," with "B" following close behind. Or, some will advocate certain made-up word patterns that simply do not exist. Test writers do not arrange their correct answer choices in any kind of pattern; their choices are randomized. There may even be times where the correct answer choice will be the same letter for two or three questions in a row, but we have no way of knowing when or if this might happen. Instead of trying to figure out what choice the test writer probably set as being correct, focus on what the *best answer choice* would be out of the answers you are presented with. Use the tips above, general knowledge, and reading comprehension skills in order to best answer the question, rather than looking for patterns that do not exist.

FREE DVD OFFER

Achieving a high score on your exam depends not only on understanding the content, but also on understanding how to apply your knowledge and your command of test taking strategies. **Because your success is our primary goal, we offer a FREE Study Tips DVD. It provides top-notch test taking strategies to help you optimize your testing experience.**

Our simple request in exchange for the strategy-packed DVD is that you email us your feedback about our study guide.

To receive your **FREE Study Tips DVD**, email freedvd@apexprep.com. Please put "FREE DVD" in the subject line and put the following in the email:

a. The name of the study guide you purchased.

b. Your rating of the study guide on a scale of 1-5, with 5 being the highest score.

c. Any thoughts or feedback about your study guide.

d. Your first and last name and your mailing address, so we know where to send your free DVD!

Introduction to the PHR

Function of the Test

The Professional in Human Resources® (PHR) exam is one of the HR Certificate Institute's® (HRCI®) recognized HR credentials. Earning PHR certification can advance one's human resource management career, demonstrate a command of the skills and knowledge of the technical and operational aspects of HR management work, and convey a commitment to the field. The PHR is intended HR professionals with career experience focused on implementing HR programs and services and working with other HR professionals. It is not intended for entry-level professionals.

There are three possible paths to achieve eligibility status for the PHR exam. To be eligible to take the PHR exam, candidates must meet one of the following three conditions concerning career experience and formal education:

- Have accrued a minimum of one year of experience in a professional-level HR position and hold a master's degree or higher

- Have accrued a minimum of two years of experience in a professional-level HR position and hold a bachelor's degree

- Have accrued a minimum of four years of experience in a professional-level HR position and hold a high school diploma

Degrees do not need to be in human resource management. "Professional-level" HR experience is specifically defined by the HRCI® on their website; candidates should review these requirements and be prepared to document evidence of their eligibility.

Test Administration

Candidates must apply to take the PHR and obtain approval prior to registering to test. The exam is administered year-round via computer at Pearson VUE testing centers around the United States. International locations are available as well. Exams must be scheduled no later than 120 days from the date of approval from HRCI®. Candidates are required to bring a government-issued ID to their testing appointment.

Requests for special accommodations are available at the tie of registration for test takers with documented disabilities.

Test Format

The PHR exam contains 150 scored questions and 25 unscored pretest questions mixed in throughout the exam. Test takers will not know which questions count toward their official scores. HRCI® includes the pretest questions to gauge their usefulness as scored questions on future iterations of the PHR. Test questions are of a variety of formats including standard multiple-choice questions with only one correct response and multiple-choice questions with multiple responses required, fill-in-the-blank questions, drag and drop questions, and scenarios. Test takers are given 3 hours to complete the exam.

There are five main domains of content on the exam, termed "Functional Areas." The topics and breakdown for these functional areas is as follows:

Functional Area	Approximate Percentage of Exam
Business Management	20%
Talent Planning and Acquisition	16%
Learning and Development	10%
Total Rewards	15%
Employee and Labor Relations	39%

Within each functional area, questions are classified into one of the three cognitive levels listed in order of increasing difficulty: knowledge/comprehension, application/problem solving, or synthesis/evaluation. It should be noted that employment laws covered on the exam and candidates are responsible for knowing the most current laws at the time of their exam administration.

Scoring

Unofficial scores are available at the test center upon completion of the exam. Official scores are released 24-48 hours after exam administration.

Minimum passing scores are established based on the modified Angoff method, which involves a team of field experts who determine the difficulty of each question and assign the scaled score of 500 as the cutoff score, indicating a score that corresponds to the lowest score that a candidate possessing the minimally acceptable level of knowledge and skills is likely to achieve. Scaling allows different versions of the exam to be compared.

Upon successfully passing the exam, test takers earn PHR certification, which is valid for three years. To remain credentialed, either 60 recertification credits must be earned over the three-year period, or the exam must be retaken and passed anew.

Business Management

General Business Environment and Industry Best Practices

Strategic Planning Process

A company's strategic planning process comprises the following four steps:

Strategy Formulation

During this first step of the strategic planning process, a company focuses on the business it is in and develops its vision statement, mission statement, and values accordingly. Plans are also made for how best to communicate the company's mission and when it may be necessary to change the company's mission or adjust its strategy. This first step can be summed up by identifying where a company currently is and defining where it wants to be in the future and how it can arrive at that place.

Strategy Development

Environmental scanning and a SWOT (Strengths, Weaknesses, Opportunities, Threats) analysis are performed during this step of the strategic planning process (both of which are described in greater detail below). Additionally, long-range plans are established that will set the company's direction for the next three to five years. This second step can be summed up by collecting information that is both internal and external to the company, along with developing alternative strategies.

Strategy Implementation

During this step of the strategic planning process, short-range plans are created that will set the company's direction for the next six to twelve months. Additionally, there is a focus on motivating employees by developing action plans and allocating the necessary resources in order to achieve objectives (i.e., human, financial, and technological). This step can be summed up by implementing a plan for the strategy that is chosen.

Strategy Evaluation

During this last step of the strategic planning process, a company agrees to continue reviewing an implemented strategy at specific intervals by performing a SWOT analysis and taking note of any changes. In the event of changes, corrective action may be necessary. This step can be summed up by evaluating the success of the implemented strategy while continuing to monitor it and make any necessary tweaks.

Environmental Scanning

An environmental scan is used to collect the necessary information from a company's internal and external environments to develop its strategic plan. A SWOT analysis is a tool used during the environmental scan as a company examines its internal strengths and weaknesses, along with any external opportunities and threats it may be facing. Porter's Five Forces is another analytical tool a company may utilize during the environmental scan to examine its competition.

SWOT Analysis
Strengths

Identified, internal strengths are hard to copy and give a company a competitive advantage, which improves its position in the marketplace. A company's internal strengths also create value for its customers. Examples of strengths are brand recognition, strong employee skill sets, a high level of innovation, and solid financing.

Weaknesses

Any internal weaknesses can potentially reduce a company's ability to reach its objectives and place it at a competitive disadvantage. Outdated equipment, unreliable suppliers, ineffective leadership, and insufficient marketing campaigns are examples of weaknesses.

It is important to note, when assessing a company's strengths and weaknesses, it is much easier to analyze its physical and financial assets than to assess examples of its intangible assets mentioned above.

Opportunities

A possible way for a company to identify opportunities is to analyze the weaknesses of its competitors. Opportunities are identified, external factors that enable a company to become increasingly profitable and grow. Examples of opportunities are advances in technology, depth in supplier relationships, consumer trends, and potential new markets.

Threats

A possible way for a company to identify threats is to analyze the strengths of its competitors. Threats are identified, external factors that a company must strive to overcome. Regulatory constraints, a labor shortage, a declining economy, and a changing political climate are examples of threats.

Porter's Five Forces

Michael Porter is a professor at the Harvard Business School. He authored two textbooks that are still widely used in MBA classes today. In one of those textbooks, *Competitive Strategy*, he outlined the Five Forces model companies should use to form strategies on how to deal with their competition. His model is built on the notion that power exists within five forces of relationships.

1. Threat of new entrants

A company must create a plan to deal with new competition when the barriers to enter an industry are low. However, an industry is protected from new rivals when the barriers to enter that industry are high. Therefore, Michael Porter identified the following barriers to entry:

- High economy of scale—This refers to a company's high production-to-profitability threshold.

- Product differentiation—This refers to a company's need to create a distinct or unique service or product that customers are willing to pay a premium for.

- Capital requirements for entry—This is when a company must make a significant investment of up-front capital.

- Switching costs—This refers to customers incurring a high cost to switch to a new company's product or service.

- Access to distribution channels—A new company must establish its distribution channels in a new market.

- Cost disadvantages independent of scale—A new company must obtain access to things such as raw materials, favorable locations, and government subsidies.

2. Bargaining power of suppliers

A company must ensure it has all the materials needed to create its products and services for its customers. A company should refrain from relying solely on one key supplier in the event the supplier is unable to meet demand or unexpectedly goes out of business. Additionally, if a supplier decides to

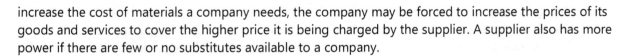

increase the cost of materials a company needs, the company may be forced to increase the prices of its goods and services to cover the higher price it is being charged by the supplier. A supplier also has more power if there are few or no substitutes available to a company.

3. Bargaining power of company's customers

A company's strategy is often driven by the needs of its customers. Customers tend to have the most bargaining power when they desire to purchase a higher-quality service or product and are willing to pay the associated price. They are purchasing a product or service that is pretty much standard across an industry and the switching costs are low, and they are fully aware of the supply and demand for the product. The bargaining power of a company's customers can pit competitors against each other and force lower prices.

4. Threat of substitute products

Substitute products are items that fulfill the same need for a customer but are not the exact services and products a company currently sells. An example of a substitute product is a customer choosing to travel on a high-speed train instead of an airline to get from one city to another. Substitute products limit an industry's profitability.

5. Industry competitors

Companies compete with one another through advertising, introducing new services and products, and pricing. In some cases of intense competition, companies will even lose out on their profits by cutting costs by extreme measures with the goal of "winning."

The Organization's Core Values, Ethical and Behavioral Expectations Through Modeling, Communication, and Coaching

In order for ethical behavior and a company's values to be demonstrated by employees at the lower levels of an organization, these expectations must be modeled by individuals at the top (the members of the board of directors and executive management). Once a company establishes its core values, it is important for management to abide by them because employees are always watching their leaders, especially in difficult times. Management loses credibility with employees when it only "talks the talk" but is not willing to "walk the walk."

The following are some ways management and human resources (HR) personnel can incorporate a company's values into daily business activities:

- HR can train hiring managers to interview candidates to determine if they are going to be the best cultural fit based on the company's values (in addition to their skills and abilities). For example, if teamwork is one of a company's values, it is important to ask a candidate interview questions related to his or her ability to work well as part of a team.

- Managers can reinforce the values during a new hire orientation presentation.

- Managers and HR can reinforce the values in company communications.

- Managers and HR can develop a system to recognize and reward employees for demonstrating the company's values. This may include something as simple as a manager verbally recognizing an employee during a staff meeting, featuring an employee who demonstrates the company's values on the website, or a web-based system where employees nominate their peers for a "spot award" and one lucky winner each month gets a $50 Amazon gift card.

- Managers can integrate the company's values into the performance review process. For example, in addition to evaluating employees on their annual project goals, a manager can also assess them on how well they demonstrate the company's core values. The performance review may be set up so that, even if an employee achieves all of his project goals, he cannot receive an overall review rating of "exceeds" if he has not demonstrated the company's core values over the past year.

- Mangers and HR can decide to terminate employees who ultimately fail to follow the company's values.

Organizations committed to ethical practices typically develop a code of conduct and/or a code of ethics to communicate the expectations to their employees. Some organizations combine these two codes into a single document. A code of conduct details the behaviors a company requires of its employees as well as the behaviors that are prohibited and subsequently result in disciplinary action. A code of ethics details the ideal set of standards a company intends to uphold in its business dealings. The following is a list of sections typically found in a company's code of ethics:

- Confidentiality
- Conflicts of interest
- Gifts, entertainment, and contributions
- Personal use of company assets
- Workplace privacy
- Outside employment
- Ownership of intellectual property
- Fair dealing
- Standards of business conduct
- Reporting code violations

Some organizations have hired individuals known as **ethics officers** who are charged with ensuring employees maintain the ethical standards that were initially developed by executive management and informing the executive team about any ethical issues that may arise. Some essential job functions of the individuals performing this role include the following:

- Create and distribute ethics statements and supporting documentation.

- Periodically review the company's other policies to ensure they are consistent with the ethics message.

- Develop and facilitate ethics training for all levels of the employees within the company.

- Conduct ethics violation investigations and prepare all associated reports.

- Lead annual corporate governance audits with members of the legal team to minimize company risk.

- Conduct confidential employee hearings about matters concerning conflicts and ethics.

- Stay up to date on corporate governance requirements and the company's compliance and reporting responsibilities.

Cross-Functional Stakeholders in the Organization

Individuals who have an interest in what a company does or how well it performs are known as **stakeholders**. They are called stakeholders because they have something at stake, or at risk, in the company. Therefore, a company's activities can result in their loss or gain.

Companies have both internal and external stakeholders. Cross-functional stakeholders are simply internal stakeholders that are representative of different areas of the company, such as finance, information technology, legal, customer service, research and development (R&D), and manufacturing. It is important to note that internal stakeholders also have a direct claim on a company's resources.

HR personnel are focused on building strategic relationships with cross-functional stakeholders to contribute to the work they are doing and to make decisions to meet the company's goals. The strategic relationships are built over time as the character and actions of HR personnel increase their credibility with a company's employees, managers, top executives, and board of directors. For example, HR employees work alongside management on a daily basis performing the following labor-management tasks, which helps to form these strategic relationships:

- Adhering to federal, state, and local regulations and laws

- Creating new policies, procedures, and rules in the workplace

- Developing and revising job descriptions

- Establishing salary ranges and position grades

- Conducting a training needs analysis

- Retrieving data for a reduction in force (RIF) and preparing corresponding employee packets/severance packages

- Creating a succession plan

A company's internal stakeholders typically remain motivated to participate in company activities if they are rewarded (i.e., power, personal accomplishment, salary, bonuses, and stock options) in an amount greater than the value of their contributions (i.e., expertise, skills, and knowledge). If this is not the case, the support of internal stakeholders may be withdrawn, and they may even choose to exit the company.

Therefore, HR personnel should stress to cross-functional stakeholders the importance of collaboration leading to successful outcomes, from which they will ultimately benefit from meaningful contributions, and perhaps a bonus program. Cross-functional stakeholders working together toward a common company goal can help break down silos and allow the whole to be greater than the sum of the parts. This will also enable all staff within a company to make a contribution, thus enhancing the organization's level of inclusiveness.

Best Practices to Mitigate Risk

Managing Risks
Organizations face countless internal risks (i.e., workplace violence, employee substance abuse, and ill or injured employees) and external risks (i.e., cyber vulnerability, changes in market conditions, and natural

disasters) on a daily basis. In order for organizations to be prepared, they must proactively manage their risk using the following four-step process:

- 1. Identify assets that may be subject to risks. This can include failing to have a succession plan in place and a candidate identified to move into the vice president of sales position when the current individual in that role steps down. This can also include liability issues the company can be sued over, such as a disabled employee who feels she was discriminated against and overlooked in a hiring decision.

- 2. Assess possible risks. This involves utilizing a formula to determine the probability of a risk occurring and the associated consequences to the company (risks = probability x consequences). For example, if a company does not train its managers on proper interviewing techniques, it is at risk of lawsuits, due to failing to comply with employment law. However, the probability of that risk would be much lower if the company provided its managers with a training course on interviewing skills.

- 3. Manage risks. Once the risks are recognized and prioritized, they can be managed in one of the following ways:

    - Elimination: An example of a company eliminating a risk is moving a piece of equipment that previously had its cords laying across the floor employees had to walk over every day to a new location where the cords are out of sight. This eliminates the risk of employees tripping and falling.

    - Mitigation: Introducing employees' use of personal protective equipment when working with a dangerous chemical is an example of mitigation. This measure reduces employees' exposure to a known hazard.

    - Transfer: An example of a company transferring risk is outsourcing a specific type of work to a vendor. For example, a company knows it needs to provide employees with a training class on sexual harassment. However, management does not have the expertise surrounding laws about sexual harassment in all of the locations in which it conducts business. Therefore, outsourcing the creation of this class to a training vendor transfers the risk of providing employees with inaccurate information.

    - Acceptance: Deciding to purchase a new, innovative piece of equipment whose long-term performance and maintenance needs are not yet known is an example of acceptance. This is when a company knows the risk and decides to live with it as a cost of conducting business. Although this means there are no controls in place to manage this particular risk, the benefit is that it will allow a company to allocate more resources to focus on more serious risks.

- 4. Review and monitor. It is important for organizations to continuously monitor their risk management decisions in order to identify and handle any new risks as well as to check to see that the current strategies are still working effectively.

Significance of Data for Recommending Organizational Strategies

Diversity in Hiring

Organizations have become more global in nature, which has, in turn, made diversity in hiring a true priority. Management understands that having a diverse workforce is a reflection of the customer base their companies serve. Diversity in hiring also brings more creativity to the table in regard to employees working together on new ideas for products and services, as well as solving problems and making decisions. Additionally, the candidate pool is automatically increased when striving to hire a diverse workforce. This practice will aid in replacing baby boomers headed toward retirement and a current shortage of skilled workers.

Cost per Hire

The cost per hire is calculated by adding the external and internal recruiting costs and dividing the total by the number of new hires during a specific period of time. Examples of external recruiting costs include items such as advertising a position on job boards, recruitment technology, background checks and drug testing, and pre-hire assessments. Examples of internal recruiting costs include in-house recruiting staff, payment of referral rewards, and internal recruiting systems.

Time to Hire

This metric lets companies know how quickly they found their best candidate and were able to move them through the hiring process. The time to hire is calculated by subtracting the day the employee (who was eventually hired) entered a job's pipeline from the day he or she accepted an offer for the position. For example, if a job position is posted on Day 1, a candidate applies for the job on Day 5, and he accepts the job offer on Day 12, the time to hire is 12 − 5 = 7.

Time to Fill

This metric lets companies know when their hiring process is taking too long. Time to fill is the number of calendar days it takes a company to fill a position, and the clock may start ticking before a job is posted, such as when HR approves a job opening. Time to fill typically ends when a candidate accepts a job offer. It is important for a company to track the time to fill consistently across various positions.

Attrition Rate

Attrition rate is the percentage of employees that left a business for some reason (i.e., resignation, retirement, or death) and were not replaced during a period of time, typically a calendar or fiscal year. The attrition rate is calculated by dividing the number of employees that left the company during the year by the total number of employees at the beginning of the year and then multiplying that amount by 100. A high attrition rate can serve as a red flag to HR that policies may need to be changed.

Success of Training

Following completion of training, it is important to study the efficiency and productivity of the program and its materials. Some questions that may be asked are: Were the primary objectives met? Were the learners' specified goals achieved? What (if any) were the most arduous aspects of the program or its materials, and how could those problems be addressed? The following list consists of tools used in success training:

- Participant surveys are a common way for employers to learn to what degree participants react favorably to the training program.

- Pre/post-testing can be a vital tool when analyzing the efficacy of a training program. A pretest assesses the knowledge of students prior to the start of a training program, and a posttest determines the knowledge students have acquired during a program.

- Performance metrics, such as an increase in sales, are utilized to determine the degree to which targeted outcomes have occurred as a result of employees completing a training program.

Vision, Mission, Values, and Structure of the Organization

After a scan of a company's external and internal environments has taken place, the executive team can turn their focus to developing the vision statement, mission statement, and values to guide the company over the long term.

Vision Statement

A vision statement can be best described as a concise statement that reflects organizational confidence and long-term aspirations regarding how a company will achieve more than economic success (it is forward-thinking). Some questions that can be addressed in a vision statement are: How does this company fit into the world? How would it positively change the world? Institutionally, how does the company plan to deliver its product or service less expensively and more efficiently than its competitors? Ultimately, vision statements serve the purpose of boosting trust and confidence, and creating an image that the company is engaging in a task larger than itself.

Mission Statement

A company creates a mission statement to detail how it will work toward obtaining its vision. A mission statement tells employees what the company does, where the company is going in the mid to long term, and how the company is different from other organizations. A company's mission statement should stay constant throughout a company's life cycle.

Items that may be addressed in a company's mission statement include:

- Where does the company compete geographically?
- What are the company's top products or services?
- Who are the company's customers?
- What is the company's competitive advantage?
- How responsive is the company to environmental concerns?
- Does the company consider its employees to be a valuable asset?
- Is the company committed to financial stability?

Values

A company's values, such as integrity, open-mindedness, respect, safety, and teamwork, communicate to employees the standards by which they are expected to adhere to while conducting business. Values are the things that are most important to a company, which is why they should be deeply ingrained in the corporate culture and demonstrated in employees' daily business interactions with stakeholders and customers. HR can play an important role in reinforcing a company's values by leading by example and communicating them to employees.

Organizational Structure

Organizational structure is used to help companies achieve their goals by defining the hierarchy of employees and allocating resources through decisions surrounding the following factors:

- **Chain of command**: This clarifies who employees report to. It is the continuous line of authority from senior-level managers to employees at the lowest levels of the company.

- **Centralization**: A company where lower-level employees carry out the decisions made by senior-level managers is highly centralized. The opposite of this is decentralization or employee empowerment.

- **Span of control**: This refers to the number of employees a manager can effectively supervise. This can be affected by such things as a manager's skills, the physical proximity of the employees, the employees' characteristics, and the complexity of the work being performed.

- **Formalization**: An organization with jobs that are standardized, allowing for little discretion over what is to be done because the work is guided by rules, has a high degree of formalization. The opposite of this is a low formalization, where employees have more freedom to decide how they can complete their tasks.

- **Work specialization**: This is also known as **division of labor** and refers to the degree a company divides tasks into separate jobs that are completed by different employees. This allows employees to become very proficient in a specialized area, such as painting or framing.

- **Departmentalization**: This comes into play when a company divides up its work by the specialization of its departments. Companies are known to departmentalize by function, product, geographic, or division.

Functional Structure
This is the most common type of organizational structure where jobs are according to function, such as finance, IT, sales, purchasing, and HR. Efficiencies are gained from grouping together individuals with common knowledge and skills. This type of organizational structure is good for a company that has one product line that can benefit from specialization. However, employees can have a limited view of the company's goals, and there can be poor communication across the various functional areas.

Product Structure
This is a type of organizational structure where jobs are grouped by product line. For example, a product organizational structure for a transportation company might be grouped by rail products, mass transit products, and recreational and utility vehicle products. Organizing by product allows managers to become experts in their industry and for specialization in certain products and services. However, employees can have a limited view of the company's goals, and there is a duplication of functions within each product line.

Geographic Structure
This is a type of organizational structure where jobs are grouped according to geographic location. For example, a company's sales directors for various regions (Eastern, Western, Midwestern, and Southern) may each be responsible for the business functions in their areas and report to the company's vice president of sales. This type of structure is the best way to serve the unique needs and issues that may arise in different geographic markets. Since most decisions are made at the location level, decision making is decentralized. However, employees may feel isolated from other organizational areas, and there is a duplication of functions within each geographic region.

Division Structure
This is a type of organizational structure where jobs are grouped by industry or market. A divisional organizational structure also experiences decentralized decision making and is similar in nature to the geographic structure.

Matrix Structure
Employees report to two managers in this type of organizational structure. Typically, one manager has functional responsibility, and the other manager has a product line responsibility. Employees have a primary manager they report to and a second manager they also work for on specified projects. In order

for a matrix structure to be successful, there must be a high degree of trust and communication among the employees involved. This type of structure is a good way to share resources across functions.

Legislative and Regulatory Knowledge and Procedures

Lobbying

HR personnel sometimes serve in the role of lobbyists. They attempt to influence government leaders in an effort to create legislation that will benefit their companies and employees. The professional organization many HR personnel are members of (the Society for Human Resource Management, or SHRM for short) also coordinates lobbying efforts and forms local and national legislative affairs committees. These committees are geared toward monitoring changes that have been proposed to legislation that are employment related in nature and provide information that may be helpful to assist with the proposed changes.

The Federal Legislative Process

Ideas that eventually become federal laws can come from a U.S. representative, U.S. senator, professional organization, company, special interest group, or an individual. Since a member of Congress must introduce and support an idea for a new law, if the idea comes from someone outside of Congress (such as from an individual), it must first be presented to a U.S. representatives or U.S. senator who will decide whether or not to move forward with it. Once the idea for a new law is introduced by a member of Congress, the following steps are followed before it becomes law:

- The idea becomes a bill and is assigned to a committee in the House of Representatives (since that is where it was introduced) to be researched, studied, and discussed.

- The committee is responsible for determining how likely the bill is to pass a full vote in the House of Representatives. The bill may not make it past this point if the committee agrees it is unlikely to pass.

- A subcommittee is assembled to study the bill that has been determined to pass. During this phase, additional input is requested from subject matter experts and citizens who are both for and against the bill.

- The subcommittee will mark up the bill with any changes they feel are necessary, and they will vote on whether or not to return the bill to the committee. The bill may not make it past this point if the subcommittee does not vote to return it to the committee.

- The committee will vote whether or not to accept the changes that have been made by the subcommittee. If the changes are accepted, the committee will send the bill to be voted on by the entire House of Representatives. This is known as ordering the bill reported to the entire body.

- Prior to voting, the U.S. representatives are presented with an opportunity to present their views on the bill, and some representatives may suggest amendments to the bill that would go into effect after it has passed.

- Once the bill has successfully passed the vote in the U.S. House of Representatives, the process described above begins all over in the U.S. Senate. The U.S. Senate may take any of the following actions:

    o Pass the bill in its current state.
    o Table the bill—the bill will not become law.
    o Vote the bill down—the bill will not become law.
    o Make changes to the language of the bill.

- If the members of the U.S. Senate pass the bill, a conference committee is formed to reconcile any major differences in the versions of the bills that were passed between the U.S. House of Representatives and the U.S. Senate. The bill will die and will not become law if the conference committee cannot reach an agreement on the bill's final form. It the conference committee is able to successfully incorporate the changes, the U.S. House of Representatives and the U.S. Senate will vote to approve the changes.

- The bill is presented to the president of the United States for consideration. He or she can veto the bill, approve the bill and sign it into law, or fail to sign the bill. Congress, in some cases, can override a veto, allowing a bill to still become law. However, if the president fails to sign a bill when Congress is still in session, it still becomes a law after ten days. If Congress has adjourned prior to the ten-day period, the bill does not become law. This is known as a **pocket veto**.

Administrative Law

In addition to federal law, HR personnel should be familiar with administrative law, as it regulates the operation and procedures of government agencies.

- **Agency regulations**: The passing of the Occupational Safety and Health Act of 1970, which, in turn, created the Occupational Safety and Health Administration (OSHA) in 1971, is an example of an agency regulation. OSHA is a federal agency designed to protect employees from working in hazardous and dangerous conditions. The agency is concerned with the welfare of employees in the workplace, and it continues to establish stringent regulations employers must follow.

- **Agency orders**: This is when federal agencies, such as the Equal Employment Opportunity Commission (EEOC) and the National Labor Relations Board (NLRB), are able to order companies in administrative law courts to be compliant with federal laws. In these courts, administrative law judges issue orders.

- **Executive orders**: The president of the United States creates these directives that do not require the approval from members of Congress. A current president has the ability to overturn an executive order that was put into place by a previous president by issuing a new executive order to that effect. An example is executive order 11246, which was signed into law by President Lyndon Johnson in 1965 to establish affirmative action requirements for those companies that do business with the federal government.

Corporate Governance Procedures and Compliance

HR personnel frequently become involved in corporate governance issues, which deal with balancing the interests of a company's stakeholders (i.e., shareholders, customers, employees, suppliers, the communities in which it conducts business, the government, and creditors).

Fiduciary Responsibilities

A company's leadership is charged with making decisions that are in the best interests of its shareholders versus making decisions that are in their own best interests. In staying in line with this, a company's board of directors is held to two fiduciary responsibilities. The responsibility known as the **duty of care** ensures that members of the board of directors take a rational and informed approach to decision making. The responsibility known as the **duty of loyalty** ensures that members of the board of directors forgo their own personal gain and instead act in the best interest of their company at all times.

Fiduciary responsibilities also come into play when considering a company's compensation and benefits programs. For example, the Employee Retirement Income Security Act (ERISA) of 1974 contains a section dedicated to fiduciary standards. These are rules surrounding how plan fiduciaries, or individuals who have a legal duty to act in another party's interest, should be conducting the operation of the benefit plan. According to ERISA, an employer must follow what is known as the **prudent person rule**. This means the employer cannot take more risks than a reasonably knowledgeable prudent investor would under similar circumstances. Additionally, the benefit plan assets must be kept separate from other company assets. This rule was established to prevent employers from misusing funds set aside for the purpose of providing benefits. Finally, the employer must follow minimum funding standards that apply to retirement benefit plans.

Corporate Social Responsibility

Companies must decide where they will fall on the spectrum of **corporate social responsibility** (CSR). For example, some companies only have a **social obligation**, which means they do nothing in addition to meeting their legal and economic responsibilities. Other companies experience a **social responsiveness** and choose to respond to some popular social needs by engaging in social actions. Still other companies bear a **social responsibility**, which is a set intention to act in ways that are good for society and to do the right things.

Companies that practice CSR do not just view themselves as independent entities that are solely responsible to stockholders. Rather, these companies feel they have a moral responsibility to society at large and that it is necessary to become involved in legal, political, and social issues. Some arguments companies have for social responsibility include the following:

- CSR can be profitable and a good way for companies to attract top talent and build good public relations.

- Companies practicing CSR may help prevent new government regulations.

- Companies' stock prices will increase in the long run.

- Companies have the resources available to help solve problems found in society, such as pollution.

Environmental Responsibility and Sustainability

Environmental responsibility is when a company's leadership takes into consideration the impact its products and processes have on the natural environment. **Sustainability** means the ability to maintain at a certain level. Thus, the concept of sustainability involves a company's ability to avoid depleting the natural resources it uses as part of its daily operations in order to maintain an ecological balance. Environmental responsibility and sustainability is often referred to as a company "going green."

There are four approaches to companies going green, depending on the level of involvement:

- Light green approach: Companies do nothing beyond what is required by current laws, regulations, and rules.

- Market approach: Companies choose to respond to their customers' preferences for products that are environmentally friendly.

- Stakeholder approach: Companies strive to meet the environmental demands of many stakeholders, such as their customers, their staff, the community, and their suppliers.

- Activist approach: Companies actively search for ways to be environmentally responsible, such as finding ways to preserve the environment in which they do business.

Employee Communications

Communication Strategy

A successful communication strategy incorporates opportunities for management to share information with employees using a top-down approach, while still affording staff an opportunity to express their concerns via bottom-up communication methods.

Top-Down Communication

In a **top-down communication** channel, communication takes place in a downward direction. This tends to be the traditional view of communication where information is transmitted from individuals in positions of higher authority (leaders and managers) to individuals in positions of lower levels of authority (employees). This type of communication tends to be unidirectional in nature and does not require a response from the recipient. Examples of top-down communication include an upper-management presentation to staff on the company's mission and vision and managers receiving an email from the board of directors on a new objective they will be required to meet. Occasionally, differences in status, knowledge, and levels of authority can lead to misinterpretations or misunderstandings in top-down communication. Since a company's success relies on effective top-down communication, individuals delivering these types of messages must make an effort to use clear and concise wording with a respectful tone and ensure that employees understand the information.

Bottom-Up Communication

In a **bottom-up communication** channel, communication takes place in an upward direction. In this type of communication, information is transmitted from individuals in positions of lower levels of authority (employees) to individuals in positions of higher authority (leaders and managers). An example of bottom-up communication is a brown bag lunch program, which is a type of informal meeting held between employees and management to discuss company problems. The lunch setting and company-provided meal can help create a relaxed setting for exchanging ideas. Staff meetings, which are more formal gatherings of employees and management from a given team, typically take place on a set day and time allow everyone involved to meet to talk about project updates and offer each other support and suggestions. In addition, all-hands meetings, which are formal gatherings for the entire company, tend to focus on sharing information that concerns the overall organization. An open-door policy is used to establish a relationship where employees feel comfortable speaking directly with management about problems and suggestions. In essence, an open-door policy allows a supervisor or manager to be a "human suggestion box." In certain situations, it can be difficult to create an environment where employees feel comfortable discussing problems in person with management. In addition, depending on the problem reported, it may not be possible to maintain confidentiality. However, in the right situation, an open-door policy can help companies identify problems quickly, almost in real time, without having to wait for a formal meeting to address an ongoing issue.

Horizontal Communication

In a **horizontal communication** channel, communication takes place in a horizontal direction. In this type of communication, information is transmitted between individuals who are working on the same level of a company. Examples of horizontal communication include two managers who are working together on a project rollout and two employees on the same team who are working together to try to solve a customer's issue. Horizontal communication is great for collaborating, sharing information, and solving problems between employees who work together in the same environment. However, sometimes differences in personalities, territoriality, and rivalry between employees can negatively affect this form of communication.

Communication Methods

It is important to answer the following questions before deciding on an appropriate communication method to use:

- Who is the intended audience for the communication?
- What is the objective of the communication?
- Who is providing the information for the communication?
- Is the information contained within the communication time sensitive in nature?
- What information is going to be provided in the communication?

There are multiple means a company can use to communicate with its employees. Each method has its own potential advantages and drawbacks.

Email makes it easy to get information to a lot of people very quickly. However, this communication method can result in employees suffering from "information overload" from too many emails, making it more likely that important information is overlooked. Also, there is a danger that confidential information may be accidentally communicated to the wrong people.

The intranet (internal website and computer network) has the benefit of no risk of important information being accessed by someone outside the organization. Intranets can be very effective at communicating important ongoing information about the company, such as policies and procedures. In addition, companies often store necessary workplace documentation such as HR-related forms on an intranet, allowing employees to access that information when they need it. However, if outside parties need information on the intranet, they cannot access it. In addition, intranet communication is often "top-down" and does not allow for feedback from employees. It is also important to note that some intranet systems are not user-friendly, and employees can be discouraged from using them.

Newsletters can provide a variety of information and have the potential to do so in an engaging, welcoming manner. However, newsletters can be labor intensive. Since they are relatively infrequent (compared to the ease of sending an email), newsletters are not always useful for communicating urgent or immediate information. In addition, newsletters do not allow for formal two-way communication from employees (although this can be remedied by involving employees in the creation of the newsletter).

Word of mouth can quickly spread information throughout a group of people. However, as in the children's game, Telephone, information can become muddled, misinterpreted, and downright unrecognizable as it is passed from person to person. A manager or supervisor has no control over misinterpretations and misunderstandings that can result from word-of-mouth communication.

Finally, taking into consideration an organization's culture, generational differences that may be present within a company, and gender differences can also help with selecting an appropriate method to ensure improved communication.

Ethical and Professional Standards

Fairness and Justice
HR personnel are charged with advocating for fairness and justice for employees within their companies. In order to create this type of work environment, HR personnel work with managers to:

- Respect all employees, for each employee is unique and has worth.

- Afford each employee an opportunity to develop his or her skills.

- Ensure the work environment is free from discrimination and harassment by treating everyone with dignity and respect.

- Remain committed to diversity and inclusion in the workplace.

- Ensure equitable and consistent treatment of employees by creating and implementing fair policies and procedures.

Board of Directors Training
The board of directors cannot simply be briefed on the company's code of ethics or take part in the ethics training employees receive. Rather, the board of directors should be provided with specific training that details areas of risk that directly affect them, such as receiving gifts, personal conflicts of interest, and consequences that may result from their unintended influence (i.e., passing a friend's resume on to a manager at the company who then feels like he has to hire the individual whether or not she is a good fit). In addition, members of the board should also receive training on their responsibility to set an ethical tone at the top of the company, as they oversee upper management and interpret compliance data and future ethics trends.

Whistle-Blower Protection
The Sarbanes-Oxley Act, or SOX, is federal legislation passed in 2002 designed to establish higher levels of accountability and standards for a company's senior executives. The act was passed in reaction to the global corporate and accounting scandals of WorldCom and Enron. A particular section contained within SOX (806) provides protection for employees who have knowledge of, or have been a witness to, actions that are in direct violation of federal securities laws or Securities and Exchange Commission (SEC) regulations and wish to report their concerns. Examples of such actions include fraudulent financial reporting and billing for goods that were not delivered. OSHA is charged with enforcing the whistle-blower protections.

Employers cannot retaliate against employees who serve in the capacity of whistle-blowers. This means that, as a result of providing information, whistle-blowers cannot be disciplined, have their work hours or pay reduced, be laid off or terminated, or be blackmailed. This also applies if an employee is assisting other employees with providing information or if an employee is assisting with a SOX investigation. In addition, employees' identities must remain confidential whenever possible.

HR personnel must ensure there is a system in place to handle the following components to guarantee whistle-blower protection:

- Employee training on recognizing unethical or unlawful activities
- Policy on the procedure to follow when there is a need to report unethical or unlawful activities
- Manager training on maintaining employee confidentiality and preventing retaliation
- Tracking system for complaints, investigation records, and complaint resolutions
- Procedure to follow for investigations, including the associated disciplinary actions

Copyrights

The Copyright Act of 1976 is the foundational law in the United States regarding property ownership of literary and pictorial works, radio, film, musical and dramatic works, and architectural structures. The statute supersedes all local and state copyright laws.

In order to lawfully reproduce, disseminate, modify, publicly display, or perform copyrighted material, one must hold a copyright over such material—published or unpublished. Stipulated by the Copyright Act of 1976, a copyright lasts for the duration of the author's life, plus an additional 70 years after his or her death.

However, the law incorporates a policy of "fair use." Fair use enumerates some instances in which a person may use copyrighted material and is determined by the following:

- The intended purpose of the work (i.e., commercial gain or nonprofit education)
- The nature or type of work in question
- The amount or proportion of the copyrighted work being used
- The potential variation in market value

Educational purposes, research, scholarship, teaching, or news reporting are the categories that would determine the applicability of fair use.

When employees create original works in the course of their employment at a company, they are unable to claim ownership of copyrights. Since their employer paid them to complete the work, the employer owns any associated copyrights. Additionally, in some instances, an employer hires freelance employees to complete work on behalf of a company (i.e., freelance marketers). In this case, the employer also owns any associated copyrights for the end work products because the employer commissioned the work to be completed. This is known as a **work-for-hire exception**. HR personnel can assist management with any confusion that may occur surrounding intellectual property ownership.

Insider Information

Insider information can relate to any type of information (not just securities trading information) a company's employees have access to that has not yet been made available to the general public. HR personnel can assist management by providing education on the criminal repercussions associated with using insider information, whether lower-level employees or those in higher-level positions who may benefit from trading in equities or stocks with the inside knowledge they have gained before it becomes public.

Bribes, Payoffs, and Kickbacks

In the workplace, a **bribe** takes place when an employee promises a gift in some form, such as money, in return for an individual agreeing to act in a specific manner. A **payoff** occurs when an employee receives money or a gift in some form following a bribe. Finally, a **kickback** takes place when an employee receives a partial sum of money as the result of a confidential agreement. HR personnel can assist management with eliminating this type of corruption from the workplace by designing and implementing an anti-bribery program. This type of program details the importance of ethical behavior in recruitment, interviewing, training, and contracts, along with the associated disciplinary procedures for failure to abide by the standards.

Business Elements of an Organization

Internal Functions and Departments
It is important for HR personnel to have an understanding of their company's internal environment and a general perspective of their business partners (BPs). This enables them to identify any emerging issues or needs and aid in collaboration and communication. The following is a list of the common functions and departments found within most companies, regardless of their size:

Finance and Accounting
These functions are closely related in that they are focused on how money is transferred in and out of a company.

The **finance** function assists the business units within a company with financial needs, such as:

- Developing financial models
- Establishing prices for products
- Granting credit to customers
- Projecting any future financial needs

The **accounting** function is charged with recording a company's financial transactions, such as:

- Payroll

- Accounts receivable

- Accounts payable

- Expense reimbursements

- Preparation of budgets for managers to understand and keep control of the costs associated with the company's operation

The budgeting the account function performs can take place in different ways:

- **Incremental budgeting**: This type of budgeting is based off of the prior year's budget, and the basis of funding is any newly identified needs.

- **Formula budgeting**: This type of budgeting is simply a percentage decrease or increase to general funding.

- **Zero-based budgeting**: In this method, the budget for the year starts off at zero. Then, expenses are justified by listing all of the objectives for the year and ranking them. Funds are allocated based on the ranking that is assigned.

Marketing and Sales

These functions are closely related in that they are focused on how a company creates demand for its products and services and then gets those products and services to its customers.

The **marketing** function is concerned with making decisions around the four P's:

- **Product**: This involves making decisions about what a company's product or service will look like or how it will perform, the type of warrantee that will be offered, the type of customer service that will be offered, and how the product or service will be packaged for sale.

- **Price**: This involves establishing a price for a company's product or service that is attractive to its customers while still earning a profit. This also includes considering any discounts that may be offered to customers.

- **Place**: This involves making decisions about where potential target customers can locate a company's product or service. In order to determine the proper place, the marketing group must have an understanding of where the target customer will shop for the product or service (on the phone, at a brick-and-mortar store, on the internet, etc.).

- **Promotion**: This involves establishing how a company's product or service will be promoted. This may include contests, discounts, rebates, advertising, or personal selling.

The **sales** function is charged with selling the company's product or service to the customer.

Operations (Production)

The terms *operations* and *production* are used interchangeably. The **operations** function assists a company with providing products and services to its customers. This is accomplished by focusing on the five elements listed below. It is important to note that operations can be affected by supply chain management.

- **Capacity**: This involves determining the amount of a product or service that can be produced with a company's available inputs (equipment, materials, and labor).

- **Scheduling**: This involves ensuring that a company's products and services are available in the marketplace during times of high customer demand (i.e., during the Christmas holiday season).

- **Inventory**: This element deals with a company's ability to have enough inventory on hand to fill its customers' orders in a prompt manner. Since a company does not want to incur the cost of maintaining a large inventory, this is where a just-in-time (JIT) inventory management system comes into play.

- **Cost control**: This involves a company's ability to provide quality products and services at the lowest possible cost.

- **Standards**: This element deals with a company's products and services meeting the standards that were established by its quality assurance processes and procedures.

Information Technology

This function assists a company with utilizing information to support its strategic goals. For example, an airline company may have a goal to achieve competitive superiority, and its information technology department is able to help it achieve that goal by building a world-class airline reservation system. A different company may have a goal of reducing costs by eliminating rent in an expensive downtown high-rise building. Its information technology department is able to help it achieve that goal by establishing systems for employees to telecommute from their home offices.

R&D

This function assists a company with innovation by responding to market research findings or advancements in technology and designing new products and services or refining the design of existing products and services. Employees in the R&D group also test new products and services to ensure they perform as expected before they are offered to a company's customers. In some companies, the R&D group is part of the marketing function.

Employees

The combination of employees' knowledge, skills, and abilities makes up a company's human capital, which can lead to creativity and a competitive advantage. Since employees are a company's most valuable asset, it is important to keep them engaged. Employee engagement is the willingness of employees to remain with a company, "go the extra mile" when completing their work, and speak highly of the company when outside of its doors. Employees tend to be more engaged when they understand how their daily responsibilities affect how the company reaches its goals. The following elements are important for employee engagement to occur as well:

- **Leadership**: It is important for employees to work for managers who support the company's goals and follow through on their commitments to them. It is also important for managers to clearly communicate employee expectations in regard to a company's goals.

- **Professional development**: It is important for employees to feel they are being invested in and groomed for higher-level positions.

- **Employee recognition**: It is important for employees to receive monetary and nonmonetary rewards in exchange for performing above expectations.

Existing HRIS, Reporting Tools, and Other Systems for Effective Data Reporting and Analysis

Balanced Scorecard

David Norton, PhD, and Robert Kaplan, PhD, developed the **balanced scorecard**. It is a tool companies can use to report on all of the elements that impact their success instead of only focusing on their financial results. The scorecard contains metrics that are financial and nonfinancial in nature that span across four perspectives: financial, customer, internal business processes, and employee learning and growth.

- The **financial perspective** addresses traditional financial measures to ensure a company is managing its bottom line in the most effective manner, such as operating margins, utilization of capital, profit and loss, and return on investment.

- The **customer perspective** looks at elements such as customer satisfaction and customer loyalty to ensure a company is meeting the expectations of its customers and can depend on receiving their repeat business in the future.

- The **internal business processes perspective** examines the processes that will need to be modified or improved to ensure a company is achieving its customers' objectives. Examples of scorecard metrics in this area are cycle time, number of hours of rework, supplier quality, number of defects, and volume shipped.

- The **employee learning and growth perspective** addresses elements such as mentoring programs, employee training and development, and succession planning to ensure a company is securing the human capital pool it will need to maintain success in the future.

A brainstorming session is typically held to determine the scorecard metrics. As the performance period progresses, the balanced scorecard metrics are labeled as red (results are below target and require immediate attention), yellow (results are within a tolerance interval below target and need to be monitored), and green (results are at or above target) and reported on in meetings. These colors alert management and HR about areas that require fast attention. Metrics in red must be addressed in a timely manner to prevent other areas from being adversely affected by poor performance. For example, a metric marked as red in the internal business processes perspective (i.e., a manufacturing bottleneck that leads to a longer cycle time), if not addressed quickly, can result in a metric turning to yellow or red in the customer perspective (i.e., lowered customer satisfaction ratings). The balanced scorecard approach serves as a powerful communication tool for all members of the company.

HR Audit

An **HR audit** is a tool used by companies to assess the state of their HR practices. Different areas of HR, such as compensation and benefits, staffing, and health and safety, are assessed to see how they have been performing. This allows management to uncover any possible areas for improvement. The following is a list of the different types of HR audits:

- **I-9 audit**: This type of audit checks to see if a company is being compliant with the I-9 form requirement and immigration regulations. For example, this would involve checking to see that HR is retaining completed I-9 forms for three years after employees begin their employment or for one year after they are terminated, whichever comes later.

- **Compliance audit**: This type of audit ensures that a company is maintaining appropriate records for state and federal paperwork requirements. For example, this would involve checking to see that HR is using the correct forms when employees take leave under the Family and Medical Leave Act (FMLA).

- **Benefits programs audit**: This type of audit checks to see if a company is being compliant with its benefits administration and reporting as well as associated regulatory compliance. For example, this would involve reviewing a company's health plan's most current summary plan description (SPD) to gain an understanding of its provisions and operations.

- **Specific program audit**: This type of audit ensures that a company is maintaining appropriate records for a specific HR subarea, such as EEO. For example, this would involve reviewing a company's employee selection procedures, such as interview questions and tests, to ensure that minorities, older workers, and women are not adversely affected by selection procedures or criteria that are not job related.

- **Full HR audit**: During this type of audit, all of the above-mentioned areas are reviewed, along with any remaining HR functions, such as learning and development.

Human Resource Information System

A **Human Resource Information System** (HRIS) assists HR with storing information, such as employee documents versus physical paper files, and making effective decisions. This type of system also aids HR personnel with pulling the data needed to compile various reports for federal and state agencies, such as the EEOC. The following is a list of ways a company's HRIS can be used:

- Tracking employees' service awards
- Tracking recruitment efforts
- Allowing for automated benefit administration
- Compliance reporting
- Tracking employees' time and attendance
- Administering training programs
- Eliminating any data entry duplication
- Compensation administration
- Sharing payroll information with the finance group

When selecting and implementing an HRIS, it is important to consider if it will need to be integrated with other company systems and to make decisions as to who will see what information, which determines the number of levels of access.

HR Accountability Measures

There are some HR accountability measures that are meaningful for strategic management purposes.

HR-to-Employee Ratio

This ratio is a measure of the HR full-time equivalents for every one hundred full-time employees in a company. It is an indicator of the HR department's overall efficiency. However, it is important to note the following:

- When using this ratio for comparison purposes, only companies similar in size should be compared.

- Outsourcing of any HR functions may lead to an improved ratio.

HR Department Expenses per Employee

This ratio is calculated by adding the direct and indirect HR department expenses and dividing that amount by the total number of employees. This measure ensures that HR's expenses remain in line with other company expenses. **HR expenses as a percent of operating expenses** and **HR expenses as a percent of total revenue** are two additional measures that are variations on this calculation.

Change Management Theory, Methods, and Application

Change Management

Organizational changes can come about as the result of internal forces (i.e., exit interviews revealing low job satisfaction, a rebranding initiative, or an effort to create a flatter organization by removing levels of management). Organizational changes may also be the result of findings from an environmental scan (i.e., regulatory and legal changes or discovering the need for a new service or product). **Change management** refers to an organization's ability to implement changes in a diligent and comprehensive manner. This concept of change is holistic and encompasses sweeping change of an organization.

Change agents are individuals who are charged with implementing organizational change effectively. These individuals tend to wear many hats. For example, they:

- Investigate. They need to understand the organization's dynamics as well as employees' attitudes and behaviors surrounding the change.

- Advocate. They must be persistent and continually supporting the change initiative when employees have forgotten about it and are busy with their full-time jobs.

- Encourage. They are skilled at listening to employees who are experiencing a wide range of emotions and may not feel comfortable taking risks or going outside of their comfort zones.

- Facilitate. They design and utilize processes, tools, and forms to assist employees when going through the change.

- Mediate. They manage conflict and help employees find common goals to assist them in collaborating to implement the change.

- Advise. They build credibility with employees through their knowledge and ability to assist them and point them in the right direction.

- Manage. They are conscientious and hold employees accountable to ensure they are on track to meet the due dates and goals for the project.

Executive sponsors, such as senior executives or the CEO, are also critical to the success of change initiatives, as they show employees they are committed to the change at their level of the organization. By being enthusiastic about the change, executive sponsors inspire employees to commit to the implementation process.

Kurt Lewin's Change Model

Kurt Lewin was a social psychologist who presented a change management model back in 1947. His change process theory is a three-step organizational program that seeks to explain how entities change, the catalysts that precipitate change, and how change can be successfully accomplished. Fundamental to the theory is the notion that an entity will respond to the need for change when there is an external stimulus that compels it.

The first phase of the theory is **unfreezing**. The need for change is identified and communicated during this stage, which creates the motivation for change. During unfreezing, it is important to create a clear vision for the outcome that will follow the change while creating a sense of urgency for obtaining that new outcome. The second phase is **changing**. Communication is key during this phase as resistance to the change is managed and the organization comes into alignment with the change. Training on new processes may also take place during this phase. The final phase is **refreezing**. In this phase, the new adjustments are solidified and cemented into the functions of an entity (the change becomes the new norm). During the refreezing phase, evaluation of the outcome takes place, which may lead to some additional fine-tuning. Positive reinforcement is very important during this phase to ensure employees will not backslide into old behaviors they engaged in prior to the change.

Kurt Lewin Change Model

Unfreeze

Create the correct atmosphere for change

Change

Come into alignment with change

Refreeze

Solidify change

John Kotter's Change Model

John Kotter was a well-known change expert and professor at Harvard Business School who introduced an eight-step change model in 1955 that was built upon the previous model by Kurt Lewin. The steps in his model are described below:

- Create urgency. This step involves developing a strong business case around the need for change so employees will buy into the change.

- Form the change coalition. In this step, key stakeholders and true leaders in the organization who will be able to lead the change effort with their influence and authority are identified. The coalition should be made up of a mix of individuals from various levels and departments throughout the organization.

- Create a clear vision for the change. This step involves identifying the purpose for the change.

- Communicate the vision. Since it is important to keep the vision for the change in the forefront of employees' minds, in this step, a communication strategy is developed from the top down.

- Empower action. This step involves removing barriers to change and encouraging or rewarding employees who are thinking creatively and are willing to take risks.

- Create short-term wins. Instead of having a single, long-term goal, this step involves finding some short-term targets that can motivate employees as "wins" when they are achieved and celebrated.

- Build on the change. This step involves utilizing the short-term wins in step 6 to reinvigorate aspects of the change process that have stalled somewhat and to involve employees who have been resistant to the change effort thus far.

- Root the change. In an effort to make the change stick and replace old habits, in this step, discussions about the connections between the successes that have been experienced and the new behaviors continue.

Peter Senge

Peter Senge was the founder of the Society of Organizational Learning and continues to serve as a senior lecturer at the MIT Sloan School of Management. He is a proponent of systems thinking, where managers spend more time focusing on the big picture than on individual actions, since actions and consequences are all correlated with each other. In this same manner, Peter Senge believes organizations should seek out and embrace change versus waiting and responding to changes in crisis mode.

Risk Management

As with nearly all aspects of business, there are risks that an HR department may face and should preemptively work to minimize and manage. At its very core, the HR management department is focused on hiring and training the right people for the right jobs, ensuring they have the skills, attitudes, and knowledge needed to advance the organization and, importantly, not hamper its future. To accomplish this, the HR department must ensure their hiring, training, and support programs and policies are robust and aligned with the organization's mission, values, and needs. It is critical for the HR management professionals to have their fingers on the pulse of the company such that they can anticipate changing needs for workforce staffing and planning. For example, if the company has an aging workforce, comprised primarily of those on the brink of retiring, strategic workforce planning might involve succession planning and hiring new employees who will have ample time to train with the seasoned employees before they retire. Similarly, high turnover is another pertinent risk for HR risk management. In addition to the critical role of hiring the right people committed to the job, the company can take strides to reduce turnover rate by offering competitive salaries and benefits, rewarding hard-working employees, building the company culture, offer flexibility with schedules, etc.

In addition to the risks inherent in staffing, HR management professionals will be integral in managing other risks for the company. For example, worker-related injuries and Occupational Health and Safety violations must be prevented, both to prevent legal and financial obligations, but also long-term health problems and lost productivity of workers. Proper safety procedures must be in place and checked routinely, staff must have proper training and equipment, etc. Other risks include financial abuse, property risks, embezzlement and theft, reputation risks, environmental risks, etc. When considering the risks a company faces, both general risks (applicable to all or nearly all organizations) and company-specific risks need to be identified.

After a comprehensive list of risks is compiled, the next step is to evaluate the likelihood of occurrence of each risk and assess the severity of the consequences should that risk come to fruition. Then, for each identified risk, strategies must be assigned to manage the risk. Usually, one of the following four categories of strategies is most appropriate:

- Avoiding: A service or activity deemed too risky is ceased or no longer offered.

- Accepting: While still deemed risky, the activity or service is still offered or provided because it is key to the organization.

- Modifying: To reduce the likelihood that an adverse event or risk will occur, and/or to reduce the severity of the consequences if it does, the activity is changed in some way, typically via modifying policies and procedures.

- Transferring/Sharing: Risks are shared or transferred to other company's by buying insurance or signing contractual agreements with other companies.

Selecting the most appropriate risk management strategy for each risk also involves considering the costs (financial and otherwise) of changing the policies and procedures in place, and/or taking on the risk. Once the strategies have been determined, a concrete plan naming the specific individuals responsible for each element in the plan should be created, communicated, rehearsed, and assessed/evaluated.

Qualitative and Quantitative Methods and Tools for Analytics

Reliable and accurate information is needed for managers to make good, solid business decisions.

Inductive and Deductive Reasoning

There are two types of reasoning. **Inductive reasoning** takes place when a generalization is made from specific incidents that were witnessed. For example, a manager looks at the backgrounds of his top sales representatives and discovers they all have degrees in accounting. He designs a rule for future hiring around this observation that an accounting background is needed for success as a sales representative. On the other hand, **deductive reasoning** takes places when a general rule guides specific actions. For example, HR has identified the ability to work with pivot tables in Excel as a key task for an open position. They decide to have all candidates complete a "test" demonstrating their pivot table skills as part of their second-round interviews.

Primary and Secondary Research

There are two types of research. **Primary research** is data gathered firsthand and includes interviews, surveys, focus groups, direct observation, and pilot projects. **Secondary research** is data gathered by others and includes benchmarking, historical data, purchased data, best-practices reports, and secondhand reports.

Scientific Method

The **scientific method** is a formal method of primary research that can be used to solve HR problems. The steps in the scientific method, along with a corresponding example, are listed below.

- 1. Problem analysis → Turnover is too high.

- 2. Hypothesis formulation → The turnover rate is higher with employees who have been at the company for less than one year.

- 3. Experimental design → HR can use a correlation analysis of length of employment and turnover data to determine if the hypothesis is confirmed.

- 4. Data collection → HR will review employee files and exit interview notes to correlate the hire and exit dates of employees.

- 5. Data analysis → HR will say if the correlation analysis verifies the hypothesis. The analysis will prove or disprove the turnover rate is higher with employees who have been at the company for less than one year. HR personnel may also uncover other issues that contributed to the problem during the process detailed above, which can be helpful to the company moving forward.

Quantitative Analysis

Quantitative analysis is based on statistics and facts.

Measures of Central Tendency (averages)

- **Mean**: The mean is calculated by taking the sum of the values in a data set and dividing that total by the number of values in the set. The mean for the set of numbers below is (60/8) = 7.5

- **Median**: The median is calculated by placing the values in a data set in sequential order and selecting the value that falls directly in the middle. If there is an even number of data points (which means that no value falls directly in the middle), the median is found by taking the average of the two numbers that fall in the middle. The median for the set of numbers below is ((6+9)/2) = 7.5

- **Mode**: The mode is determined by finding the number that occurs the most frequently in a data set. The mode for the set of numbers below is 9.

Number Set: {1,3,6,9,12,15,9,5}

Time-Series Forecasts

Time-Series Forecasts is predicting future values based on previously observed values using some type of model.

- **Trend analysis**: This type of analysis looks at the changes in a single variable over time. For example, HR personnel can utilize trend analysis to provide them with information about a company's seasonal staffing requirements.

- **Simple linear regression**: This type of analysis looks at the relationship between two variables and the change in one variable in response to the other variable. For example, HR personnel can utilize simple linear regression to compare manpower requirements with production output. This type of analysis would allow HR to forecast the number of employees a company will need to meet an increase in its demand.

- **Multiple linear regression**: This type of analysis looks at the relationship between multiple variables to predict another variable. For example, HR personnel can utilize multiple linear regression to determine if a relationship exists between lower employee morale, absenteeism, lower production output, and higher turnover.

Qualitative Analysis

Qualitative analysis is more subjective in nature and is based on feelings, opinions, and attitudes. This type of analysis is used when depth of information is important, along with uncovering individuals' underlying values, motivations, and perceptions. The following are some of the tools that can be used when performing a qualitative analysis to generate ideas:

Brainstorming

Brainstorming is a simple method used to generate a large number of ideas in a relatively short period of time. The necessary individuals are gathered together. The problem is clearly stated by the group leader, and the participants suggest any alternatives they can come up with in a given period of time. During brainstorming, no criticism of ideas is allowed, which encourages the participants to think "outside of the box." All of the ideas are recorded for further analysis and discussion.

Nominal Group Technique

The nominal group technique can be used as an alternative to brainstorming. A problem is presented to the group. However, before any discussion takes place, each individual writes down ideas about the problem independently. Then each of the participants presents one idea to the group. After all of the participants' ideas have been presented and documented, a group discussion takes place. Following the discussion, each participant silently rank-orders each of the ideas. The final decision is reached by the idea with the highest aggregate ranking.

Delphi Technique

The Delphi technique is unique in the fact that the participants involved do not meet. Instead, they contribute their input only in written form. A group of individuals utilize their expertise to answer multiple rounds of questions regarding an issue. Their results are collected, combined, prioritized, and returned to the participants following each round in the form of a new questionnaire. This format continues until some type of consensus among the participants can be reached.

Dealing with Situations that are Uncertain, Unclear, or Chaotic

HR professionals are often faced with uncertain situations in which they must assist management in reassembling the company's workforce to rise above the current challenge. Below are some of the ways in which this is accomplished.

Business Process Reengineering

With the end goal of delivering more value to a company's customers, business process reengineering involves rethinking existing processes to eliminate waste and increase efficiency. Often this work is accomplished in cross-functional teams who share end-to-end responsibility for a designated process. For example, consider a manufacturing engineer who walks to a copier every hour to make multiple copies of protocols for her lab. The copier is located on the other side of the large building she works in. If this step was part of a business process that was being reengineered, it would be deemed wasteful. The copier may either be moved closer to the engineer, or the engineer may be told to make her copies only once or twice a day to save time.

Organizational Restructuring

In an effort to eliminate redundancy or layers of bureaucracy, a company may engage in corporate restructuring activities. HR will assist management with looking at individual business units to reduce costs by removing management layers, offering employees early retirement buyouts, laying off employees (RIFs), or changing reporting relationships among staff. These actions will ultimately result in an increase in production.

Divestitures

This is another form of organizational restructuring where a company makes the decision to sell off some of its investments, business units, or subsidiaries. Divestitures occur when businesses are no longer in line with a company's core competencies, are redundant following a merger or acquisition, are experiencing financial duress, and no longer profitable. For example, Nestlé is in the process of selling its chocolate business that is based in the United States, as it is currently underperforming, and the company wants to focus on healthier products.

Shared Service Models

This is another form of organizational restructuring where a company's administrative staff positions in specific groups, such as HR or information technology, are consolidated across business groups so as not to be redundant. This allows for these types of overhead costs to be distributed across various geographic locations. For example, Bayer Group moved to an HR shared services model several years ago to allow their HRBPs to be more strategic in nature. By doing so, the HRBPs were able to focus on human capital development instead of on managing employee leaves of absence and administering tuition reimbursement. Benefits of an HR shared services model include the following:

- Internal resources placing focus on strategic tasks
- More efficient HR operations
- Greater continuity of HR operations
- Economies of scale gained from combining HR software and tasks
- Higher-quality HR services

Offshoring and Outsourcing

When a U.S.-based company wants to lower its production and manufacturing costs, **offshoring** is a process it can use to accomplish that goal by moving those parts of its organization to another country, such as Mexico, in order to experience a cost savings. For example, offshoring takes place when an American automotive company shifts production of a certain passenger car to a factory in China to benefit from the lower cost of labor. When a company no longer wants to perform a particular function in-house, such as payroll, **outsourcing** can be used to contract a specific internal business service to a third party known for having expertise in a particular skill set. For example, a small business owner may outsource the payroll of its employees to Automatic Data Processing (ADP), which is well known for its payroll expertise. Both offshoring and outsourcing result in staff reductions at a company.

Mergers and Acquisitions (M&As)

These are different means of combining two organizations into a single company. A **merger** takes place when two or more companies form a single entity with the goal of leveraging their assets to become more successful. An example of a merger occurred when Sirius merged with XM Radio. On the other hand, an **acquisition** takes place when one company purchases another company. An example of an acquisition occurred when Disney acquired Pixar. Acquisitions can take place under friendly or hostile conditions, and the organization that is purchasing the other company can do so with either stock or cash.

HR personnel assist management with the **due diligence** process that takes place prior to M&A. This process involves examining the following aspects to learn more about the worth of the company that may be purchased to ensure that no financial or nonfinancial aspects are questionable:

- EEO compliance records
- Employee handbook
- Collective bargaining agreements
- Employee relations practices
- Grievance history
- Compensation practices
- Employee contracts
- I-9 forms and visa documentation
- OSHA compliance
- Employees on leave
- Any pending legal exposure

HR personnel also assist management with integrating the workforces of the two companies following M&A. This may involve identifying gaps in employment, reducing or transferring staff, and efforts to assimilate the two cultures. Throughout the M&A process, continuous communication from HR is essential for maintaining employees' morale.

Global Expansion

A workforce expansion of this type occurs when a company has made the decision to expand into global markets as a result of a business strategy, acquisition, or merger. This type of expansion affects a company's organizational structure and requires meticulous planning, coordination, and resource allocation.

Practice Questions

1. During which step of the strategic planning process does environmental scanning take place?
    a. Strategy Formulation
    b. Strategy Development
    c. Strategy Implementation
    d. Strategy Evaluation

2. Which of the following is an example of a weakness that may be uncovered during a SWOT analysis that can affect an organization's ability to reach its objectives?
    a. Outdated equipment
    b. Consumer trends
    c. A labor shortage
    d. A changing political climate

3. Under Porter's Five Forces, the reality that a company's customer can decide to stream movies from their Smart TV instead of purchasing DVDs is an example of which of the following?
    a. Bargaining power of a company's customers
    b. Threat of new entrants
    c. Industry competitors
    d. Threat of substitute products

4. Risks can be managed in one of four ways: elimination, mitigation, transfer, and _____.

5. If a job position is posted on Day 1, a candidate applies for the job on Day 7, and she accepts the job offer on Day 15, what is the time to hire?

_____ days

6. Which of the following is used to determine if targeted outcomes have occurred as a result of employees completing a training program?
    a. Pretests
    b. Participant surveys
    c. Performance metrics
    d. Posttests

7. Which of the following statements is used by a company to explain what it does differently from other companies?
    a. Code of conduct
    b. Mission statement
    c. Corporate values
    d. Vision statement

8. Teamwork, respect, safety, and integrity are examples of a company's _____.

9. An organization where employees have the freedom to make decisions on how they complete their tasks has a low degree of _____.

10. If twenty-three employees left a company during the course of the year and sixty-seven employees were working at the company at the start of the year, what is its attrition rate?

_____ days

11. Which of the following types of organizational structures groups jobs according to industry or market?
    a. Division
    b. Geographic
    c. Product
    d. Functional

12. An employee will report to a primary manager and also a second manager for work on specified projects in an organizational structure known as a/an _____.

13. Which of the following best describes a pocket veto?
    a. The president decides to veto a bill he receives from Congress immediately.
    b. The president does not sign a bill within ten days of Congress submitting it to him.
    c. The president vetoes a bill from Congress. Congress holds a vote but does not have the necessary quorum it needs.
    d. The president does not sign a bill within ten days of Congress submitting it to him and then adjourns.

14. Human resources attempting to influence government leaders in an effort to create legislation that will benefit their companies is known as _____.

15. Which of the following is a type of administrative law used by the president of the United States to create directives that do not require the approval of Congress?
    a. Agency order
    b. Pocket veto
    c. Executive order
    d. Agency regulation

16. A presentation from upper management to staff on the company's mission is an example of _____.

17. Which of the following is an example of bottom-up communication?
    a. Managers receiving an email from the board of directors
    b. Staff participating in an all-hands meeting
    c. Two employees on the same team sharing information to solve a problem
    d. Two managers in the same group working together on a project rollout

18. Individuals who are charged with implementing organizational change effectively are referred to as _____.

19. During which phase of Kurt Lewin's Change Model is the motivation for change created?
    a. Unfreezing
    b. Changing
    c. Refreezing
    d. Monitoring

20. In John Kotter's Change Model, which step involves identifying the key stakeholders and true leaders in the organization who can guide the change effort with their influence and authority?
    a. Create a clear vision for the change.
    b. Communicate the vision.
    c. Create short-term wins.
    d. Form the change coalition.

21. Which of the following is a way human resources can incorporate a company's vision into daily business activities?
    a. Develop a system to recognize and reward employees who demonstrate the values.
    b. Reinforce the values during employee exit interviews.
    c. Mention the values once a year during the annual holiday party presentation.
    d. Interview candidates only to ensure they have the right mix of skills and abilities.

22. Which of the following sections would typically be included in a company's code of ethics?
    a. Personal privacy
    b. Ownership of intellectual property
    c. The ability to run a small business at work
    d. Using your personal computer at work

23. An individual who is charged with ensuring employees maintain the ethical standards that were initially developed by executive management and informing the executive team about any ethical issues that may arise is known as a/an _____.

24. Which of the following is an example of the types of cross-functional stakeholders human resources personnel work with on a daily basis?
    a. Creditors
    b. Government agencies
    c. Customer service
    d. Suppliers

25. The balanced scorecard contains metrics that span across four perspectives: customer, financial, employee learning and growth, and _____.

26. Which of the following is a way a company can most effectively utilize a human resource information system (HRIS)?
    a. Providing for duplication of data entry
    b. Restricting payroll information from the finance group
    c. Allowing for only managers to track their attendance
    d. Enabling reporting for compliance purposes

27. When a manager looks at the backgrounds of his top human resources personnel and discovers they all have degrees in counseling and he designs a rule for future hiring that says a counseling background is needed for success as a manager, it is known as _____.

28. For the given data set {1,3,9,8,7,7,4,10}, the mean is _____.

29. For the given data set {1,3,9,8,7,7,4,10}, the mode is _____.

30. Which of the four P's of marketing is concerned with where a target customer will shop for the company's product or service?
    a. Place
    b. Product
    c. Price
    d. Promotion

Answer Explanations

1. B: Environmental scanning and a SWOT analysis are performed during the Strategy Development step of the strategic planning process. During this step, long-range plans are also established that will set the company's direction for the next three to five years.

2. A: Outdated equipment, unreliable suppliers, ineffective leadership, and insufficient marketing campaigns are examples of weaknesses that can be uncovered during a SWOT analysis. Internal weaknesses can potentially reduce a company's ability to reach its objectives and place it at a competitive disadvantage. Consumer trends are an example of an opportunity. A labor shortage and a changing political climate are examples of threats.

3. D: This is an example of the threat of substitute products. Substitute products are items that fulfill the same need for a customer but are not the exact services and products a company currently sells.

4. Acceptance: Once a company's risks are recognized and prioritized, they can be managed in one of the following four ways: elimination, mitigation, transfer, and acceptance.

5. 8: The time to hire is calculated by subtracting the day the employee (who was eventually hired) entered a job's pipeline from the day he or she accepted an offer for the position. In this example, a job position was posted on Day 1, a candidate applied for the job on Day 7, and she accepted the job offer on Day 15. Therefore, the time to hire is 15 − 7 = 8 days.

6. C: Performance metrics, such as an increase in sales, are utilized to determine the degree that targeted outcomes have occurred as a result of employees completing a training program. Participant surveys are used to find out the degree to which participants react favorably to a training program. Pretests assess the knowledge of learners prior to the start of a training program, and posttests determine the knowledge students have acquired following a training program.

7. B: A mission statement tells employees what the company does, where the company is going in the mid to long term, and how the company is different and unique from other organizations. A code of conduct is a set of principles a company is committed to follow. Corporate values, such as integrity, open-mindedness, respect, safety, and teamwork, communicate to employees the standards by which they are expected to adhere to while conducting business. A vision statement is a concise statement that reflects organizational confidence and long-term aspirations regarding how a company will achieve more than economic success.

8. Values: Teamwork, respect, safety, and integrity are examples of a company's values.

9. Formalization: An organization that has jobs that are standardized, allowing for little discretion over what is to be done because the work is guided by rules, has a high degree of formalization. The opposite of this is a low formalization, where employees have more freedom on how they can complete their tasks.

10. 34.33%: To calculate attrition rate, divide the number of employees that left the company during the year by the total number of employees at the beginning of the year, and then multiply that amount by 100. In this example, the calculation is (23/67) x 100 = 34.33%.

11. A: A division organizational structure groups jobs by industry or market. A geographic organizational structure groups jobs according to geographic location. A product organizational structure groups jobs by product line. A functional organizational structure groups jobs according to function.

12. Matrix structure: An employee will report to a primary manager and also a second manager for work on specified projects in an organizational structure known as a matrix structure.

13. D: If the president fails to sign a bill when Congress is still in session, it still becomes a law after ten days. However, if Congress adjourns prior to the ten-day period, the bill does not become law. This is known as a pocket veto.

14. Lobbying: Human resources attempting to influence government leaders in an effort to create legislation that will benefit their companies is known as lobbying.

15. C: An executive order is a type of administrative law used by the president of the United States to create a directive that does not require the approval of Congress. An agency order is when a federal agency orders a company in administrative law court to be compliant with a federal law. A pocket veto occurs when the president does not sign a bill within ten days of Congress submitting it to him and then adjourns. An agency regulation is when a federal agency passes a stringent regulation employers must follow out of its concern for the welfare of employees in the workplace.

16. Top-down communication: A presentation from upper management to staff on the company's mission is an example of top-down communication.

17. B: Staff participating in an all-hands meeting is an example of bottom-up communication. Managers receiving an email from the board of directors is an example of top-down communication. Two employees on the same team sharing information to solve a problem and two managers in the same group working together on a project rollout are examples of horizontal communication.

18. Change agents: Individuals charged with implementing organizational change effectively are referred to as change agents.

19. A: During the unfreezing phase of Kurt Lewin's Change Model, the motivation for change is created. During the changing phase of Kurt Lewin's Change Model, communication as resistance to the change is managed, and the organization comes into alignment with the change. During the refreezing phase of Kurt Lewin's Change Model, evaluation of the outcome takes place, which may lead to some additional fine-tuning.

20. D: In John Kotter's Change Model "form the change coalition" step, key stakeholders and true leaders in the organization who will be able to lead the change effort with their influence and authority are identified. The coalition should be made up of a mix of individuals from various levels and departments throughout the organization.

21. A: Human resources can incorporate a company's vision into daily business activities through all of the following activities:

- Train hiring managers to interview candidates to determine if they are going to be the best cultural fit based on the company's values.
- Reinforce the values during a new hire orientation presentation.
- Reinforce the values in company communications.
- Develop a system to recognize and reward employees for demonstrating the company's values.
- Integrate the company's values into the performance review process.
- Decide to terminate employees who ultimately fail to follow the company's values.

22. B: The following sections are typically included in a company's code of ethics:

- Confidentiality
- Conflicts of interest
- Gifts, entertainment, and contributions
- Personal use of company assets
- Workplace privacy
- Outside employment
- Ownership of intellectual property
- Fair dealing
- Standards of business conduct
- Reporting code violations

23. Ethics officer: Some organizations have hired individuals known as ethics officers who are charged with ensuring employees maintain the ethical standards that were initially developed by executive management and informing the executive team about any ethical issues that may arise.

24. C: The following are examples of cross-functional stakeholders human resources personnel work with on a daily basis:

- Finance
- Information technology
- Legal
- Customer service
- Research and development
- Manufacturing

25. Internal business processes: The balanced scorecard contains metrics that span across four perspectives: customer, financial, employee learning and growth, and internal business processes.

26. D: The following are ways a company can most effectively utilize a human resource information system (HRIS):

- Tracking employees' service awards
- Tracking recruitment efforts
- Allowing for automated benefit administration
- Compliance reporting
- Tracking employees' time and attendance
- Administering training programs
- Eliminating any data entry duplication
- Compensation administration
- Sharing payroll information with the finance group

27. Inductive: The scenario given is an example of inductive reasoning, which takes place when a generalization is made from specific incidents that were witnessed.

28. 6.13: The mean is calculated by taking the sum of the values in a number set and dividing that total by the number of values. The mean for this set of numbers is (49/8) = 6.13.

29. 7: The mode is determined by finding the number that occurs most frequently in a number set. The mode for this set of numbers is 7.

30. A: Place involves making decisions about where a target customer will shop for the company's product or service (on the phone, at a brick-and-mortar store, on the internet, etc.). Product involves making decisions about what a company's product or service will look like or how it will perform. Price involves establishing a price for a company's product or service that is attractive to its customers while still earning a profit. Finally, promotion involves establishing how a company's product or service will be promoted.

Talent Planning and Acquisition

Federal Laws and Organizational Policies on Hiring

Hiring programs must comply with all federal hiring laws; these include Title VII of the Civil Rights Act of 1964 (Title VII), the Americans with Disabilities Act (ADA), the Age Discrimination in Employment Act (ADEA), and the Fair Labor Standards Act (FLSA). These laws ensure that all individuals—regardless of their gender, race, ethnicity, religious affiliation, physical ability, or age—are afforded the same rights for a fair hiring opportunity. Additionally some states have their own hiring laws to comply with. Sometimes the state law differs from the federal law; in these situations, the law that is the most generous to the individual is the law that should be followed. Human resources professionals must ensure that recruitment and hiring methods comply with the most generous level of protection.

Disparate impact is an important hiring practice concept. **Disparate impact** means policies or practices disproportionately impact a specific group of individuals. Artificial recruitment barriers can increase the likelihood of disparate impact. An **artificial recruitment barrier** is a qualification that is not truly necessary for a particular position, which could cause applicants to be disqualified from consideration. If an audit shows that a particular protected class now has been screened out from consideration due to this barrier, a disparate impact has occurred. Organizations should strive to regularly audit their hiring and selection processes to ensure that all qualifications are appropriate and screening processes are fair and equitable.

An organization's policies should ensure that all candidates are provided with a fair and equitable opportunity to be considered for employment. Policies should clearly communicate rights as well as responsibilities of the employer and the candidate. These policies are especially important when making decisions to disqualify or remove a candidate from consideration. One such reason for disqualification is nepotism. **Nepotism** is defined as favoritism based on a personal or familial relationship such as friendship, marriage, or family connection. If a candidate has a familial or personal relationship with a hiring manager or supervisor, it may present a conflict of interest. In circumstances such as this, it is important to have a policy that identifies which relationships—both personal and professional –disqualify a potential candidate from consideration. A nepotism policy should clearly define which exclusions and exceptions will be made. Although a husband may not be able to report directly to his wife as a manager, he may be able to be employed in a different department where he has no direct reporting relationship or connection to his spouse. Some organizations may stipulate that spouses simply cannot work for the organization, in an effort to mitigate any potential conflicts of interest. Nepotism policies should clearly outline any and all exceptions so that there is no confusion. Candidates should be asked about nepotism early in the application process. Many organizations have a standard question in the initial application, such as "Do any of your relatives work for this organization? If yes, who?" These questions enable an immediate review of the nepotism policy in relation to each specific circumstance. Any decision to disqualify an applicant from consideration should be connected to and supported by a specific written policy.

Sourcing Methods and Techniques

Recruitment uses sourcing methods to generate a robust, qualified candidate pool. There are numerous ways to source candidates, and some methods may work better for particular positions or markets. Human resources professionals should understand the positions they are recruiting for and how best to find candidates. Specialized positions in information technology may require postings on a niche IT-focused job board. Positions in maintenance and operations may need online postings in the local newspaper or on Craigslist.com. Each position should be reviewed before advertising, so that an appropriate sourcing method can be established to ensure the best possible candidate pool. A sourcing method helps to limit costs and decrease the time needed to build a qualified candidate pool.

Job boards and social media are among the most common sourcing techniques. Candidates do not generally visit individual company websites to see if there is a hiring opportunity. There are job boards on many social media platforms, and many organizations use targeted advertising on particular sites to appeal to prospective candidates. From LinkedIn to Indeed, job boards can provide a large audience for job opportunities. Organizations also have corporate accounts on Twitter, Facebook, Instagram, and other social media platforms. Having an inviting corporate profile and a list of open job opportunities on a social media platform can increase the number of applicants.

Some organizations use an internal program for employee referrals. By entrusting the workforce with referring individuals for open positions, organizations let employees play a part in the hiring initiative. Many programs reward the referring employee with an initial bonus if their referred candidate is hired and then a secondary bonus if their referred candidate remains employed after a certain period of time. This encourages employees to engage with their network and assist in the recruitment process by being ambassadors and champions of the organization. Current employees who are working in the culture and climate of the organization can be the best recruiters.

Some positions are harder to fill than others, and in these cases, an executive recruiter may be the most appropriate sourcing option. Executive recruiters can specialize in certain fields, markets, or levels such as executive leadership. While contracting with a recruiter can be an increased cost, it can also serve to fill a position with the best, most qualified candidate, one who otherwise would not be sourced. Executive recruiters can tap into established networks and passive job seekers, sometimes yielding a candidate pool that an organization would otherwise not be aware of.

Regardless of the sourcing methods used, organizations must ensure that recruitment is fair and equitable, affording all qualified candidates the same opportunity to be considered for an open position. By initiating multiple sourcing methods to search for candidates, an organization can increase its candidate pool.

Talent Acquisition Lifecycle

The talent acquisition lifecycle is a multi-step process that begins with a hiring need—usually a job opening—and ends with the hiring and onboarding of an employee. This process should be objective and standardized, ensuring that it is free from discrimination or other unethical and illegal practices.

The first step in the recruitment lifecycle is to determine the need of the department. If an organization has an opening due to a resignation, promotion, or transfer, the recruitment need must be evaluated. Once the need has been assessed, a job posting should be created that communicates the job description, company information, employee benefit information, and other information that a prospective employee would need to determine whether to submit an application.

The second step in the process is to source candidates and assess the candidate pool. By utilizing various sourcing methods, such as social media platforms, niche job boards, and other appropriate methods, a robust candidate pool can be gathered for the initial screening review. The initial screening review should group candidates into two basic initial categories—meeting required qualifications and not meeting required qualifications. The third step in the process is to further screen the candidates who have the required qualifications. These candidates should be further screened into such groups as "most qualified" and "least qualified." Then candidates should be selected for invitation to interview for the position. Candidates should be selected on criteria such as education, years of experience, accomplishments in previous positions, and leadership experience.

The fourth step in the process is to assess the most qualified candidates via assessment tests or interviews. Assessment tests should be conducted to determine the validity and strength of the candidates' skills. When candidates are invited to interview with the organization, the interviews should be conducted by individuals who are familiar with conducting interviews. Interviewers should be able to assess responses to score and rank the candidates for the hiring manager to review. Once the initial interviews have been completed, finalists should be selected. Hiring managers should then conduct final interviews with the most qualified candidates to make a final selection to offer the position.

The fifth step in the process consists of the employment offer and orientation. The employment offer should include not only the job title and salary, but also the name of the hiring manager, potential start date, necessary background checks or screening required prior to starting, and any pertinent employee benefit information. Benefit information often makes or breaks an offer, so employment offers should include information regarding vacation time, sick leave time, holiday schedules, medical insurance, (including when coverage starts and whether the organization assists with premiums), and any other pertinent information. If the prospective employee has other needs and wishes to negotiate the terms of the offer, it is appropriate at this point to engage in these conversations. Relocation expenses, deferred compensation, additional vacation time, or signing bonuses are all potential benefits that a prospective employee could negotiate. Once the offer has officially been accepted; and the background, references, or medical screening has been conducted; and the individual has been cleared to start employment, then an official hire date should be established. Once the new employee has begun working for the organization, it is important to immediately orient the individual to the company culture and procedures such as benefits enrollment, payroll, safety, work-related injuries, union participation, policies and procedures, and any other important information for a new employee to be exposed to.

Talent Planning and Acquisition Activities

Federal laws and regulations have been passed to ensure that all applicants for an employment opportunity are treated fairly and equitably. These laws and regulations protect individuals from discrimination on various levels, and they include Title VII of the Civil Rights Act of 1964 (Title VII), the Age Discrimination in Employment Act (ADEA), the Americans with Disabilities Act (ADA), the Pregnancy Discrimination Act of 1978 (PDA), and the Genetic Information Nondiscrimination Act (GINA). Human resources professionals are responsible for understanding all pertinent federal and state laws and applying them to hiring policies and practices. Discrimination is illegal throughout the entire employment process, including selection and hiring, offer negotiation, disbursement of raises and merit increases, transfers, promotions, training opportunities, termination, and in any other terms or conditions of employment. It is also important to stay informed about updates to current legislation as well as new legislation.

Title VII was passed in 1964 and originally prohibited discrimination in employment based on race, color, sex, religion, or national origin. After multiple amendments, the following protected classes were added: age, disability, pregnancy, and genetic information. Title VII was amended in 1972 to add educational institutions and again in 1991 to provide remedies for individuals who have been discriminated against. The Equal Employment Opportunity Commission (EEOC) is responsible for investigating complaints of Title VII violations and making determinations to file a lawsuit in federal or state court. Additionally, individuals who believe they are the victims of discrimination can also file a lawsuit directly. It is important to understand that harassment is a form of discrimination and Title VII therefore prohibits harassment on the basis of race, color, sex, religion, national origin, age, disability, pregnancy, or genetic information.

The ADEA was passed in 1967 and prohibits discrimination on the basis of age. The ADEA stipulates that an employer may not fail or refuse to hire an individual based on age. An employer may not terminate an individual based on age. An employer may not fail to provide or offer employment opportunities such as promotions or transfers based on age. An employer may not reduce an individual's wage based on age. No employment action may be taken simply due to an individual's age. Originally, this law protected individuals from ages 40 to 65. In 1986, the upper age limit was removed completely.

The ADA is a civil rights law that was passed in 1990 and prohibits employment discrimination on the basis of disability. A disabled individual can request reasonable accommodations to allow them to perform the essential functions of their job. Employers are required to provide these reasonable accommodations as requested; however, the accommodations must be reasonable. If the accommodations create an undue hardship or change the job substantially, the employer may have the right to decline the accommodations.

The PDA was passed in 1978 as an amendment to Title VII and bans employment discrimination against women who are pregnant. The PDA requires employers to treat pregnancy just like any other medical condition. In doing so, pregnancy is therefore covered under the ADA and afforded the same protections. An employer may not refuse to hire a woman or terminate a current employee because she is pregnant. Additionally, employers may not force a pregnant employee to take pregnancy leave prior to the birth of her child if she is able to work. During the recruitment process, the PDA prohibits an employer from asking questions about family plans or other personal details such as marital status and number of children.

GINA was passed in 2009 and prohibits discrimination in employment based on genetic information. Employers may not ask an applicant or employee to provide genetic information, submit to a genetic test, or discuss family genetics. An employer may never use genetic information to make an employment decision as this information is not relevant to an individual's ability to do the work. This law has been especially important relative to health insurance coverage because a genetic condition may be considered a pre-existing condition and some insurance companies may deny coverage. Between GINA and the Affordable Care Act (ACT), individuals are now protected from being discriminated against from both angles of being employed and being provided with insurance coverage.

It is important to realize that as the workforce and corporate climate change and evolve, so will the laws and protections afforded to individuals. Amendments will be made and new laws created to protect individuals and afford everyone the same opportunities based on their qualifications. For example, evidence has shown that eliminating applicants merely on the basis of a criminal record may have a disparate impact on minority candidates. This is because the criminal justice system disparately affects minorities. Many agencies are reviewing and updating their policies regarding hiring individuals with criminal records to ensure that equal opportunities are afforded to all. Instead of a sweeping policy of not hiring any applicant with a felony conviction, the agency may have specific guidelines as to when an applicant would be removed from consideration. One example of this would be that the felony conviction has a direct nexus, or correlation, to the position. If the position involves handling cash and deposits and the applicant under consideration has a conviction for theft, the agency could legitimately disqualify the applicant; however, if the position involves repairing water main breaks, the organization may consider the applicant because the conviction does not have a direct nexus to the work.

Planning Concepts and Terms

In a recruitment process, it is important for human resource professionals to fully understand planning concepts and terms. It is equally important to ensure that all stakeholders involved in the process understand the concepts and terms. This enables open and clear communication, allowing all parties to be on the same page throughout the process and minimizing misperceptions or misunderstandings.

Workforce planning is the complete strategic process that forecasts an organization's current and future workforce, determines the most effective practices and processes to fill these needs, and implements the plans to deliver results. Workforce planning includes the following components at various stages in the process:

- Forecasting
- Critical skills gap analysis
- Recruitment
- Onboarding
- Succession planning

Human resources professionals should ensure all parties have a clear understanding of each of these concepts.

Forecasting is the process of deciding which positions must be filled and how to fill them. Forecasting is generally used to determine the overall personnel needs of an organization as well as the applicant pools of both internal and external candidates. Then forecasting is used to implement the appropriate methods to align the personnel needs and the applicant pools. During the forecasting process, it is important to understand company trends such as sales, growth, and market opportunities. If growth is such that additional employees are needed, a recruitment plan may be needed to address this need. Additionally, it is also important to understand current company demographics, such as when employees are eligible for retirement. This information is useful when determining future attrition and the needs of the organization if such attrition is realized.

A **critical skills gap analysis** is a process by which an organization defines its personnel needs in terms of the skills required to achieve the organization's goals. Having a complete and thorough understanding of the skills available and the skills needed allows an organization to make better decisions in recruitment, training, and succession planning. This analysis also allows employees to understand the skills needed to be successful and to progress within the organization throughout their career. Additionally, critical skills gap analysis can assist in the recruitment process by allowing hiring managers to home in on the required skill sets for applicants. It is also important to thoroughly define a critical skill. A **critical skill** is one that must be present in order to achieve the results necessary. If the critical skill is not present, problems can occur in the completion, accuracy, quality, and other aspects of the task. Critical skills should be identified in the job description and validated through reviewing the work being done on a day-to-day basis.

Recruitment refers to the entire process of filling an open position. Because there are various elements to recruitment, it is important to outline and describe each step so that everyone involved understands the overall process, timing, and responsibilities. The recruitment process includes advertising the position, screening the applicants, setting up interviews, developing the interview questions, selecting the most qualified candidate, and negotiating an offer, as well as completing the background and medical screening, reference checks, and onboarding process. It is important to note that internal recruitments can be substantially different from external recruitments and may require less time to select, hire, and onboard the successful candidate; however, the recruitment should still be outlined thoroughly to ensure complete understanding.

Onboarding is the process of acclimating newly hired employees to an organization. Onboarding introduces employees to several essentials, including the company, culture, and products. Onboarding can last a few hours or a few days and can include introductions with executive leadership and the workgroup. These introductions can then provide new employees the opportunity to discuss the organization and begin the course of forming strong working relationships. One piece of onboarding is the **new employee orientation (NEO)**. The NEO includes relaying information to new employees about paychecks, direct deposit, benefits and retirement information, safety and workers' compensation programs, holidays, and other important information that new employees should have after beginning a job with a new organization. Onboarding should also include an opportunity to receive the tools and resources necessary for employees to complete their work. Laptops or desktop computers, phones, printers, and software should be provided with appropriate instruction so that employees can immediately begin to acclimate to the working environment. Studies have shown that when a robust onboarding process is implemented, employees are almost 70% more likely to stay with an organization for longer than three years.

Succession planning is the process of identifying required critical positions within an organization and determining if there is an internal talent pool to fill these positions in the future. Succession planning enables continuity of leadership, increases employee morale as it displays the organization's commitment to employees, and creates a culture of recognizing, developing, and retaining top leadership talent. Plans can show short- and long-term readiness and include specific, tailored training plans for individuals to ensure they are prepared when the opportunity is available. Succession planning is most effective when top leaders are involved, accountable, committed, and invested in the future. When employees see leadership engaged in this process, they are more likely to be committed to their professional development within the organization. While most organizations engage in the succession planning process for executive leadership, many organizations use this process to identify future opportunities for employees at lower leadership levels, such as department or team managers. Planning for these roles is as beneficial as planning for higher-level positions, and planning here can have an even more positive impact because the effects can be seen at all levels of the organization. Although a maintenance worker may not be aware of succession plans for the CEO, they definitely are aware of succession plans for their team manager and may even have opportunities to be considered for this role within the process.

Current Market Situation and Talent Pool Availability

The current market situation and the available talent pool are constantly evolving. Organizations must keep themselves informed about trends in several markets—industry, city, state, and country. Depending on the needs of the organization, it may be necessary to expand recruitment efforts into new markets. Market expansion assists by providing a larger applicant pool that is also more diverse. Locating qualified candidates is a common concern for any organization. Human resources professionals can assist with this issue by having an understanding of the immediate surrounding market as well as other opportune markets. Having knowledge of the educational programs, both collegiate and skilled trade, professional associations, and networking affiliations, recruiters can tap into the most appropriate areas to locate potential candidates. Establishing partnerships with these groups can allow for recruiters to have immediate insight and knowledge into potential talent pipelines that can feed directly the organization's applicant pools. Another resource to take advantage of is talent pool reports provided by agencies such as LinkedIn. These reports show the supply and demand of the prospective employees an organization is looking for and the demographics of these individuals.

One current area of concern is the talent pools for fields related to science, technology, engineering, and math (STEM). Efforts have been made to increase the number of women studying STEM fields and to increase the opportunities for these women. From specific marketing to government funding, concerted efforts are being made to increase participation in these fields. The future result will be more qualified applicants to hire in related positions. Another area of concern is the talent pools for skilled trades such as carpentry, machinery, and maintenance related fields including construction, electrical, plumbing, and heating and cooling. The shortage of skilled trades workers across the country is becoming more demanding as current workers are moving closer to retirement. Many organizations hiring skilled trades professionals are offering apprenticeship programs to new employees who have little to no experience. By offering incentives such as in-house training, professional development, career paths, and competitive wages and benefits, many organizations are meeting their recruitment needs through these efforts.

Human resources professionals can work with leadership to understand the organization's skill shortages and align those with the current labor surpluses. Using the same supply and demand principles as economics, organizations can work to fill the recruitment gaps and meet needs based on the current and potential available workforce. This is becoming harder to do in today's marketplace, but it is possible. The first step is to look at the incentives that allow potential candidates to consider working in certain fields. Incentives such as free training to learn a specific trade, sign-on bonuses, career advancement within a certain time frame, or educational reimbursements may entice an individual to consider a particular career. In some cases, the more creative the offer, the more potential applicants submit their credentials for consideration. By bringing in new employees with little to no experience, organizations can develop these individuals professionally and based on future needs, have experienced candidates in the pipeline to promote to new opportunities.

In order to fully understand prospective applicants and their needs, it is critical that human resources professionals and hiring managers be aware of generational differences in the talent pool. Many organizations have three to four generations working as employees at any given time, and each generation has different values, goals, motivators, and needs. Understanding this enables recruiters to gain a better understanding of how to incentivize individuals to consider some of the hard-to-fill positions as possible career choices. In general, the generations have distinct values and objectives. Baby boomers—individuals born between 1946 and 1964—value dedication, one-on-one time, and working in teams, and they are focused on the health and wellness of their family. Generation Xers—those born between 1965 and 1980—value work/life balance, independence, flexibility, experiences, and a global perspective. Generation Yers or millennials—individuals born between 1981 and 2000—value constant feedback, recognition, personal fulfillment, fun, happiness, advanced technology, and diversity. Generation Zers—those born after 2000—value equality, activism, collaboration, sustainability, and flexibility.

By looking at the needs of the organization and aligning these with the values of each generational dynamic, human resource professionals can create a plan to market and promote the available opportunities to each group of potential applicants. When marketing these opportunities, it is necessary to ensure multiple communication platforms. Generation Xers and Generation Zers will need different information. Organizations should adapt, using various communication methods to ensure that employees in each demographic receive the information they need. While a recruitment flyer posted to the corporate website may be the best way to communicate with a Generation X candidate, it may not be the best method for Generation Z candidate. Posting information on a social media platform such as Twitter or Instagram may be the better method for the Generation Z candidate.

The employment market will constantly evolve and change. While there is no way to know for sure how this will directly affect the talent pool, human resources professionals can stay informed about how the changing market and attempt to update recruitment plans to address this. Some of these changes may not result in a marked improvement in sourcing candidates; however, it is beneficial to continue to evolve recruitment strategies so that organizations can stay informed and show a willingness to adapt. Social media is a great example; recruitment trends in using social media platforms have changed substantially in the past few years. Research shows that in 2011, 56% of organizations used social media for recruiting; in 2015, this number increased to almost 90%. Organizations that evolve with current trends stay relevant with both passive and active job seekers and are more likely to be seen as potential employers. This is one way for an organization to maintain an active role in the talent pool that they are sourcing candidates.

Staffing Alternatives

There are two situations in which staffing alternatives are considered: employee surpluses and employee shortages. Each circumstance has unique challenges and human resources professionals can provide a wide array of options for management to consider. **Employee surpluses** occur when there is not enough work for all the employees, or when the number of employees is greater than needed. **Employee shortages** occur when there are not enough employees to perform all the work, or when the number of employees is less than needed. Some organizations have a naturally occurring business cycle and see both circumstances, depending on the time of year. If this type of business cycle occurs, an organization should familiarize itself with short-term options for both circumstances to allow employees the opportunity to adjust to the cycle. Some organizations see these changes, however, on a more permanent basis and must take more drastic long-term options to adjust the employee headcount to match the workload. The goal of any staffing alternative should be to minimize disruption to the organization, employees, and customers.

When the number of employees is greater than the number needed to perform the workload, an employee surplus can be dealt with on a short-term or long-term basis. Selected solutions should be thoroughly reviewed, including the benefits and drawbacks, before implementation. Short-term solutions to deal with employee surpluses can include the following:

- Freezing hiring activity and using attrition to manage employee headcount
- Reducing overtime opportunities
- Allowing volunteering employees to reduce their position to part-time
- Transferring work in to the department
- Reducing the work week to less than the standard 40 hours
- Temporarily shutting down operations or laying off employees for a period of time
- Approving excused absences, with or without pay
- Temporarily assigning employees to different positions within the organization
- Retraining or training employees to enhance their skill sets

Long-term solutions to deal with employee surpluses can include the following:

- Freezing hiring activity and using attrition to manage employee headcount
- Permanently transferring employees to different positions
- Permanently laying off employees
- Offering retirement incentives
- Retraining employees
- Transferring work in to the department

When the number of employees is less than the number needed to perform the workload, an employee shortage can be dealt with on a short-term or long-term basis. Selected solutions should be thoroughly reviewed, including the benefits and drawbacks, before implementation. Short-term solutions to deal with employee shortages can include the following:

- Increasing overtime opportunities
- Increasing subcontracts or outsourcing
- Increasing productivity and efficiency
- Offering vacation buybacks or holiday buybacks to decrease the amount of leave time taken
- Temporarily assigning employees to different positions where more employees are needed
- Temporarily hiring employees to assist with the workload until caught up
- Transferring work out of the department

Long-term solutions to deal with employee shortages can include the following:

- Issuing recalls or limiting production
- Increasing the recruitment efforts to hire more employees more frequently
- Permanently transferring employees to different positions
- Retraining employees to transfer to the hard-to-fill positions
- Transferring work out of the department

Some solutions for short-term and long-term are the same; they can be implemented for the length of time needed to adjust the employee headcount to the appropriate level. If certain short-term solutions do not achieve the results needed, additional solutions can be implemented or continued until the organization achieves the desired outcome. Human resources professionals should understand the demographics of the affected employees to propose the best solutions. While certain employees may not respond to a retirement incentive or a vacation buyback program, they may be susceptible to a change in overtime opportunities or a temporary assignment elsewhere in the organization. It may not be feasible to offer multiple solutions, but consideration should be given to offering more than one solution. Each employee is motivated by different factors, and having an understanding of this can assist when determining which options to implement.

Regardless of the circumstances that need to be addressed, leadership should be open with employees and communicate as much information as possible. It may not be appropriate to share all information due to confidentiality issues, but when leadership offers opportunities to communicate with employees, it can greatly affect the success of any program. The solutions listed above are not the only options. Employees may be able to assist leadership with new, creative, and innovative solutions that address the overall issue. Additionally, once the options are finalized and ready to implement, it is important to communicate the details of the options to the affected employees. Providing as much information as possible and an appropriate amount of time to adjust to the change is vital.

If options are afforded to employees, it is important to provide clear directions and instructions as to how employees can research their options and what needs to be done to select the option that works best for the individual. Engaged employees who feel valued, respected, and treated with integrity will be more open to working together to come up with solutions to solve any issue, including employee surpluses and shortages. Difficult times call for difficult decisions to be made but when leadership works together with employees, the circumstances can be less difficult for all involved. There will be times though that this collaboration and discussion is not possible and the leadership must make the best decision with the information at hand. When there is not an opportunity to openly communicate with employees about the process and discuss options, leadership should still strive to provide as much information as soon as possible. Leadership may have to choose the best solutions to implement to address the issue quickly. In these circumstances, it is still vital to communicate to employees the situation. Expedient communication works to minimize gossip, fear, and rumors. Human resources professionals can offer assistance and guidance to employees to help work through the impacts of the changes. Employee assistance programs (EAPs) can be an excellent resource in these situations, or individual coaches and counselors can be brought into the organization to help employees manage this change.

Interviewing and Selection

There are various styles and techniques of interviewing. It is important to have an understanding of each type of interview to ensure that most appropriate can be selected for each open position. Having the best and most appropriate technique applied to the interview process can help enhance the process and provide the hiring manager with the most beneficial insight to the candidates, allowing for the best selection to fill the position. Four common interviewing techniques are focus groups, in-depth interviews, dyads or triads, and paired interviews.

Focus groups are interviews that are primarily discussions, led by a moderator, that focus on the specific work and how this work affects the group present in the discussion. Focus groups are often defined as assessment centers. They generally last one to two hours, with the candidates working with the group to solve real issues and concerns of the job. Candidates are scored on their teamwork, innovation, communication, and other factors which allows the hiring manager to assess the most qualified candidate.

In-depth interviews are formal, one-on-one conversations that can last anywhere from a half hour to two hours or so. In-depth interviews can focus on the scope and range of the position, with questions being pointed and specific to certain issues the candidate has handled in their previous work or broader in definition as to the work ethic and prioritization of work tasks. In-depth interviews are meant to assess the chemistry and "fit" between the candidates and the hiring managers as well as gain an understanding for the candidate's experience and skills.

Dyads or triads are similar to in-depth interviews, but with two or three individuals, respectively. The individuals conducting the interview may be employees who will be working with the new individual. These interviews assess the chemistry and "fit" within the workgroup to gain an understanding of the team dynamic. The in-depth interviews, both with one individual or more, should be structured with the interview questions outlined and discussed prior to conducting the interview. All applicants should receive the same questions and afforded the same opportunities to discuss their experience and skills.

Paired interviews are consecutive interviews with two employees who will work with the new employee. This interview allows a joint opinion of how the applicants experience and skills will fit within the process and workflow.

All interviews techniques have benefits and drawbacks; human resources professionals should review the position to determine which technique is best suited. Ultimately, the interview technique that provides the most accurate information about the most qualified applicant should be the goal. Some recruitment processes incorporate multiple interview techniques—starting with an assessment center to narrow down the applicants, followed by a dyad interview with two senior level employees who work within the team, ended with an in-depth interview with the hiring manager. Each interview technique should be implemented in the same way with each applicant. Interview questions and process should be standardized and structured so that all applicants are afforded the same opportunity. Human resources professionals should work with the hiring manager early in the process to determine what assessments should be made during each step and what the interviewers should be looking for.

Another interviewing technique is to structure the applicant's responses. While many recruiters simply ask a question and allow an applicant to respond however they like, other recruiters provide a framework for each applicant. Applicants are provided with this structure at the beginning of the interview and are scored according to how they answer within this structure. A common interview technique to apply to applicant's responses is the STAR technique. **STAR** stands for Situation, Task, Action, Results. For each question asked, applicants should answer in the following format:

- Situation: provide the context and background of a situation, problem, or issue
- Task: describe the problem and challenges taken on to solve the problem
- Action: discuss and explain the steps taken to implement a solution
- Results: discuss the impact of the action(s) and what was learned

By engaging applicants in this way during the interview, interviewers can better assess the applicants' skills and behaviors. This allows better scoring of applicants, showing which qualified individuals should be forwarded on in the process. The STAR technique is commonly used to assess an applicant's actual behavior when faced with issues and problems. Past performance is an indicator of future performance, and by having applicants answer interview questions in this format, interviewers can gauge the behaviors that the applicant will bring to the table in the new role.

It is extremely important that interviewers be trained in these techniques and understand their role and responsibilities in the interview process. Most organizations request that existing employees participate in the interview process. However being a subject matter expert may not translate to knowledge of interviewing and applicant scoring. Human resources professionals should ensure that individuals who conduct the interview receive training—either in house or externally—in the fundamental techniques of interviewing. Interviewers should understand the interview structure and which questions are not allowed during the interview. Human resources professionals should be present as a participant or as a facilitator to ensure the interviews stay on track relative to time, questions, appropriateness, and structure.

Interviews should be structured so that applicants all receive the same opportunity; however, a recent trend gaining traction is providing applicants an open-ended panel interview. An **open-ended panel interview** is an interview with multiple individuals, such as an entire department or work group, that provides the applicant a certain time period to communicate to the group why they are the best candidate for the position. While there is no structure to this type of interview, it can be an excellent method to show certain specific skill sets such as quick thinking, communicating a clear message with little time to prepare, communicating to a large group while connecting with each individual, and being able to summarize a large amount of information. Leadership and management positions must have these characteristics, and this interview technique, although new, can be an excellent way to assess an applicant in a different way.

Applicant Tracking Systems

Applicant tracking systems (ATSs) are software applications that manage an organization's recruitment processes. These applications can track various components of the recruitment process, including hiring requests submitted, applications received, interviews scheduled, and offers extended. ATS applications also provide various reports specific to tracking recruitment information. Most organizations utilize an ATS to handle applications, resumes, and candidate data; however, some organizations may use a simple tool such as Microsoft Excel® or Access® to create a customized database. Some companies receive a large number of applications on a daily basis, and an ATS application can provide the capability to manage these applications efficiently. The ATS can perform initial screenings, separate qualified and unqualified candidates, and screen out candidates that do not have the required skill sets.

An ATS provides functionality in multiple areas such as applicant workflow, candidate communications, interview management, skills assessments and tests, background checks, and on-boarding. Human resources professionals manage the ATS for the organization, and, through the ATS, provide information specific to the recruitment process. Reports can include information such as how long it takes to fill a position from the initial request to the date of hire, the number of applications received, and the number of qualified candidates for each position. This information can assist in making decisions for future recruitments.

While most ATS applications are customized, the basic structure should incorporate the following:

- Search engine optimization
- Job posting distribution and resume collection
- Advanced candidate search
- Employee referral management
- Integration capabilities
- Robust candidate relationship management
- Advanced reporting and analytics

The ATS application should provide an organization with the specific tools required for their recruitment needs. Most ATS applications can be integrated into an organization's existing website. An example of a widely used ATS that is integrated into corporate websites is Taleo. Taleo offers the ability for the organization to incorporate all recruitment elements into the branding and culture of the organization. Once an organization has determined a recruitment need, the request, often referred to as a **requisition**, is submitted by the hiring department. The requisition is approved and the job posting is created and managed directly within the ATS. Job postings should include the complete description of work, including the scope, roles, responsibilities, examples of work, supervisory duties. Additionally, the job posting should indicate required qualifications, preferred qualifications, educational requirements, and previous experience necessary to be qualified for the consideration. Timeframes should be clearly communicated on the job description so that candidates understand when the posting will close. The ATS will publish the job description to the corporate website, job boards and other organizations as structured within the ATS platform. Organizations can also add supplemental questions for candidates to answer as part of the application process. Candidates who are interested in submitting an application are guided through a structured, customized, electronic process in which they can attach additional documentation or other information to be considered. After applications have been submitted, the ATS can be programmed to send out standard communications, such as receipt of the application and next steps. Once the application window has been closed, the ATS can then screen the applications to determine which candidates meet the qualifications and which do not. Their status can then be updated in the ATS, and, again, standard communications can be sent to candidates indicating the status of their application. Throughout all steps of the interview process, the ATS can facilitate screening and communication.

Organizations should implement an ATS that maximizes the recruitment process for the hiring managers, leadership, recruiters, and candidates. ATS applications that provide robust and expansive services offer benefits on a financial, operational, strategic, and technical level. Financial benefits can include increases in productivity, elimination of manual processes, and freeing up more time to focus on projects that improve profitability and achieving goals. Additionally, positions can typically be filled in less time, which can improve employee morale, customer service, and overall satisfaction. Organizations can see substantial costs when recruiting for and filling an open position. Costs, such as overtime to fill the opening, can add up to much more than anticipated. An effective ATS can assist in decreasing these costs by streamlining the process and reducing the time needed to fill an open position. Operational benefits can include having a standardized and automated recruitment process, providing advanced reports and statistics, and identifying continuous improvement opportunities. By having a standardized process, organizations implement the same hiring practices across all positions. This is highly recommended by the Equal Employment Opportunity Commission (EEOC) and can dramatically reduce the risk of discrimination in hiring. Strategic benefits can include improved compliance with regulations, having access to larger, diverse, and highly qualified candidate pools which results in highly qualified new hires, providing an excellent candidate recruitment experience, and increasing the employment brand with prospective employees. Technical benefits can include minimizing information technology support when using a web-based system as well as affording unlimited data storage to maintain the records. Additionally, by maximizing the technical capabilities of the ATS application, organizations may see opportunities to re-purpose resources that are now available.

An effective ATS can also enhance the candidate experience throughout the recruitment process, potentially resulting in an immediate effect on the new employee and a commitment to the organization. **Candidate experience** refers to the feelings, behaviors, and attitudes a job candidate faces when they interact with a hiring manager and organization during the recruitment process. Candidate experience begins with the organization's webpage, job description, and initial information available to prospective employees. Studies show that candidate experience is vital to an organization's recruitment efforts. Over 90% of candidates are more likely to apply for future positions if they have a positive candidate experience. Almost 100% of candidates who had a positive recruitment experience would refer others to apply for employment. Almost 90% of candidates with a positive recruitment experience would purchase the products manufactured or sold by the organization. Over 50% of candidates with a positive experience would communicate with their social networks about the experience. Even seasoned marketing professionals with a targeted advertising campaign could not have this kind of reach. With potential talent pool shortages and hiring challenges, organizations cannot afford to lose highly qualified applicants due to a bad candidate experience that is announced over a social media platform.

Impact of Total Rewards on Recruitment and Retention

Total rewards is defined as the financial and non-financial rewards package that an organization offers to its employees. Financial rewards include, but are not limited to, salary, bonuses, specialty pay, overtime, and benefits such as medical insurance, retirement, and paid time off. Non-financial rewards include, but are not limited to, performance management, training opportunities, excellent working environments, work/life balance programs, and career growth and enhancement. Offering a robust total rewards package has a substantial impact on recruitment and retention, by enticing applicants to apply and join an organization to keeping employees fulfilled and more likely to stay with an organization.

Total rewards can affect an organization's recruitment in various ways. With a robust total rewards package, an organization can attract candidates who are highly qualified, bringing with them the values, skills, knowledge, and abilities that most closely match the hiring need. Candidates can assess an organization's commitment to employees and the cultural dynamics of the organization by the strength of the total rewards offered. An organization's website should clearly describe all rewards offered to employees. This enables applicants to review the information prior to submitting an application for consideration. After a candidate is selected to receive an offer of employment, the organization should provide a complete and thorough informational packet to the potential new hire. This information should include full details of all programs offered. Details should include information such as vacation and sick leave accruals and rollover information, a calendar with the list of approved and paid holidays, and medical insurance plan options, costs, and coverage. The more information that is provided to an individual who is considering an employment offer, the better and more informed their decision can be.

Total rewards can impact an organization's retention in various ways. A robust total rewards package that is flexible and evolving can motivate employees to reach new goals and objectives within their position and career. Organizations should ensure that the total rewards offered to employees continue to be the most appropriate and cost effective, and that they meet the needs of as many employees as possible. Individual needs change as personal circumstances change, and an organization should make an effort to ensure that various programs and benefits options are available to meet current and future needs. Additionally, it is important to continually communicate with employees to ensure they are aware of programs—both current programs and new programs being introduced. An organization should take a proactive approach to assessing the effectiveness of the total rewards program. From assessing the amount of compensation offered for each position to determining if additional insurance plans should be considered, human resources should be aware of all possible options to consider. A benefit survey can help ensure that the most appropriate benefits are offered to an employee population. Such a survey enables employees to provide feedback on how current programs meet their needs and if there are other programs to consider that would meet employee needs in a better way. Having information directly from employees can assist human resources in making the best recommendations for programs to offer. Additionally, this method makes employees a part of the process of designing the total rewards for the organization. This involvement and engagement can increase employment satisfaction and lead to better employee retention.

An excellent best practice for human resources professionals to incorporate into a training program is to have a robust new employee orientation (NEO) to review all programs offered as well as an annual training session to review all programs and any potential changes. An excellent time of year to conduct these annual sessions is during open enrollment. **Open enrollment** is the time frame during the year in which employees are able to make changes to their benefits such as medical insurance. By ensuring employees have updated, accurate, and timely information about benefit programs, an organization can take an active role in retaining employees versus being reactive when employees leave the organization. Human resources should also be available to meet with employees as needed to discuss programs that are needed at specific times. While a new employee may not need information about pregnancy disability leaves during the NEO, it may be needed later during their employment. Being able to offer this information at the time when it is needed is important to ensure employees are informed and understand the programs offered and available.

Communication is the key in all aspects of recruitment and retention, especially regarding total rewards. There are numerous components to total rewards, each ranging in various levels of complexity. Additionally, because each employee values programs differently, it is important to be clear, concise, and thorough when communicating. Incorporating various methods of communication ensures that all employees receive the same information in a manner that is specific to their style and needs. From in-person meetings, print communications such as brochures, emails and memos, online portals, social media, and training sessions, human resources can incorporate multiple modes of communication as necessary. An important factor to consider when implementing a communication plan is the differing employee demographics within the organization. Many organizations have multiple generations as a part of the workforce and each learns differently. Some employees may want a flyer with contact information whereas other employees may want an online portal to find the information as it is needed. Human resources should incorporate various methods of communication and offer in-person meetings to discuss employee's individual needs. Employees can provide information as to their personal circumstances so that human resources professionals can ensure all information is provided and understood. Many organizations have a third-party administrator deliver certain programs such as voluntary insurance programs or employee assistance programs. **Employee assistance programs** (EAPs) are a non-financial reward that provides confidential services at no cost to employees, helping them to deal with challenges of everyday life. EAPs can assist with family counseling, legal discussions, reducing stress and conflict, and many other challenges. Having representatives from these companies offer to meet with employees in person is also a great way to ensure employees are informed and understand the benefits offered.

Testing Processes and Procedures

Many organizations implement testing procedures in the recruitment process to ensure candidates meet the required qualifications for a position. Depending on the position, certain tests may assist the hiring manager in determining which applicant best fits the needs of the organization. There are numerous examinations that an organization can incorporate into the hiring process, including the following:

- General knowledge
- General intelligence or IQ
- Personality
- English proficiency
- Second language proficiency
- Technical or mechanical proficiency
- Cognitive ability
- Reasoning
- Quantitative ability
- Physical ability

The examination selected should be appropriate for the position, such as a typing test for an administrative office position, a personality test for a senior leadership position, or a physical ability test for a law enforcement officer.

A general knowledge test shows an applicant's knowledge in certain areas that relate specifically to the open position. A typing test allows applicants to be scored in their specific ability related to their typing skills including the number of words per minute, number of errors and time needed to make corrections, and certain formatting techniques. General knowledge tests can also be specific to the subject of the position to ensure the applicants have the knowledge and understanding required of the position. A skills test that shows an applicant's expertise in how to create complete spreadsheets, pivot charts, or formulas would be appropriate for accounting positions that use Microsoft Excel® frequently.

A general intelligence test, or IQ test, shows how quickly an applicant can process complex problems with the information provided. These tests can also examine how applicants process available information, determine next steps, gather new information, formulate conclusions, and provide solutions and recommendations.

A personality test shows the type of personality of each applicant. The Myers-Briggs Type Indicator (MBTI) is the most common and widely used personality test. It assesses eight dimensions: extroverts or introverts, sensors or intuitives, thinkers or feelers, judgers or perceivers. From these eight dimensions, sixteen separate personality styles emerge in the MBTI method. After answering a series of questions, individuals can be provided with an assessment of their personality, which can be highly useful when constructing a team. This information can assist the team in understanding each other better, resulting in a cohesive, functional team. The MBTI test is an excellent tool to incorporate into the recruitment process when hiring high-level executives, and it can also be an excellent tool to assist current employees in working better within a team.

An English proficiency test is one that shows an applicant's knowledge and understanding of the English language. This test is useful for recruitments in communications or marketing as these applicants will be writing, speaking, and communicating on multiple platforms. Assessing applicants in their proficiency of the use of language, grammar, syntax, and parallel writing can be helpful in determining the most qualified candidate for positions that require this skill set. The ability to speak multiple languages is becoming a more sought-after skill set, and if an organization has a need for a second language in a particular, it may be appropriate to provide a language proficiency test for the second language.

A technical or mechanical proficiency test is one that focuses on an applicant's ability in handling tools, machinery, equipment, or other specialized components. These tests are effective in assessing applicants' ability and knowledge in positions such as maintenance, construction, carpentry, plumbing, or other specialized fields. If a position requires this knowledge, it is appropriate for an organization to initiate a test to score applicants on their knowledge to ensure the most qualified applicant is selected for the opening.

A cognitive ability test assesses an applicant's mental abilities in both verbal and non-verbal skills, memory, and speed of processing information. This test includes a series of questions that include puzzles, remembering certain details, and solving complex problems. Applicants receive scores in their ability to reason, solve problems, and learn strategies. These tests are commonly used in standardized testing for students in multiple grades throughout their education experience. These tests are also popping up on social media, encouraging users to complete them and share their scores.

A reasoning test allows an organization to assess an applicant pool based on how they determine the right answers to a problem after receiving a situation and a number of certain conditions. Having knowledge of how an applicant thinks allows the hiring manager to understand how the applicant would work through specific issues that they will face in their role.

A quantitative ability test specifically assesses an applicant's ability to process numbers. These tests provide applicants with a series of number problems to solve. Some of these tests are timed to determine how quickly applicants process and solve the problems. These tests are excellent sources of information for applicants in areas such as accounting, actuarial, and other math-focused positions.

A physical ability test scores applicants based on their physical ability specific to the position. These tests should be standardized with minimum passing requirements. Common elements of a physical ability test include running a mile, sprinting 40 meters, and doing pushups, pull ups, and sit ups in a specific time frame. Generally each element is given a pass or fail score, and if the candidate fails one element, he or she is dismissed from further consideration. Applicants who pass all elements of the physical ability test will then be ranked based on the best scores in each category. These tests are specific to positions that require physical ability as a qualification of the position. Law enforcement officers, fire fighters, personal trainers, and security officers are examples of positions that should require a physical ability test.

Employment tests must be directly related to the open position. Regardless of the employment test used to assess the knowledge, skills, and abilities of applicants, it is important to have a standardized test that assess all applicants fairly and equitably.

Verbal and Written Offers and Contracts

When extending an offer of employment to a candidate, it is important to have as much information available to ensure a complete discussion. A best practice is to have all information available that will be written into the final job offer or contract. Additionally, understanding which items can be negotiated is also important. This allows both parties an understanding of where flexibility is available in the offer. Suppose a particular item is not negotiable, such as when eligibility for health insurance starts. If the candidate asks about negotiating this item, the human resources professional can tell them there is no flexibility to negotiate it. This allows for a more efficient and productive conversation about the offer of employment. Extending a verbal offer with these details can allow for discussion and negotiation, resulting in a final and formal offer extension in the form of an offer letter or official contract.

An offer of employment should include the following items, if appropriate based on the position:

- Job title and summary of position
- Base salary and bonus potential
- Fair Labor Standards Act (FLSA) status and overtime eligibility, if applicable
- Benefits, including all insurance offered with eligibility and leave accruals
- Additional benefits if appropriate, including relocation and signing bonus
- Miscellaneous allowances such as car, phone, and clothing
- Probation terms, if any
- Contingency terms such as medical screenings and background checks
- Supervisor and reporting relationships
- Start date, work schedule, and weekly hours
- Location, work environment such as dress code, and company culture
- Growth and professional development opportunities
- Acceptance terms including consideration time and a date to officially accept
- Direct contact for additional questions

If an employee is receiving an official employment contract, it may be necessary to include additional items. These could include non-complete clauses, confidentiality or non-disclosure agreements, severance terms, copyright and trademark ownership, and other specific terms negotiated between the organization and candidate. Additional items such as the annual calendar showing holidays and days off, company newsletters and articles, health insurance availability, and other information should be provided as well. It is also important to communicate escalating benefits as well. **Escalating benefits** are benefits that increase over time, based on length of employment time. An example of this would be that a new employee accrues eight hours of paid time off for each month worked; once the employee reaches five years of service, this increases to twelve hours of paid time off.

Salary negotiation is the beginning of the employment relationship. There are generally four stages of negotiation:

- Preparation
- Exchanging information
- Bargaining
- Closing and commitment

Depending on the discussions, it may be necessary to navigate back to exchanging information after bargaining to ensure both parties on the same page throughout the process.

Four Stages of Negotiation

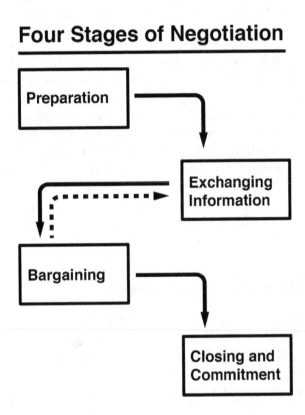

Items that may be appropriate to negotiate are base salary, bonus potential, leave accruals or receiving a balance of hours immediately upon hire, miscellaneous allowances, start date, work schedule, and potentially other items that a candidate requests to incorporate into the offer. It is important to have an understanding of which items are negotiable, along with the level of flexibility for each item. To expedite hiring, it may be appropriate during the verbal process to allow the individual extending the offer to agree to the candidate's counteroffer immediately. The organization may want a consolidated and complete list of the counteroffer to determine which, if any, items will be considered and potentially agreed upon. Once there is a verbal agreement of the terms and conditions, a formal letter should be prepared to detail all the agreed upon items. It is important to note that some organizations may prefer to prepare an initial offer letter and then rescind and redraft a new, updated offer letter. This new offer letter would include the newly agreed upon terms and conditions after negotiation. Having thorough documentation of the employment terms at each step of the offer and negotiation process may be more appropriate based on the organization and the position. Offer letters or contracts should be signed by the organization's hiring authority. The offer letter or contract should also include a section indicating that the individual agrees to the terms and conditions of the offer with their signature and date.

A common and successful salary negotiation technique is summarized as the five P's: proper preparation prevents poor performance. This technique is can be used by the hiring manager and recruiter as well as the candidate to assist with the negotiations process. Being properly prepared for the upcoming negotiations will result in successful outcomes for all parties. Prior to extending the offer of employment, it is important to be prepared with an understanding of why certain terms are being offered, specifically, the proposed salary amount. In general, most candidates are interested in this piece of information and will ask questions about how this amount was determined. Having an understanding of the qualifications required for the position, the specific experience of the candidate, and growth opportunity within the position are all excellent pieces of information that can be used to convey how the salary offer was calculated. Additionally, communicating the salary range can allow the candidate insight as to the growth opportunity within this position. This information can also assist the candidate when considering a counteroffer.

The goal in extending employment offers and negotiations is for all parties to be satisfied with the terms. The organization, hiring manager, recruiter, and candidate all have different needs and perspectives regarding what constitutes a successful offer negotiation. Depending on how the discussions progress however, it may be appropriate to end negotiations and formally rescind the initial offer of employment if the candidate's requests are unreasonable or inappropriate. During these circumstances, understanding which items are negotiable and the flexibility for each can assist in making the decision to end the negotiation discussions. For example, if the candidate requests to negotiate a different job title and responsibilities or a salary outside of the range established for the position, it may be appropriate to end the negotiations. Once an offer of employment has been negotiated and agreed upon by both parties, documents have been updated and signed, and a formal agreement is in place, the organization's focus should shift to an onboarding mentality and bringing in the new employee to the workplace culture and environment.

New-Hire Employee Orientation Processes and Procedures

New employee orientation (NEO) is the first formal experience that an individual has as an employee with an organization. An NEO is part of the overall onboarding process that is initiated when an employee joins an organization. The NEO can range from a few hours to several days of initiation into the new organization. In addition to showing employees their new workspace, restrooms, exits, and the breakroom or lunch area, the NEO should cover several main areas of focus:

- Organization overview
- Human resources basics
- Health and safety
- Policies and procedures

The organization overview should discuss the corporate mission and vision, company history, executive management, and organizational structure. Employees should gain an understanding of where their position is located in the overall hierarchy of the organization. Additionally, separate locations should be identified and a complete directory provided.

Human resources basics should also be provided to new employees immediately upon hire. These basics include a complete tour of the corporate intranet. The **corporate intranet** is the internal website provided only to employees; it includes an employee portal for access to information such as medical information and summary plan descriptions, change forms for personal contact information and beneficiaries, policies and procedures, and important information. Some organizations incorporate the payroll portal into the corporate intranet; other organizations maintain a separate payroll portal. During NEO, employees should receive a full tutorial about the payroll system. This tutorial should provide training in how to submit a timecard, request leave time, and, if the manager is a supervisor, how to approve timecards and leave requests. Employees should receive an overview of the paycheck to explain compensation, deductions, and other information provided on the paystub. Employees should also know how to access leave accruals and request time off. Employees should also receive all paperwork necessary to enroll in benefits such as health insurance, life insurance, deferred compensation and retirement programs, and union membership, if needed. Employees should have a full understanding of the deadlines for returning these documents to ensure enrollments can be completed. Other items such as signing up for direct deposit, finalizing new hire paperwork such the I-9, and taking a formal picture for the corporate directory should be conducted during the NEO.

Health and safety also constitute an area of focus that should be discussed at length to ensure new employees are aware of and understand the organization's policies and procedures. Health and safety items include the workers' compensation program, workplace injuries, personal medical leaves, and safety policies should be reviewed in depth. Procedures such as reporting a workplace injury, applying for a personal medical leave, understanding the safety protocols specific to the organization and the position, and knowing evacuation plans for the location are important pieces of information that all new employees should be aware. Policies and procedures should be thoroughly reviewed and a copy of the employee handbook provided. Many organizations request employees complete and sign an acknowledgement form to indicate that the handbook has been received, read, and understood. Policies and procedures such as sexual harassment, workplace violence, harassment, performance management, and other significant policies should be discussed at length during the NEO.

If the new employee is a supervisor or manager, additional time should be spent orienting the employee to this specific role. New supervisors should receive an informational report about the employees who will be directly supervised. Standard information such as job title and duties, salary, and seniority can be provided as well. Approving timecards, leave requests, and running reports are standard job responsibilities for supervisors. Performance evaluations are also standard job responsibilities for new supervisors, as are providing an overview of the documents used, timeframes necessary for providing the evaluations, and resources available for performance management.

A new employee needs a lot of information. Therefore an NEO best practice is to break up the information into blocks or sessions. This allows the employee to absorb the information in a more complete way and ensures a higher retention rate. The four main areas discussed above may be broken down into separate blocks offered on multiple days or provided in one long session. Additionally, new employees should receive a tour of the workplace, including other locations if appropriate, introductions to the team and other employees, and a list of local resources such as local restaurants, coffee shops, post office, banks, gyms, and other amenities. If local businesses offer discounts, specials, or incentives to employees, this information should also be provided.

Some organizations provide a mentor or buddy to new employees during the NEO. The mentor is responsible for going to lunch with the new employee, meeting informally to discuss the organization and answer questions, and in general be a resource and friendly face to the new employee. Depending on the working relationship between the new employee and mentor, it may be appropriate for the mentor to bring the new employee along to meetings or other events that would be helpful and informational. Depending on the size of the organization and resources available, multiple mentors may be assigned to allow for various viewpoints. Assigning a mentor from different departments such as payroll, information technology, human resources, customer service, and the hiring department can provide insight to the internal operations, lending to a more informed employee.

Finally, it is a best practice for human resources to schedule frequent NEO follow-up discussions with the new employee. Some organizations schedule these discussions for 30 days, 60 days, and 90 days following the start date. These discussions allow for specific questions that a new employee may realize were not addressed during the original NEO. New employees should be aware of the resources available through human resources and the mentor assigned during NEO. If an employee has a specific question due to a certain life event or for information, human resources should be available to meet on an as-needed basis to ensure employees have the information needed at the time it is needed.

Internal Workforce Assessments

Organizations must be strategic when assessing the workforce to ensure readiness and preparedness for both expected and unexpected staffing changes. Workforce assessments should be holistic, thorough, and broad in scope to ensure planning is as effective as possible. While forecasting is basically a guess, if a robust process is defined and supported with data, these guesses can be useful and in many cases accurate in addressing the organizational needs. Workforce planning should include a series of steps to ensure all available information is utilized in this process.

The first step in the workforce planning process is to understand the business objectives and goals and translate them into personnel needs. Every action taken or program implemented should be directly or indirectly aligned with the business objectives and goals. The work that employees complete is directly aligned with the organization's accomplishments. It is vital to understand how this work is being done and if opportunities are available to increase efficiency and productivity. An excellent tool in assessing the gaps within the personnel needs is a SWOT analysis: Strengths, Weaknesses, Opportunities, Threats. Strengths and weaknesses are usually internal factors, and opportunities and threats are usually external factors. Regardless, this information can be used to determine where resources are available, are needed, and should be deployed relative to personnel needs.

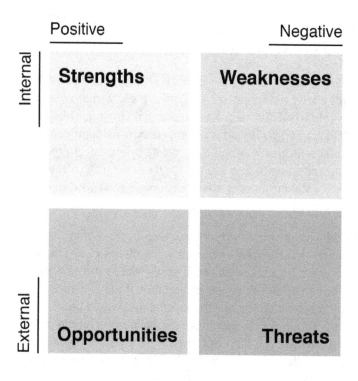

The second step in the workforce planning process is to analyze data. Gathering various pieces of information and analyzing the data will help to provide a complete and holistic view of the organization's personnel needs—both currently and in the near future. Employee demographics, staffing levels, skill mix, turnover trends, retirement opportunities, assumed growth, and available talent pools are all vital pieces of information that can be used to identify the risks and concerns to be addressed. If the majority of the employee population is eligible to retire within the next three years, it is vital that steps be taken immediately to ensure there is an internal talent pool with the necessary training to accept internal promotions. Additionally, understanding the external talent pool is also vital to ensure that any recruitment needs not met by internal promotions can be met by external hires. Engaging in partnerships with trade schools, universities, professional organizations, or other networks for internships, mentoring, or job training can assist an organization in preparing the external talent pool for future recruitment needs. It is important to note that employee demographics in the context of workforce planning should include more information than is available in a standard system report. While standard information such as years of service, current position and department, former positions and departments, and salary information is important, additional information should be gathered to understand the complete picture of employee demographics. This information should include the following:

- Highest degree received
- Special certifications
- Total years of experience
- Total years of supervisory experience
- Special skills
- Computer software and program proficiency
- Recognition and awards received
- Performance review history

By obtaining and reviewing this information, human resources can conduct a robust assessment of the workforce, and human resources will be able to better assess any skills gaps. This will then enable training and development programs to be implemented to provide the current workforce with growth opportunities or for a specific recruitment plan to be deployed to recruit candidates with the specific skills needed.

The third step in the workforce planning process is to assess the organization's current recruitment and retention practices. This step includes identifying short-term and long-term risks of recruitment and retention. The data gathered in the second step of the process can be further reviewed to ensure that hiring practices identify the strongest, most qualified candidates. Reviewing recruitment timeframes and the number of days that positions remain unfilled can assist the organization in determining new strategies and methods.

The fourth step in the workforce planning process is to recommend and implement programs to address any risks and concerns identified. Training programs, professional development opportunities, external candidate sourcing, and other programs may be necessary to address the current and future needs of the workforce. If an organization sees that a majority of high-level management will be eligible to retire in the next three years, it may be appropriate to work with an educational program to deliver an on-site degree program in management, leadership, or other appropriate fields. Understanding the program and the details such as cost, resources needed, interest, and time required to implement should be a part of the proposal for consideration.

The fifth and final step in the workforce planning process is to prioritize and adjust programs based on the actual results. Once the recommended programs have been implemented, metrics should be developed and reviewed on a reasonable basis to determine the success of each. Certain programs may take longer to see a level of success and this should be taken into account when reviewing the data. If a program is not meeting the required milestones and delivering the results anticipated, discussions should determine whether it is necessary to implement an immediate change or course correction. It may be necessary to end a particular program if there are no reasonable results that justify the expenditure of resources.

Organizations that implement a strong workforce planning process are more likely to see the following benefits, which also yield benefits:

- Readily available talent pool
- Optimized employee investments
- Protected historical knowledge

Organizations that have an available talent pool of candidates have shorter recruitment periods, filling open positions faster. This talent pool can be formed by both internal and external candidates. Having an understanding of the current employee dynamics, as addressed in the second step above, human resources can regularly determine the talent pool of employees who have promotional or advancement opportunity. Organizations that optimize employee investments in areas such as training, growth, and development realize lower turnover and increased employee morale. Employees that feel valued and supported are more likely to remain with an organization. Organizations that protect the historical knowledge of their employees are more likely to be able to address the impact of employee retirements. Creating programs and tools that facilitate the transfer of knowledge are best practices that should be incorporate at all levels within an organization. All these benefits provide costs savings to the organization, increase employee morale, and ensure staffing needs are properly met.

Transition Techniques for Corporate Restructuring, Mergers and Acquisitions, Due Diligence Processes, Offshoring, and Divestitures

Organizations experience change often. Whether the change is due to restructuring, mergers and acquisitions, divestitures, expansions, or outsourcing, each change should be accompanied by a full due diligence process and a communications plan. **Due diligence** is an audit or investigation conducted by an organization of the changes being considered. Due diligence should include reviews of multiple facets including legal, financial, process, operations, products, consumers, information technology, human resources, and department functions. Each area will be impacted by a transition change and it is important to understand the impacts prior to implementing any change. This will ensure that each impact is fully vetted and liabilities can be minimized. A **communications plan** is the complete plan for all communications that should be delivered, when, and to whom. Multiple platforms may be appropriate including in-person meetings to deliver the same message to multiple employees, written memos or question and answer documents, and frequent updates via email. Each platform should be appropriate to the message and its importance.

Human resources has a key role in the due diligence process with the specific focus being the employees of the organization. Human resources serves as a business partner to senior leadership in the following areas:

- Identify human resource management risks
- Establish appropriate resolutions and options to mitigate the risks

- Determine costs associated with employment changes such as severance
- Assess the organizational structure
- Assess the human resource management process

By fully vetting each of these areas during the due diligence process, senior leadership can make the best, most informed decision possible. Once the decision has been made, this information will also lend to a well-planned workforce transition strategy. This strategy should address all possible personnel actions, including changes in position, supervision and leadership, compensation and benefits, transfers, or layoffs. Fully vetted and well planned strategies will assist in the transition by providing the following:

- Fair treatment of all employees impacted by the change
- Strong commitment to the transition
- Transfer of critical knowledge and process
- Minimal disruption to the customer
- Stability to _____ ~th transition for employees
- Effective t_____ ~os and procedures for employees

The goal of any t_____ and insecurity for employees, customers,
investors, or ver_____ that communications are accurate,
timely, and tarc_____ iors, misunderstandings, and
misperception

In order for l_____ issues related to a transition, it is
important t_____ individual processes change and
transition c_____ h step of managing change can assist
employee_____ sition successfully. There are two main
phases o_____ efore the transition, individuals who receive
the new_____ ty, shock, resistance, fear, anger, frustration,
confusi_____ ough new stages of emotion while processing
and ac_____ after the transition are creativity, skepticism,
accep_____ ch stage of emotion and the time that it takes
to ac_____ dual. Being understanding and offering resources
for_____ enefit to the organization. This allows employees
to_____ their current position and accept the new
cha_____ practice that many organization implement during
time_____ ugh an employee assistance program (EAP). EAP
servic_____ cessible materials, an on-site counselor that
commu_____ ws for one-on-one sessions. Communicating the EAP
services_____ during the transition may be an excellent starting point
to the co

Individuals_____ cultural, personal, and behavioral changes in others. This
can quickly_____ misunderstandings if not addressed immediately. While
many details a_____ in points in time, it is vital to begin communicating with
employees as soon as app_____ will understand that some details may not be appropriate
to share, but they will appreciate the_____ ation taking a proactive approach in communicating. The
most important technique, one that should be incorporated early and often, is communication. Being
open and honest, even if there are details that cannot be provided or questions that cannot be answered,
is key to the communications plan. Outlining steps within the communication plan, including when

meetings will be held, memos distributed, and individual opportunities for discussions will assist the senior leadership with employees and gain support for assisting with the transition. This support will lead to a more successful transition for the organization and individual employees. An important element to consider when drafting communications for written memos, presentations, or other formats is that the writer or senior leadership is not the audience of the message. Understanding this element and the fact that employees at various levels of the organization may require a different level of information, it is important to tailor the message to the individuals receiving the message. It may be appropriate to employ a communications professional to ensure that messages are clear, concise, tailored, and specific to those receiving the message. Another practice that organizations can incorporate into the communications plan is to identify champions for each department or area of the organization. The champions are responsible for communicating the approved messages to employees and collecting or answering questions that arise during the meeting. The champions would be available when needed and assist employees working through the stages of emotion when dealing with the upcoming changes. Communicating early, frequently, openly, and honestly can make a substantial difference in how employees process and work through a transition that could have extensive and significant impacts.

Assessing Past and Future Staffing Effectiveness

A dashboard that clearly communicates metrics and provides an overview of effectiveness is an excellent tool to show the effectiveness of a staffing program. Additionally, it is important to convey how the staffing program is aligned with the overall human resources program. Basic information can be incorporated into the dashboard, such as total salary, average salary, average age, average years of service, total headcount, turnover rate, absenteeism rate, new hires, and the number of employees who left the organization. These are all important pieces of information that tell the story of the organization. Dashboards are typically updated on a quarterly basis. Configuring each dashboard to show particular periods of time then enables an organization to display informational trends to indicate success or opportunities. Each program in human resources can also have a separate dashboard for their metrics.

Multiple metrics can be used to measure staffing effectiveness. Organizations should select metrics that are appropriate and effective for their specific needs. Metrics should also be selected for which the data can be obtained without a substantial undertaking or extensive resources. There are four primary areas that metrics should focus on:

- Cost
- Timeliness
- Outcomes
- Reactions

Metrics should be focused in each of these areas to convey the effectiveness of staffing elements such as the overall staffing system, recruiting, selection, final match, and retention. Any metric implemented should be measured against specific targets so that success against the target can be determined.

Staffing systems can be evaluated for effectiveness by incorporating the following metrics:

- Cost: staffing budget including actual expenditures, staffing-to-employee ratios, and staffing expenses for full-time hires

- Timeliness: amount of time to respond to requests

- Outcomes: evaluation of employee readiness for achieving objectives

- Reactions: communication and satisfaction with services

Recruiting can be evaluated for effectiveness by incorporating the following metrics:

- Cost: advertising budget including actual expenditures and cost per applicant
- Timeliness: recruits per week, month, or quarter based on actual hiring needs
- Outcomes: number of recruits
- Reactions: quality of applicants

Selection can be evaluated for effectiveness by incorporating the following metrics:

- Cost: test costs per candidate, interview expenses, and cost per candidate
- Timeliness: time to hire and days to fill
- Outcomes: competence and workforce diversity
- Reactions: candidate quality and satisfaction with tests

Final match can be evaluated for effectiveness by incorporating the following metrics:

- Cost: training costs per hire and cost per hire

- Timeliness: number of days to start and time-to-perform

- Outcomes: number of positions filled and job performance after 30 days, 90 days, 6 months, and one year

- Reactions: new employee satisfaction

Retention can be evaluated for effectiveness by incorporating the following metrics:

- Cost: exit interview expenses and replacement costs
- Timeliness: amount of time to response to external offers
- Outcomes: voluntary separation rate, involuntary separation rate, and overall attrition rate
- Reactions: employee job satisfaction

An organization should select the metrics appropriate to the story being told about the program. Some staffing dashboards call out specific items that are important to the organization and dive into more detail for others. A recruitment funnel is a specific metric that shows the number of overall applicants who progress to each step of the recruitment process, beginning with the application, progressing to the phone screen and then the on-site interview, and finalizing the offer and eventual hire.

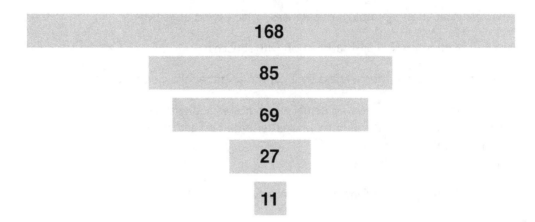

Three other specific metrics that some organizations choose to include in the staffing dashboard are the application sources, the decline reasons, and the pipeline efficiency of hiring. The application sources metric provides the main areas where applicants locate a job posting and then apply for the open position. This metric also shows the number of applicants hired from these sources. This metric allows the organization to pinpoint the most effective sources and dedicate additional resources in order to source more qualified candidates. The decline reasons metric provides the main reasons that applicants are disqualified or declined from consideration. This metric allows the organization to pinpoint areas that could be improved or clarified to ensure qualified candidates are applying for the open positions. Changing the language in a job description may be the solution needed to ensure candidates are receiving the most accurate information about the position and its qualifications. The pipeline efficiency of hiring metric shows the average number of days taken for each stage in the process as well as the overall process. Each step of the recruitment process is broken down in this metric to show where the process is slowing down and taking more time. Screening applications, conducting phone screens, initiating in-person interviews, interviewing with the hiring manager, extending the offer, and hiring the new employee are all steps in the process that can be viewed as separate timeframes as well as one larger overall timeframe. This metric shows the organization where efficiencies can be gained within the process.

Organizations review staffing data from an organization-wide viewpoint to show the effectiveness of the entire program. Many organizations also present staffing data from a department-wide perspective to communicate with department directors and managers specific to their hiring needs. Having departmental breakdowns of this information also allows human resources to identify areas that need additional focus or change in direction to meet the specific staffing needs of each area. The Finance department may meet all their staffing needs through advertising with a specific website; however, the maintenance department may meet all their staffing needs through career centers and jobs events. Each department and position may require a different recruitment plan to reach and attract qualified candidates for the open positions. By reviewing this data, human resources is able to pinpoint areas that can be improved or areas that are effective. Understanding the status and results of implemented is the primary reason to track this information. Without an understanding of where the issue actually lies, it is impossible to accurately determine the best course of action to recommend. By using data to locate issues and make decisions, human resources professionals can implement solutions to increase the effectiveness of the program.

Using data allows human resources professionals to provide solutions to actual issues rather than guessing and hoping a solution works. Implementing effective solutions that result in meeting the needs of the hiring department and the organization is the ultimate goal of human resources. Dashboards are an important and highly useful tool that can result in effective solutions.

Practice Questions

1. _____ describes the situation when policies or practices affect one specific group of individuals.
    a. Nepotism
    b. Artificial recruitment barrier
    c. Disparate impact
    d. Recruitment

2. Which of the following relationships would be a potential violation of a standard nepotism policy? (Select all answers that apply.)
    a. Sibling
    b. Neighbor
    c. Spouse
    d. Parent

3. Which of the following statements accurately describes sourcing methods in a recruitment process? (Select all answers that apply.)
    a. Sourcing methods should ensure that recruitments are fair and equitable.
    b. Employee referral programs are an excellent way to source candidates and engage current employees in the recruitment process
    c. Job boards and social media platforms are the only method to fully engage potential applicants.
    d. Sourcing methods should afford all qualified candidates the same opportunity for consideration.

4. Drop and drag the talent acquisition lifecycle steps in the appropriate order:
    a. Assess candidates with tests or interviews   1.
    b. Source candidates and assess the talent pool   2.
    c. Offer employment and orient new employee   3.
    d. Conduct further screening   4.
    e. Determine the hiring needs of the department   5.

5. _____ prohibits discrimination in employment based on race, color, sex, religion, national origin, age, disability, pregnancy, or genetic information.
    a. Genetic Information Nondiscrimination Act (GINA)
    b. Age Discrimination in Employment Act (ADEA)
    c. Title VII of 1964
    d. Pregnancy Disability Act (PDA)
    e. Americans with Disabilities Act (ADA)

6. Match the workforce planning process with its focus:
    a. Forecasting   1. Orient a new employee to the organization
    b. Critical skills gap analysis   2. Determine the positions to be filled and how to fill them
    c. Recruitment   3. Fill an open position
    d. Onboarding   4. Identify required critical positions and assess internal talent pools
    e. Succession planning   5. Define and refine personnel needs

7. Which of the following statements about the current market situation is true? (Select all answers that apply)
   a. The employment market will constantly evolve and change.
   b. Generational differences should not be a consideration that is taken into account.
   c. Incentives may be necessary to attract potential candidates into new fields.
   d. When recruiting, it is important to focus solely on the region and market that the organization is located.

8. Drop and drag the short-term solutions to match them with the appropriate circumstance, either employee surplus or employee shortage.
   a. Offering additional overtime opportunities
   b. Offering vacation buybacks or leave buybacks
   c. Freezing hiring activity and managing headcount through attrition
   d. Transferring work out of the department
   e. Approving additional absences and time off
   f. Reducing the number of hours worked in the work week

   Employee Surplus

   Employee Shortage

9. Which of the following long-term solutions could be implemented to address either an employee surplus or an employee shortage? (Select all answers that apply.)
   a. Issuing recalls and limiting production
   b. Retraining employees
   c. Offering retirement incentives
   d. Permanently transferring employees to different positions
   e. Transferring work out of the department

10. _____ are excellent services that can provide various resources to help employees manage change.
   a. Employee assistance programs
   b. Employee referral programs
   c. Communications plans
   d. Onboarding programs

11. Match the interviewing technique to its format.
   a. Focus groups
   b. In-depth interviews
   c. Dyads or triads
   d. Paired interviews

   1. Formal, one-on-one conversations focusing on scope and range
   2. Consecutive interviews that allow a joint opinion of the applicant
   3. Moderator-led discussions focusing on specific work
   4. Formal conversations with two or three interviewers

12. What is the correct structure for the STAR technique?
   a. Situation, Training, Assessment, Results
   b. Strengths, Task, Assessment, Reactions
   c. Situation, Task, Action, Results
   d. Strengths, Training, Action, Reactions

13. Which of the following statements about candidate experience is true? (Select all answers that apply.)
    a. Candidate experience refers to the experiences and interactions during the interview process.
    b. Candidate experience is vital to an organization's recruitment efforts.
    c. Candidate experience has no effect on an applicant applying for future open positions with the organization.
    d. Candidates who experience a positive recruitment are more likely to refer others to apply for employment with the organization.

14. Which of the following are effects of a robust total rewards program? (Select all answers that apply.)
    a. Attracting the most qualified and experienced applicants
    b. Retaining the most qualified and experienced employees
    c. Maintaining high employee satisfaction and morale
    d. Having a highly qualified, well trained, and best-in-class workforce

15. _____ examine how applicants process information, determine next steps, gather new information, formulate conclusions, and provide solutions.
    a. Reasoning tests
    b. Cognitive ability tests
    c. General intelligence tests
    d. Personality tests

16. Which of the following statements about salary negotiation are true? (Select all answers that apply.)
    a. A common salary negotiation technique is the five P's: proper preparation prevents poor performance.
    b. The goal of salary negotiation is to satisfy the organization's needs.
    c. Salary negotiation is the beginning of the employment relationship.
    d. Four stages of negotiation include preparation, exchanging information, bargaining, and closing and commitment.
    e. Communicating all the various benefits is not necessary during the salary negotiations and can be discussed later in the process.

17. _____ is the first formal experience that an individual has as an employee.
    a. Recruitment
    b. Onboarding
    c. New employee orientation (NEO)
    d. Completing new hire paperwork

18. Which of the following is a NEO best practice? (Select all answers that apply.)
    a. Providing program or benefit information only as needed or requested
    b. Scheduling follow-up discussion with new employees
    c. Showing employees where to access information when needed
    d. Providing a mentor or buddy
    e. Reviewing the organization, human resources information, health and safety procedures, and policies and practices

19. What does a SWOT analysis evaluate?
    a. Strengths, Weaknesses, Opportunities, Threats
    b. Strengths, Workforce, Opportunities, Tasks
    c. Staffing, Weaknesses, Openings, Threats
    d. Staffing, Workforce, Openings, Tasks

20. Arrange the workforce planning process steps in the correct order.
    a. Analyze data
    b. Recommend and implement programs
    c. Assess the current practices
    d. Understand business objectives and personnel needs
    e. Prioritize and adjust programs

21. Which of the following statements about due diligence are true? (Select all answers that apply.)
    a. Due diligence is necessary to make the best and most informed decisions.
    b. Human resources plays a key role in the due diligence process.
    c. Due diligence only needs to focus on legal and financial implications.
    d. Due diligence is a complete audit or investigation conducted when assessing major changes.

22. Drop and drag the stages of emotion to the appropriate transition phase of managing change.
    a. Creativity
    b. Enthusiasm
    c. Resistance   Before transition
    d. Frustration
    e. Denial
    f. Skepticism
    g. Shock
    h. Anxiety   After transition
    i. Acceptance
    j. Impatience
    k. Fear
    l. Confusion
    m. Anger
    n. Stress
    o. Hope
    p. Energy

23. _____ are important tools that present various pieces of information, data, and trends that can be extremely useful in implementing effective solutions.
    a. Metrics
    b. Dashboards
    c. Communications plans
    d. Cost, Timeliness, Outcomes, Reactions factors

24. Match the metric with the measurement description.
    a. Recruitment funnel   1. Average number of days taken for each process step
    b. Application sources   2. Number of applicants received from each source and number hired
    c. Decline reasons   3. Number of overall applicants who progress to each step of the process
    d. Pipeline efficiency   4. Specific reasons for disqualifying candidates from consideration

Answer Explanations

1. C: Disparate impact occurs when policies or practices disproportionately affect a specific group of individuals. Nepotism occurs when favoritism is shown to certain applicants based on personal relationships. Artificial recruitment barriers are qualifications that are not necessary to perform the position, disqualifying applicants who would otherwise be qualified for consideration. Recruitment refers to the entire process involved in filling open positions.

2. A, C, & D: Nepotism policies concern the relationships that would be potential problems related to employment. Siblings, spouses, children, parents, and other familial relationships may be identified in this policy as disqualifiers for a position or to be reviewed regarding the specific circumstances. Neighbors are not generally included in a nepotism policy, although if favoritism is shown to an individual because of this relationship, it may be a violation of the nepotism policy.

3. A, B, & D: Sourcing methods should always ensure that recruitments are fair and equitable. Employee referral programs are an excellent way to source candidates while engaging the current workforce in the recruitment process. While job boards and social media platforms are an excellent method to engage potential applicants, it is one method of many that can be effective in sourcing candidates. All sourcing methods used by an organization should ensure all qualified candidates have the same opportunity for consideration.

4. A – 4, B – 2, C – 5, D – 3; & E – 1: The talent lifecycle is a multi-step process that begins with determining the hiring needs of the department, then sources candidates and assesses the talent pool, followed by conducting further screening, then assessing candidates with tests or interviews. The final step in this process is offering employment and bringing the new employee onboard.

5. C: Title VII of 1964 is the original federal law that prohibits discrimination in employment. Title VII has been updated throughout the years to increase protections to additional individuals. GINA, ADEA, PDA, and ADA are all laws that have been incorporated into Title VII or as civil rights laws to protect individuals from being discriminated against in the hiring process.

6. A – 2, B – 5, C – 3, D – 1, & E – 4: Forecasting is the process of determining the positions to be filled and how to fill them. Critical skills gap analysis is the process of defining and refining the personnel needs. Recruitment is the process of filling an open position. Onboarding is the process of orienting a new employee to the organization. Succession planning is the process of identifying required critical positions and assess internal talent pools.

7. A & C: The employment market will always be evolving and changing. Organizations may need to offer incentives to attract candidates and even create new talent pools depending on the recruitment needs and candidate availability. Generational differences are an important factor in the recruitment process and play a large role in the talent pool availability. Depending on the availability of talent, it may be necessary to expand outside of the region and market to source the most qualified candidates and have a robust and broad talent pool.

8. Employee Surplus – C, E, & F; Employee Shortage – A, B, & D: When organizations face an employee surplus, it may be necessary to implement short-term solutions to attempt to remedy the situation. These solutions include freezing all hiring activity and using attrition to manage the headcount, approving additional absences, and reducing the amount of hours worked each week. When organizations face an employee shortage, short-term solutions may include offering additional overtime opportunities, offering vacation or leave buybacks, and transferring work out the department.

9. B & D: Retraining employees and permanently transferring employees to different positions are both solutions that can be implemented in either employee surplus or employee shortage situations. Issuing recalls and limiting production and transferring work out of the department are both solutions to address employee shortages only. Offering retirement incentives is a solution to address employee surpluses only.

10. A: Employee assistance programs (EAPs) can be an excellent resource for employees who are managing change within the organization, the department, or the position. These programs can also offer resources for personal matters as well. Employee referral programs are the programs that support recommending individuals to an organization for employment consideration. Communications plans are the complete plans for communicating a particular message, which could be the details for the employee assistance program and how employees can access these services. Onboarding refers to the process to bring a new employee into the organization, which could include details for the employee assistance program.

11. A – 3, B – 1, C – 4, & D – 2: Focus groups are discussions led by a moderator that focus on specific work being done. In-depth interviews are formal, one-on-one conversations that focus on the scope and range of the position with specific questions to gauge the applicant's experience. Dyads or triads are formal conversations with two or three interviewers that focus on the candidate's ability to perform the job duties based on their previous experience. Paired interviews are consecutive interviews that allow for joint opinions and ratings of the applicant.

12. C: Situation, Task, Action, Results is the correct structure for the STAR technique, which can be used to structure applicants' responses during an interview. While it is important for candidates to highlight strengths, training, assessments (such as performance reviews), and reactions to particular circumstances, the STAR technique is specific to Situation, Task, Action, and Results.

13. B & D: Candidate experience is vital to an organization's recruitment efforts, and candidates who have a positive experience are more likely to refer others to apply for employment with the organization. Candidate experience includes more than the experiences and interactions during the interview process. The candidate experience encompasses the entire recruitment experience, from viewing a job posting, interviewing, and negotiating an offer to beginning employment. Furthermore, a positive candidate experience will have an impact on applicants applying for future open positions.

14. A, B, C, & D: A robust total rewards program has many benefits, including attracting and retaining the most qualified and experienced individuals, maintaining a high employee satisfaction and level of morale, and having highly qualified personnel.

15. C: General intelligence tests show how quickly an applicant processes complex problems with the information provided and then formulates a solution based on the steps taken. Reasoning tests assess how applicants determine the right answers to a problem after receiving set pieces of information. Cognitive ability tests assess mental abilities in verbal and non-verbal skills, memory, and information processing. Personality tests show the general personality type of applicants and provide insight into how they will work with others.

16. A, C, & D: The five P's—proper preparation prevents poor performance—is a common salary negotiation technique. The employment relationship begins with salary negotiation, which includes four stages: preparation, exchanging information, bargaining, and closing and commitment. The goal of salary negotiation is to satisfy the needs of all parties: the organization, hiring department and manager, and the candidate.

17. C: NEO is the candidate's first formal experience as an employee. The NEO includes completing new hire paperwork and is a component of a larger onboarding process. Although recruitment is the first interaction with an organization as a future employee, the NEO is the first formal experience as an official employee.

18. B, D, & E: The NEO should incorporate best practices and standards to ensure employees have as much information as possible when joining the organization. Scheduling follow-discussions for employees to ask questions or provide additional information is a best practice to incorporate, as well as providing a mentor or buddy. Standard NEO should include reviewing the organization, human resources information, health and safety procedures, and policies and practices. It is important to provide all information as part of the NEO as well as when requested. It is also important to show employees where to access information, along with providing insight and information about the specific programs.

19. A: A SWOT analysis examines the following: Strengths, Weaknesses, Opportunities, Threats. While staffing, workforce, openings, and tasks may be items that need to be assessed, they can be reviewed within the SWOT categories.

20. D, A, C, B, & E: Workforce planning is a strategic and holistic process to ensure panning is effective. Understanding the business objectives and personnel needs, analyzing data, assessing current practices, recommending and implementing programs, and prioritizing and adjusting programs are the steps in this process.

21. A, B, & D: Due diligence is necessary to make the best and most informed decisions, and human resources plays a key role in this process. Due diligence is a complete audit or investigation conducted by an organization when considering major changes. Due diligence needs to focus on various areas in addition to legal and financial implications. Areas such as process, operations, products, consumers, information technology, human resources, and departmental functions should also be reviewed.

22. Before transition – C, D, E, G, H, K, L, M, & N. After transition – A, B, F, I, J, O, & P: Before a transition of change, employees process emotion in stages—denial, anxiety, shock, resistance, fear, anger, frustration, confusion, and stress. After a transition of change, employees process different emotion in new stages—creativity, skepticism, acceptance, impatience, hope, energy, and enthusiasm.

23. B: Dashboards are important tools that present information, data, and trends that can be extremely useful in implementing effective solutions. Metrics are an important piece of information included within a dashboard, and the dashboard is a form of communications plan because it provides a message on the effectiveness of a program. Additionally, metrics should focus on four primary areas: cost, timeliness, outcomes, and reactions.

24. A – 3, B – 2, C – 4, D – 1: A recruitment funnel is a metric that shows the percentage of overall applicants that progress to each step within the process. The application source metric provides the sources that the majority of applicants locate positions and submit applications. This metric allows an organization to target marketing to specific positions and understand where applicants are locating job postings and ultimately where new hires applied. The decline reasons metric provides information about disqualification of candidates to ensure that organizations have the most accurate descriptions of positions available to applicants. The pipeline efficiency of hiring metric provides the average number of days taken for each step within the process, allowing the organization to identify areas of improvement.

Learning and Development

Professional Growth and Development Opportunities

Human resources professionals are responsible for providing consultation to managers and employees on professional growth and development opportunities. In order to provide the best recommendations, it is important to have an understanding of individual, team, department, and organizational needs. Each level is vital to the overall success of an organization's holistic training program. While training programs should be provided to ensure updated information is available, new skills and techniques are learned, and certifications are renewed, it is also important to understand individual needs for employees who may be struggling to perform their job. From individual development plans to all-employee focused training programs, human resources professionals are responsible for delivering a robust and holistic growth and development program. Additionally, training programs should be aligned with the organization's goals and priorities to ensure that employees are working toward the same goals and priorities in their specific position.

Robust training combines individual skill enhancement with overall training for the entire department. Human resources can deliver such robust training opportunities by working with department managers. Human resources departments are responsible for delivering training opportunities with either internal staff or an outside third-party agency. Even if an organization employs individuals who can offer in-house training, it may be beneficial to have a third-party agency deliver certain types of training. Examples of topics that may require a third-party agency to deliver training include legal updates, compliance issues, health and safety matters, and state certifications. Examples of topics that could be provided by internal staff include written and verbal communications, developing relationships, writing emails and reports, and building effective teams.

All employees should be trained in how the organization's systems work and how they will need to use these systems in their position. From submitting timecards for payroll or approving requisitions and purchase orders, human resources should ensure there is a standard protocol for all employees to be trained on the important systems that will be used in their job. Providing opportunities to expand employee's knowledge of these systems can also open future career opportunities for them. Knowledge really is power, and understanding how to gain this knowledge through data and utilizing the systems and programs available can potentially increase the opportunities available to an employee.

Professional growth and development can also be facilitated through access to programs such as tuition reimbursement and job shadowing. Enabling employees to further their formal education by reimbursing their tuition is a great way to show employees that they are supported. Tuition reimbursement also benefits the organization by encouraging employees to use this knowledge to increase their productivity and effectiveness. Job shadowing provides an opportunity for employees to gain exposure to different areas of the organization and the work being done to support overall goals and objectives. Whether formal or informal, job shadowing enables an employee to watch or "shadow" another employee while they work to see what is being done on a daily basis. Job shadowing can be a great tool for employees to use in gaining an understanding of how their work fits in with other employees' work and in the organization as a whole.

Human resources is instrumental in ensuring that an organization's training program is managed and delivered appropriately. When human resources has a strong working relationship with managers and employees, a holistic training program can be developed.

Career Development and Training Programs

Career development and training programs can take many different formats, and human resources professionals are responsible for understanding which programs are best for the organization and the employees. Individuals learn in different ways, so it is important to have multiple training methods to ensure that all employees can learn and grow in a way that works for their learning style. While the variety of training methods may be limited by budget and resources, it is important that human resources regularly evaluate programs to update them by incorporating new ways of learning.

Individual Development Plans (IDPs) are a great way to engage employees directly in their career growth. IDPs enable employees to work with their supervisor and human resources to discuss their current position and learning opportunities to increase their knowledge and skills specific to their current role. IDPs also enable employees to discuss future opportunities and the skills needed to achieve those opportunities and be successful. These assessments are known as skills gap assessments—they review the requirements for future positions and the skills and knowledge the employee lacks. These gaps can then be filed with training and learning opportunities, provided either in-house or outside.

Organizations can also incorporate mentoring and job shadowing to enhance an employee's opportunities. An employee may express a desire to hold a position at certain level in the future. Human resources can implement programs and policies to identify mentors for such employees. Similarly, job shadowing can enable employees to actually see the day-to-day workings of a position and take this information into account when determining their own career path and goals.

In addition to planning and implementing training programs for individuals, human resources professionals also need to incorporate specific training programs for supervisors and managers. Training in how to be a successful supervisor and manager is vital to having strong teams. There may even be an opportunity to align this training with IDPs and offer individuals the opportunity to attend a training program for supervisors BEFORE becoming a supervisor. The benefit of doing so is a clear understanding of the roles and responsibilities that are expected at the supervisory level.

Human resources professionals can structure specific training programs for each position with a pre-defined career path. Another option is to enable flexibility in designing training programs and career paths for the needs expressed by employees and departments. Both are legitimate and both enable career development and growth. Training employees at an individual level as well as at a group level is also an important component to training programs. Understanding how each individual contributes to the organization's priorities and objectives is vital to overall success. Additionally, having an understanding of how each team and group can contribute to success is an important piece of the puzzle to ensure success at an individual level and an organization-wide level.

Contribute to Succession Planning Discussions with Management by Providing Relevant Data

Human resources departments can contribute to succession planning discussions by providing relevant and meaningful data to management. Before even determining what data should be used, it is vital to establish criteria to identify which positions will be reviewed in succession planning. High-ranking positions in the organization—chief executive officer, chief financial officer, and information technology director, for example—are not necessarily the only positions to consider. Identifying the hard-to-fill positions, the positions with the highest turnover, and the positions that have the largest scope and impact on the organization are also important to review for succession planning. Tracking sheets created for each position can also be a helpful tool for those reviewing this information. The tracking sheets can include such information as position title; compensation; minimum requirements, including education and experience; primary roles and responsibilities such as supervisory and budgetary duties; and other important information. Potential candidates and their current status can be listed on this tracking sheet as well. Assessment can then determine whether the organization has viable internal candidates for the position and when those candidates will be ready. Some candidates may be ready for the position immediately; other candidates may need two to three years to transition. This is important to assess during the succession planning process so that the organization can provide training and mentoring to ensure candidates are ready for future opportunities.

A vital piece of information that should be reviewed in determining which positions are included in succession planning is attrition. **Attrition** is the percentage of employees who leave the organization. Voluntary attrition occurs when employees leave of their own accord—retirement, resignation for a new position, or relocation. Involuntary attrition occurs when employees are terminated or laid off. Attrition should be calculated on an annual basis and broken down into such categories as voluntary and involuntary, department, job classification, and rank. Analyzing this data enables a holistic view of the organization to determine which positions should be considered in the succession planning process. This data can also be used in the succession planning process to visualize gaps in the organization, such as gaps related to promotions, career paths, and other opportunities.

Organizational charts, job descriptions, and total rewards are also important pieces of data that should be incorporated in succession planning discussions. Organizational charts can show clear career paths for employees as well as positions that are significant to the organization. Job descriptions can provide an even clearer picture when aligned with the organizational charts regarding roles, responsibilities, education, and experience for each position. Total rewards can provide the information that would attract potential candidates, internal and external, to this position during a recruitment process. The total rewards information can also be aligned with the attrition data to show an area that needs additional focus. If certain positions have higher than usual turnover, it may be appropriate for human resources to conduct a total rewards review to ensure competitiveness and eliminate any potential concerns for future recruitment and retention.

Federal Laws and Regulations Related to Learning and Development Activities

Many organizations understand that offering career enhancement through training programs is beneficial to their overall success. Training opportunities that enable growth and development in current and future roles can enhance an employee's employment experience and dedication. It is important to understand that while many training programs are voluntary and based on the needs of the organization, all employees should be offered training program opportunities and not be discriminated against when seeking out these opportunities. Organizations must ensure fair and equitable learning and development opportunities for all employees. The training programs themselves should also be discrimination free in their materials and presentation to employees. Requesting feedback on the training content and instructors after each session is a best practice that can help an organization determine if changes need to be made.

Additionally, it is important to understand when employees should be compensated for training opportunities. The Fair Labor Standards Act (FLSA) provides specific details regarding when training programs should be compensated for. In general, if a training program is considered to be (1) directly related to an employee's current job and (2) is conducted during regular working hours, employees must be compensated at their regular rate of pay. If a training program is not considered mandatory but meets the two terms indicated above, employees must be compensated for the time to attend the training program. Human resources professionals should ensure they have a complete awareness and understanding of compensation requirements.

The Occupational Safety and Health Act (OSHA) is a federal regulation that requires training in various safety and health areas. Organizations are required to ensure that all employees are trained in the emergency plan. Each facility should have a specific plan that is regularly communicated and delivered to employees via a training plan. Providing practice drills along with classroom training enables employees to not only read the emergency plan's materials and maps but to physically familiarize themselves with such details as escape routes, meeting points, and signage. Many organizations require this training on an annual basis for all employees and provide additional opportunities throughout the year for newly hired and transferred employees. Emergency plans should also include information specific to natural disasters, based on the location. While all facilities should have plans for fires and other events, they should also have plans for location-specific natural disasters. Depending on the location, possible natural disasters include earthquakes, tsunamis, floods, hurricanes, and tornadoes. Employees should never have to guess about safety protocol in the case of an emergency.

OSHA also requires employees to be fully trained in all areas related to safety for their specific job. Every employee should be made aware of all safety procedures and protocols before beginning their work. Specific training related to safety procedures include, but are not limited to, machinery and equipment, fire hazards, chemicals and other hazards, hearing protection, personal protective equipment (PPE), and Automated External Defibrillator (AED) equipment. Employees should be fully trained on every piece of equipment they use to do their job. Each position should have a specific training schedule depending on the equipment being used. Organizations may even provide a separate training program for PPE alone. Some positions require multiple pieces of PPE, and training should include not only how to use the PPE in the scope of the work being performed, but also how to clean, prepare, and request new PPE. From coveralls and safety glasses to Kevlar vests and handguns, organizations are responsible for delivering the training programs that ensure employees are completely aware of and understand how to accurately use the PPE.

Many organizations require that an employee complete and sign a written notification that training has been provided and the employee understands all aspects of performing their job safely. This document can be important if an employee refuses to abide by the protocols and needs to be disciplined. Additionally, refresher training should be provided to ensure employees are aware of updates to regulations and procedures. The goal should be to ensure that employees leave work at the end of the day in the same physical condition in which they arrived. Providing consistent, frequent, and thorough safety training will decrease on-the-job injuries and accidents. Many organizations reward employees for adhering to safety practices and procedures. Another common practice is to communicate how many days have elapsed without a safety incident or accident.

The Supreme Court has ruled that organizations can be held liable for sexual harassment if there is not reasonable effort made to prevent and correct inappropriate workplace behavior. Even if the organization is unaware of the behavior, it may still be liable for an employee's inappropriate behavior. Therefore, organizations must take every action necessary to provide training about sexual harassment. This training should include definitions and examples of sexual harassment, appropriate examples of lawsuits and case law, legal standards, the workplace policy, and the process for reporting sexual harassment. Additionally, training should include prevention techniques, employee responsibilities, and how sexual harassment investigations are conducted. Sexual harassment training should occur frequently to ensure that employees understand the organization's policies and procedures as well as the legal ramifications for individuals and for the organization. Some states have passed legislation mandating sexual harassment training, and they conduct audits to ensure compliance. For example, in the state of California, Assembly Bill 1825 requires that all employers with 50 or more employees have their supervisors attend a two-hour class on sexual harassment at least once every two years. Additionally, all new supervisory employees must attend this training within six months of their hire or promotion to the supervisory role. Organizations must keep accurate records of when these trainings are offered, employees in attendance, and the content delivered.

Some organizations may choose to include diversity training in the scope of sexual harassment training. This inclusion can ensure that employees understand that, although these are separate topics, they intertwine with each other on many levels. Diversity training enables employees to be exposed to information regarding individuals with differences working together, providing different perspectives, and allowing for a more robust dialogue. Employees should understand an organization's policies regarding diversity and how each individual plays a part in creating the culture of the organization. Valuing each other's differences and treating each other with respect is vital to the success of the team, department, and organization.

Learning and Development Theories

A learning theory is a group of principles and concepts that explain how individuals gain, remember, and recall information. Knowledge of learning theories can help trainers better structure their training programs. Trainers can incorporate principles from these learning theories to create content, determine which tools to use, facilitate discussion, and test skills.

Many basic learning theories can be applied to a training program. Below are five standard learning theories:

- Behaviorism
- Cognitivism
- Constructivism
- Experiential
- Connectivism

Behaviorism focuses on what an individual does; learning delivered in accordance with this theory is led by an instructor. This learning theory is centered on behaviors, reactions, and responses to situations and events. Learners in this theory are reactive in that they are responding to information, while the instructors observe new behaviors and changes. In general, a behaviorist learning theory is used to teach basic definitions, explain concepts, or perform a certain task. This theory is facilitated through assessments, tests, repetition, and continued practice of the concepts. Behaviorism does not prepare the learner for problem solving, creative thinking, or critical thinking. Behaviorist learning is limited to the recall of information or the performance of a specific task. This kind of learning can be used as a building block for learning that adheres to the other theories.

Cognitivism, or cognitive information processing, focuses on how an individual processes information; learning delivered in accordance with this theory is led by an instructor. This learning theory centers on how new information is organized and aligned with existing knowledge. According to this theory, learners in this theory are proactive; they are reasoning and processing information at a high level. In general, a cognitivist learning theory is used to teach strategies, with an emphasis on how this information is processed. This theory is facilitated through feedback, concept mapping, use of analogies and metaphors, and providing structure. Cognitivism can build upon the knowledge learned from a behaviorist method by having participants question and discuss what they learned.

Constructivism is the learning theory that focuses on how an individual interprets new information and then applies this information to their own circumstances. Constructivism is a student-focused learning approach, with learners being very proactive, solving problems and analyzing situations critically. According to this theory, learners understand that information is constantly evolving and its applications may change frequently. In general, a constructivist approach is used to teach learners how to apply new knowledge in many contexts and perspectives. This kind of learning is facilitated through case studies, brainstorming, simulations, apprenticeships, and collaborative learning. A constructivist approach can enable participants to learn how to change their thinking and actions in response to new information. These are necessary skills when dealing with emergency situations or circumstances in which new information is constantly being provided and decisions need to be made.

Experiential learning focuses on an individual's experiences and how they learn from them. Experiential learning is instructor-led and can be a very effective learning technique when course content is lecture based or is heavy in material content. By having an individual focus on their experiences and then apply different learning techniques to each situation, individuals can then work to modify future behaviors. This learning theory assumes that individuals do, think, plan, and redo; they learn through reflecting on what they have done and what they will do. Experiential learning is facilitated through assignments that involve studying concepts, reviewing experiences, reflecting on previous actions, incorporating new ideas and concepts, and determining future opportunities.

Connectivism is a relatively new learning theory that focuses on an individual being self-directed in their learning. This learning theory is a direct response to readily available technology for individuals to access information. Connectivism is a student-focused learning approach, with learners being extremely proactive and outgoing. They are constantly looking for and educating themselves with new information. They understand the importance of sharing information and source material with others and connecting individuals together through learning. This theory is facilitated by having individuals seek out new information and knowledge in traditional and non-traditional learning settings.

All five learning theories can yield positive learning results. Because each individual learns differently, a blended training course that taps into all these learning approaches will be a robust one. By combining various components of each theory, training programs will more accurately accommodate the ways individuals learn in everyday life. Some learning happens through simple repetition and practice, while other learning happens through brainstorming, creative thinking, and discussion.

Incorporating and applying all these learning techniques is important to ensure robust learning. Adding the following tools to a training program will increase the learning for participants, and ultimately retention of the knowledge:

- Memory exercises
- Additional discussion time
- High-level critical thinking exercises
- Face-to-face interaction and conversation
- Personalized instruction to handle different paces of learning
- Various communication styles
- Virtual training including videos and simulations
- Handouts including course material and resource material for future reference

By enhancing the learning opportunities through the theories and tools above, there are multiple benefits to the participants, other employees who they will interact with, and the organization. These benefits can include the following:

- Information can be taken back to the workplace and used in the future
- Learning becomes more interesting and sought after
- Communication techniques can improve relationships and ensure clarity
- Training becomes important to employees and not just something they have to do
- Employee morale improves, resulting in positive attitudes
- Employees are presented with new ways of looking at and thinking about concepts and ideas
- Dialogue can begin or continue
- Relationships can improve, expand, or begin
- Results can improve, including efficiency, effectiveness, and profitability

Regardless of which learning theories or techniques are used in a training program, a solid program should include complete and accurate content, guidance to the participants, opportunities for the participants to practice and learn independently, and an assessment as to how the participant performed in the program. Using as much of the information regarding learning theories and techniques will enhance the quality of a training program and achieve the end result of a more educated, informed, and knowledgeable workforce.

Training Program Facilitation, Techniques, and Delivery

Before creating a training program, it is important to understand the organization's goals and needs. Training programs should be relevant and appropriate for both the organization and employees. A needs analysis can provide insight as to the training needed instead of trying to guess. The following are resources that can be used to determine training needs:

- Organization goals
- Departmental goals
- Results
- Performance measures
- Attrition
- Job descriptions
- Safety logs and performance
- Complaints
- Legal requirements and compliance needs

Additionally, interviewing or surveying employees may also provide important information. Sometimes training programs overlook speaking to and hearing from employees about the skills and training that would help them be more productive. An organization may think it knows what employees need, but unless it seeks confirmation from the employees themselves, the organization may end up providing unnecessary training. Such training can be costly, wasting time, money, resources, and energy while also undermining future training opportunities. When employees are included in the conversation about training, they are most often supportive of the training program.

Once training needs are determined, human resources professionals then need to decide which employees need to be trained and how often. Many training programs are necessary or even required for all employees and should be conducted on a frequent basis. Some training programs are specific to certain departments or employees at different levels of the organization. All employees should be trained in communication, teamwork, company policies and applicable safety, but only management employees may need training in team development and strategic planning. Knowing which employees need the training also enables insight into how the training should be developed and presented. If a software update training is being proposed for all information technology employees, understanding how these employees learn is necessary in delivering a successful training program. Allowing individuals at computer stations to practice and follow along with the instructor may ensure maximum learning for a particular group of employees. Additionally, logistics such as location, workload, schedules and coverage, work group dynamics, and cost should be taken into account when developing and delivering a training program.

As mentioned earlier, individuals learn in different ways; therefore, it is important to incorporate multiple ways of learnings in each training course. Planning flexibility into the course is important because each session will be different, based on the individuals in attendance. Each participant brings unique experiences, examples, and questions that the instructor needs to integrate into that specific training session. Group dynamics also change from session to session. Experienced instructors include these exchanges in future sessions to enhance learning for all employees. A best practice is to keep a "parking lot" or list of ideas, questions, and suggestions. At the end of the program, the instructor can then compile this information and send it to all participants, so that learning can continue after the course.

Training sessions should be as interactive as possible, encouraging conversation and engagement. Keeping participants involved and attentive can be challenging. A great way to start the session is by reviewing the course objectives. Each course should have a complete list of objectives that individuals are meant to learn by the end. This is also a great opportunity to begin engaging with the participants about their own individual objectives. Questions like "why are you here?" and "what do you want to know by the end of this class?" are great ways to start a dialogue. Breaking up a training session to include various learning methods can keep a steady flow going. Incorporating quizzes, case studies and breakout discussions, role-playing and demonstrations, and debate opportunities can also keep participants engaged. Employees tend to sit near the people they know. These are the day-to-day, naturally occurring working groups. Breaking up these groups and having employees sit with unfamiliar colleagues can facilitate new conversations and ideas.

Not every training topic is exciting. Some sessions are mandatory. Some training material is difficult to grasp or even uncomfortable to listen to. Regardless, the challenge is getting individuals to participate and be engaged in the training. By incorporating various methods of learning and discussion opportunities, an instructor can usually get maximum participation. In fact, several studies show that a training session incorporating multiple learning methods is more effective, takes less time, and results in individuals retaining the information longer. Using PowerPoint slides and handouts, asking questions and involving participants, acting out situations with different outcomes, and having fun when appropriate can all support a robust and successful training program.

Training must be supported by executive management in order to be accepted and fully integrated into the organization. Employees must see the commitment from all levels of the organization, especially executive management. If possible, having a member of upper management present in every training session will assist in showing the organization's commitment to the training programs. If a training is required for all employees, dispersing the executive team among various sessions is a great way to include different levels of thinking in every session. It is also helpful in providing an opportunity for executive management to interact directly with employees at various levels in the organization. It is important to note, though, that this strategy may not work for all organizations, depending on the personalities and culture. Having an executive manager present may stifle conversation, and employees may be less vocal than usual, for fear of retribution. It is incumbent on the human resources professional to assess whether this could be a concern and develop an appropriate and effective training plan.

Adult Learning Processes

Individuals learn differently, and instructors must ensure that training encompasses multiple learning techniques to make sure that all participants are engaged and absorbing the information. In addition, it is important to understand that adults learn differently than inexperienced people. For the purpose of this section, the term **adult** refers to individuals who are very experienced in their field and have been working in their profession for more than 15 years and/or are in the Baby Boomer or Generation X age bracket. More experienced employees may have pre-established philosophies and ideas based on their past experiences, both with the organization and others. In general, they are mature and have experiences that can be related to the course material. Instructors need to ensure they are prepared with tools to address engagement with the intent on creating an open-minded learning experience.

An important component to any training program is setting expectations and objectives. This is especially true with training adult learners. Learning objectives should be reasonable and thoughtful, and they should enable questions and feedback. Additionally, participants should be encouraged to discuss and apply the course material specific to certain situations. This enables robust discussion and can provide an opportunity for participants to learn from each other. Ground rules should also be established as a part of the expectations so that all learners feel comfortable in participating and understand what is expected of them during the class. Following along with the agenda, staying on track, staying on time, and providing periodic breaks and refreshments are also important ensuring the training program is accepted and respected by adult learners.

Adult learners generally have their own learning styles, and instructors should incorporate the following five elements in all training classes in order to fully engage all participants regardless of their experience:

- Orientation
- Motivation
- Reinforcement
- Retention
- Transference

Orientation is emphasizing to the adult learner what they are going to learn and how they will be able to apply the knowledge to their current work. Adult learners will want to know what the end game is and how they will benefit, both short-term and long-term. **Motivation** is key with adult learners. Some participants will be motivated by the additional knowledge and insights, while others will be motivated by the social interaction with their coworkers. Each individual has a different motivator and it is important to understand this when preparing a training program. A great way to have a better understanding of what will motivate the class is to review the participants who will be attending and take into account their position, experience, and background. Understanding this information enables the trainer to customize the training plan and include multiple motivators. **Reinforcement** is a successful training technique used when training adult learners. Both positive and negative reinforcement can be appropriate depending on the circumstances and the course material. **Retention** is a vital component to any training program. If participants are not retaining what they learned, then the class was ineffective and ultimately a waste of time, resources, cost, and more. Practicing new skills, challenging ideas, and ensuring various ways of presenting the course material will help participants retain the knowledge and information. Transference is one of the most important elements and refers to how participants understand the material and information in relation to their job. **Transference** is understanding what was learned and applying it to everyday life and work. The more connections that an instructor can help participants make in this area, the more successful the training program will be for the adult learners. Incorporating these five elements can enable maximum participation and effectiveness of training programs with all learners, including adult learners.

Sometimes adult learners can be averse to learning and may be resistant to participating. It is important for the instructor to overcome this issue to ensure that learning can take place. Many techniques can be used to combat resistance. Below are a few examples:

- Building on previous experience and opportunity for future experience
- Establishing relevance to adult learners' everyday life and work
- Creating and delivering on expectations
- Aligning individual objectives with those of the learning opportunity
- Acting out and applying the material with specific examples from participants

Customizing training for adult learners by incorporating all these elements is necessary to ensure a successful and effective training program. While it may not be feasible to include every element, having an understanding of each and being prepared to address issues as they arise can be helpful. Some training is mandatory, and it may be a struggle to specifically show how the training material could affect an individual's future opportunities. It may simply be a matter of showing that the individual understands the material and applies it as appropriate. This level of honesty can be invaluable when encouraging adult learners to engage and participate in a course.

Understanding the specific needs of adult learners can assist in facilitating the learning experience. Feedback can be invaluable in this regard. Request real and honest feedback on the course, what could be done better, what they learned and will incorporate in their day-to-day work, and other suggestions for improving the course. When adult learners see their feedback solicited, they see that they are contributing to future courses, which may be a motivator for some.

Instructional Design Principles and Processes

Instructional design is a multi-step process to create and deliver an effective training program. While there are many different structures available to work through, a frequently used design model is the "ADDIE" model. This model is a generic instructional design model that can be used for various subject matters in multiple fields. Each step builds on the previous one; because of the simplicity, this model can eliminate wasted time, money, and work. This model is generally seen as the foundation for other instructional design models and is easily adaptable to most training program needs. The ADDIE model follows these steps in the design of a training program:

- Analyze
- Design
- Develop
- Implement
- Evaluate

Each step is vital to the success of a training program and should be conducted thoroughly before moving to the next step. The ADDIE process is linear, meaning that before moving to step 2, step 1 must be completed. If changes occur in the timetable, content, or organizational need during step 3, the process must be started over again at step 1.

ADDIE

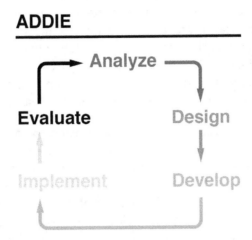

Analysis is the first step; it focuses on what is needed. A needs assessment should be conducted to determine the needs of the organization, departments, teams, and individuals before designing or delivering any training program. The analysis step determines the organization's needs and skills gaps. Having an understanding of who will be in the training is important. Defining the "audience" will help structure the training program in later steps. Additionally, understanding the goal and objectives of the training is vital to having a relevant and respected training program. Aligning training with an organization's overall goals will help employees understand their purpose in the larger organization and how their contributions affect the company.

Design is the second step; it focuses on what should be included. This step also focuses on the audience—who this training program will be delivered to and who will be learning—as well as the instructor who will be delivering this program. Design is the sketched-out plan for the program. Understanding the characteristics of the audience and instructor can help to define how the materials and course should be structured, the learning techniques applied, and how issues such as resistance to training should be addressed. During this step, course content is identified, lessons are structured, tools are selected, and assessment options are reviewed. Storyboards are a great way to visually show the training program to ensure the flow is steady and maintainable.

Development is the third step; it focuses on the actual content and materials. Development consists of the actual deliverable training program that will be implemented, including the visual tools such as PowerPoint® presentations, handouts, lecture notes, tests and quizzes, resource material, and assessments such as discussion questions and group exercises. This step uses the information gathered in the analysis and design steps to create the actual program. Development can also include running trial sessions to determine if there are issues to resolve before delivering the training to participants.

Implementation is the fourth step; it focuses on delivery of the training program. Conducting the training session is the culmination of the first three steps. Preparing the environment, delivering the course, engaging the participants, and closing out the course are all important components to the implementation step. This step is "where the rubber meets the road," and as soon as the participants enter the training room, they should be engaged with each other and the instructor. The instructor should be prepared to handle the unexpected and answer far-afield questions. The instructor is responsible for keeping the training program on track and the participants engaged.

Evaluation is the final step of the model; it focuses on two components: evaluating the effectiveness of the course and validating it for the future. Evaluation forms should be provided to all participants to gauge the overall response of those receiving the training. The evaluation forms should include rating areas such as instructor effectiveness and knowledge, content and material, if the course was helpful and will be used in the scope of work, the best and least liked parts of the training, and suggestions for opportunities to improve. Additionally, an individual may be assigned to sit in during the course to evaluate the responses received from the participants. Because the instructor will be busy delivering content and focusing on the time, agenda, participant engagement, material, and other items, an assigned evaluator for the course can observe the reactions of participants and other interactions that the instructor may miss.

The assigned evaluator can then give constructive feedback on how to enhance the training. Validating a training program is reviewing how participants take and use the information and knowledge back to their work. Frequent follow-ups and check-ins with those that attended a training to keep the material and information fresh can help retention. Taking this information into account is vital to validating a training program. Follow-up surveys can also assist in gaining information and insight related to how a training program is continuing to impact an employee and their work. Once data is compiled, trends can be potentially seen and reviewed to suggest recommendations for the training program.

Although the ADDIE model is an easy model to follow when creating a training program, there are a few drawbacks to consider. The steps are linear and build on each other, which may not work well in certain situations. Additionally, if there are multiple changes and continual evolution happening, this model may not work well. Having to repeatedly go back to previous steps due to the linear nature of this model may result in needing additional time and resources or causing set-backs and delays if training is needed by a particular time. As with all techniques, there are positive and negative aspects to each, but it is important to consider each to ensure that the model or technique that is applied is appropriate and the best method for the particular situation.

Techniques to Assess Training Program Effectiveness

A training program's effectiveness can be assessed by taking metrics and measurements. The best known and most commonly used model for assessment is the Kirkpatrick Model. Developed by Donald Kirkpatrick in the late 1950s, this model evaluates a training program on four levels: reaction, learning, behavior, and results. Each level is a more progressive and broader level of evaluation than the previous one; the model moves from individual results to organizational results. Some training programs may only need to be evaluated at the lower two levels (learning and reaction), while other training programs need evaluation at all four levels.

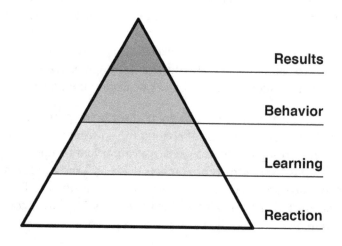

The first level of evaluation, **reaction**, measures the individual's response, determining how useful a training was to the participants. Did participants find the training challenging? Did they find the training thoughtful and organized, with appropriately structured content? This feedback can be garnered through surveys and questionnaires, participant interviews, and formal focus groups. Gathering this feedback immediately after the training program and then at certain times afterward can help to determine whether participants believe the knowledge was useful, and also whether they ultimately retained it for later use. This level of evaluation is used most by training managers.

The second level of evaluation, **learning**, measures how much individuals improve their knowledge, skills, and abilities as a direct result of the training. This level determines how effective a training is for the participants in their day-to-day work. Did participants become more efficient with their work? Did they learn a new skill that enhanced their work product? This feedback can be gained through testing or assessing participants before and after a training program, doing performance reviews and manager's reports, and making on-the-job assessments of work performed. This level of evaluation is used most by supervisors.

The third level of evaluation, **behavior**, measures how much an individual changes their behavior as a direct result of the training. This level determines how a training program affects a participant's attitude and behavior in the performance of their job duties. This level is important to assess for training programs that teach communication skills, conflict resolution, team building, and other skills specific to behavior. This feedback can be gained through having participants complete questionnaires, observing daily behaviors, and reviewing feedback provided by managers, customers, peers, and other individuals who work directly with the individual. This level of evaluation is most used by managers.

The fourth level of evaluation, **results**, evaluates how the organization as a whole benefits from the training program. This level determines how a training program impacts the organization's productivity, efficiency, effectiveness, revenues, and other high-level, organizational results. This feedback can be gained by reviewing financial reports, inspection reports, and other high level reports that indicate the success of an organization. Reviewing this information before and after a training program is delivered, as well as after certain periods of time—immediately following the program, six months after, twelve months after—can help determine actual impacts and when they occur. This level of evaluation is most used by executives and high-ranking officers in an organization.

It is important to use accurate, valid, and time-sensitive information. Because there are costs in resources, finances, and time, it is imperative to ensure that the evaluation of a training program is effective, just like the training program itself. Using inaccurate information to evaluate a program's effectiveness is a waste of resources. If the results so obtained are used to determine training recommendations, the recommendations may not be appropriate. Once the evaluation has been conducted, it is important to ask questions to determine what can be done better for future training programs. If there was little to no impact, a decision to not conduct the training program might be made, or a program could be completely reworked to attain different results.

In addition to evaluating individual training programs, training metrics are important for determining the effectiveness of a training department and all programs being delivered. Organizations should determine what is important to measure and how readily available information is to calculate these measurements. It may not be effective to track certain pieces of data due to a manual process or timely and potentially inaccurate data source. These metrics are often referred to as **key performance indicators**, or **KPIs.**

KPIs are measurements that show the achievement of a certain goal, or in some cases, the lack of achievement. KPIs add the following value:

- Clarity by showing a clear picture of the strategy being implemented
- Focus by showing what matters and what requires attention
- Improvement by showing the progress toward the goals and objectives

Below is a list of potential KPIs to evaluate a training department:

- Average training cost per employee
- Average training hours per employee
- Budget spent on training—by department and overall
- Internal training sessions offered and attended
- External training sessions offered and attended
- Return on investment

Each KPI is a valuable metric that illustrates data used to determine the effectiveness of a training department. KPIs should be clearly defined and any calculation required should be clearly established, including where and when data will be sourced. When put together to tell the entire story of a training department, these metrics can show where successes are occurring, where opportunities are available, and if there are deficiencies to address. The primary purpose of any metric or KPI is the behavior or change that the measurement creates. When KPIs are established, a training program can be discussed honestly and results-driven. These discussions then lead to focused training programs in areas that can actually make a difference.

Organizational Development Methods, Motivation Methods, and Problem-Solving Techniques

Organizational development (OD) is defined as a series of methods and techniques that are used to facilitate long-term changes in an organization. OD is a strategic, planned, interactive, and ongoing approach to improve employee and organizational effectiveness. Any OD method or process can be broken down into components: diagnose a situation; introduce solutions; monitor the progress. Throughout the process, it is important to provide feedback. This feedback may start the cycle over again to ensure that any changes include the feedback received.

Basic Organization Development Model

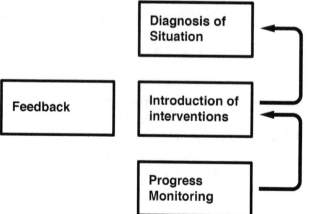

The model can be expanded to add more steps, but the core steps are always the same. A more expansive, more detailed model could include the following steps:

- Determine the needs of the organization as they are aligned with the mission, vision, and values
- Understand the current state of the programs and process being reviewed
- Propose and adopt a future state of the programs
- Design updates and changes while reviewing current resources
- Implement changes after thorough communication to ensure understanding
- Evaluate the changes and impacts to make adjustments if necessary

Even with these additional steps, the same three-step process is still the core of the OD process.

Throughout an OD process, it is important to involve employees and bring them along in the conversation, as this will increase their motivation and engagement throughout the entire process. Ensuring they are a part of the conversation can also help ensure that any new program or process implemented is successful.

OD methods focus on changing the organizational culture while engaging in continued and constant communication. Throughout this model, using OD techniques can be incorporated to engage employees and determine the changes that need to be encouraged and implemented. OD techniques include survey feedback, process consultation, team building, sensitivity training, and workgroup growth. These techniques all lend to a more effective interpersonal working environment with deeper relationships and understanding between coworkers.

One positive by-product of working through an OD model to increase efficiency and productivity among employees is creating and maintaining motivation in the workforce. When employees feel as if they are being heard and are part of a process to implement change, their satisfaction and continual motivation in the future can be substantially increased. This motivation occurs because the organization is creating an environment that values empowerment, individual growth and development, and high morale. Within the OD process, there are three main techniques that can be used to motivate employees:

- Facilitate development
- Align goals
- Communicate

By facilitating individual learning and growth, an organization creates opportunity for employees to be invested in the process and the change. When an employees is invested at this level, increased motivation can be seen. This increased motivation lends to a smoother implementation of changes and increases comfort level for individuals to come forward with additional suggestions and concerns. Ultimately, this can increase productivity and efficiently substantially while seeing higher employee retention levels.

When individual goals and objectives are aligned with the organizational goals and objectives, employees understand how their daily work supports the organization's overall work. Even if employees do not have a direct impact on meeting certain organizational goals, ensuring there is understanding of the goals enables employees to support these goals.

In an organization, when there is frequent communication, both upward and downward, transparency can be established. Communication can establish trust in the changes that will be implemented. By ensuring that messages are clear, concise, applicable, and honest, an organization can motivate employees to be engaged in the process of change and implement the change successfully. Messages should be direct and, in the case of delivering negative information, messages should also inform employees of the potential positive aspects of the challenges presented. This type of communication can also lead to employees being more open to sharing ideas and issues that may not otherwise be discovered.

A key component of OD methods is problem solving. There are various structured techniques that can be applied when solving a problem, and each technique comes down to the same basic core steps: (1) define and analyze a problem; (2) identify and choose a solution; (3) plan and implement the solution.

Problem Solving Steps

Analyze Problem

Define Problem

Identify Solutions

Implement

Choose Solutions

Plan of Action

Various structured techniques have been created to assist in the process of solving a problem. Below are three specific techniques and the corresponding steps that can be followed to solve a problem:

- P.D.C.A.: Plan. Do. Check. Act.

- D.M.A.I.C.: Define. Measure. Analyze. Improve. Control.

- A3: Clarify the problem. Break down the problem. Set a goal. Determine the root cause. Develop an action plan. Implement the action plan. Evaluate and review the results. Adjust if necessary and standardize the process.

Many organizations will adopt one technique to apply to all situations. Regardless of the technique selected, the intent and goal is always the same: solve the problem. When applying a problem solving technique, it is important to encourage teamwork and group participation. Having many individuals work through a problem allows for different perspectives to be brought to bear and can enable a deeper understanding of the problem. This can be extremely important when determining the root cause of an issue. If the root cause is not fully determined, then a solution could be implemented that will not affect the issue, or it may even cause other issues. When determining the root cause of a problem, a common practice employed is the "Five Whys" technique. This Six Sigma method is an excellent tool that can be used without needing data or other information. Asking the question "Why?" five times can assist in getting to the bottom of why a certain issue is occurring, or the root cause. Once the true root cause is determined, then real solutions can be discussed to solve the initial problem. Without understanding and addressing the root cause, solutions will not truly address the issue and affect the change needed. When this occurs, it can have a negative impact as employees could become discouraged and their engagement and motivation could suffer. There may be a future impact to engagement as well.

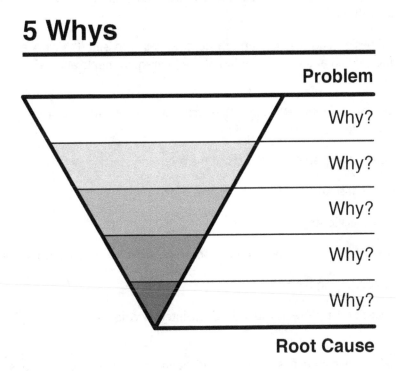

5 Whys

Problem

Why?

Why?

Why?

Why?

Why?

Root Cause

Task/Process Analysis

There are two main types of task analysis—instructional and informational. Instructional task analysis is a step-by-step process that explains how something is done. Informational task analysis is a step-by-step process that explains why something is done. Instructional task analysis can be done at any level in an organization and is an important piece of information for human resources professionals when validating job descriptions. Data gained from task analysis can justify minimum requirements and qualifications, and ensure a well-written and accurate representation of the work being done in a job.

Instructional task analysis is the process in which we study the way others perform a task in a certain environment. Task analysis is a widely accepted and commonly used process for determining valid, accurate, and appropriate job content as well as minimum requirements for positions. This information can validate a requirement for a position and clearly show the essential functions that a position performs.

The task analysis process is based on several concepts:

- Any requirement that could affect the selection and retention must be based on actual, valid job needs

- Any requirement that could affect the selection and retention must be subjected to federal and state regulations such as Equal Employment Opportunity (EEO) and the Americans with Disabilities Act (ADA), and therefore, cannot be discriminatory unless a bona fide occupational qualification (BFOQ) can be proven

    - A BFOQ is a qualification that, while discriminatory in the context of hiring, has been proven and established to be necessary and required in order to perform a particular job. An example of this would be a women's clothing company hiring only women to model their clothing.

- Any individual performing the work and those directly supervising the work are the best resources to provide information and understanding of the job requirements and daily needs to complete the work

- Any job requirements identified from a standardized and consistent analysis are most likely reliable and accurate

Conducting an instructional task analysis consists of the following steps:

1. Identify the specific task to analyze

2. Write down each specific step for the task

3. Have others perform the task following the exact steps identified in the second step

4. Observe others conducting the task

5. Research variances of the process: Did individuals interpret the steps differently? Were there missing steps?

6. Adjust task analysis to include missing steps and clarify misunderstood directions

7. Perform the task with the updated information to ensure accuracy

The information collected from a task analysis can then be used to review and streamline the process. The final, adopted process can then be implemented and used to design and create standard operating procedures (SOPs), manuals, and guides. These materials are vital to ensuring consistency and efficiency for employees and can serve as training materials for new employees. When tasks are broken down into clear steps, new employees can learn processes specific to these tasks.

An instructional task analysis process can be used for simple tasks as well as complicated ones. One way to introduce this concept to others is to engage the group in writing out a process for a simple task that everyone has done. Examples could be making a peanut butter sandwich, brushing one's teeth, or even putting gas in a car. Break employees up into small groups and have them write down the steps to the task of making a sandwich. Once the directions are complete, have another individual act out the steps as written and only those steps. Employees will quickly understand that there can be no assumptions made—if there is not a direct instruction to open the bag of bread or the jar of peanut butter, then the individual cannot move to the next step. When writing a guide or manual that clearly identifies standard operating procedures for a specific task, it is vital to ensure that any individual—regardless of their background or understanding of the work—has every piece of information needed to perform the work and that no assumptions are made. Additionally, it is important to ensure that tools, such as machinery or specific wrenches, and equipment, such as a computer with specific software, are clearly identified in the task analysis and made available to the individual performing the task. Finally, any information that can be shared regarding working and environmental conditions should be indicated in the task analysis. This information may change the tools and equipment needed to perform the tasks and may even change the outcome based on where the work is being done.

An informational task analysis process can be used to communicate a broader picture to individuals and provide information and insight as to how certain task and work flow into other areas of the organization. Understanding the bigger picture is the goal of an informative task analysis and can be gained by discussing the instructional task analysis results. An informational task analysis can also link individual tasks together and show how each process can have a direct impact on another process. This can also help to inform employees in what the ramifications are when errors occur. Impacts from errors may not be immediately discovered, causing multiple issues that could require re-work and even damage control depending on the error and impacts.

By using both instructional and informational task analysis, organizations can ensure a robust understanding of the skills required for each position and how each position builds on to the next. No position is self-contained and the relationships between positions must be understood. These tools enable an organization to have this understanding and to make corrections as new information is available and as process evolves. Additionally, strengths and weaknesses can be identified for each employee which can then result in additional training and learning opportunities to increase and enhance different skill sets or to impart their knowledge and strengths to others.

Coaching and Mentoring Techniques

There are many similarities between coaching and mentoring programs, and many techniques can be used in both programs. It is important, however, to understand the differences between coaching and mentoring to ensure that the appropriate techniques are applied. Both coaching and mentoring programs endeavor to help employees realize their full potential while making a positive impact in their current position. Both programs are built on respect, trust, integrity, and mutual interest. Additionally, both programs are incredibly beneficial for the organization and the individual. Some of these benefits include increased motivation, satisfaction, and engagement for employees, reductions in turnover, more effective interpersonal communications, enhanced relationships, increased productivity, and overall a more successful organization with successful employees.

Mentoring programs are informal programs based the goal of advising. Mentoring is an ongoing relationship that can last for an indefinite period of time. Mentoring is generally informal with meetings scheduled on an as-needed basis when guidance and advice is being requested. Mentoring programs usually focus on broader views with specific discussions about career development, personal growth, and future opportunities. A mentor is an individual who is more experienced and can offer insight in areas of leadership, career opportunities, and professional guidance.

Coaching programs are formal programs based on the goal of asking. Coaching is a relationship that is established for a set period of time to accomplish a set goal. Coaching is a more formal program with meetings scheduled on a regular basis to discuss status, milestones, and next steps. Coaching programs usually focus on specific growth opportunities and performance needs with discussions centered on work developments, issues with specific tasks, or achieving specific goals. A **coach** is an individual who is more experienced in a specific role or task and can offer training in certain skills to reach certain achievements.

The GROW model is a frequently used model of techniques that is commonly used for coaching but can also be used for mentoring. The GROW model focuses on the process shown in the illustration.

Grow Model

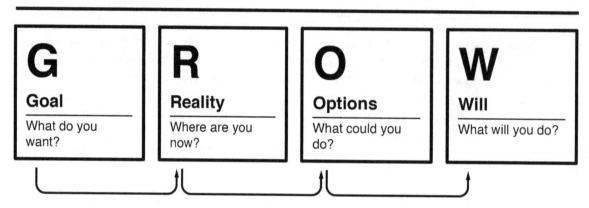

Each step in the process is important to structure the focus of the coaching and mentoring relationship. Without this information, two individuals are just having a conversation with no tangible growth opportunities and, ultimately, no outcomes. Each step of the GROW model provides an opportunity for discussion, thought, dialogue, and questions.

The Goal step focuses on defining an objective, or goal, to accomplish and identifying what success would look like. The Reality step focuses on the current situation, individuals involved, resources available, and other information that is pertinent and important. The Options step focuses on exploring and researching opportunities to solve the issue; this step should focus on the advantages and disadvantages of the options being considered and any new resources needed to accomplish the selected option. This step should also focus on any obstacles that may present themselves in the course of any proposed action or in the implementation of the action. The Will step, often known as the Way Forward or Wrap Up step, focuses on selecting the actions that will be taken and determining if these actions will meet all the goals defined in the first step.

Applying the GROW model to a mentoring program may prove to be more difficult as mentoring is generally less structured and focused on strategy and personal accomplishments. It may be more conducive to a mentoring relationship to utilize the following tools:

- Take notes and create a learning log
- Ask open-ended questions
- Listen
- Encourage conversations
- Request feedback
- Create a record of achievements

While these tools may seem simple and elementary, they are effective and can make all the difference in creating and maintaining an effective and successful mentoring program.

Regardless of the techniques or model used for coaching and mentoring, it is important to understand that a successful program requires several key skills from both parties. Both the coach/mentor and the student/mentee should demonstrate the following skills for a productive relationship and ultimately successful outcomes:

- Establishing an open and honest relationship while building trust
- Actively listening to each other
- Clearly communicating ideas, concepts, thoughts, and concerns
- Sharing constructive feedback during each step of the process
- Giving detailed and specific directions or instructions
- Asking pertinent, specific, and pointed questions
- Taking action at the right times
- Focusing on the appropriate needs of the individual and organization
- Respecting each other's time and commitment to the process

These skills enable participants to have a robust and effective experience in these programs, which can lead to increased satisfaction, morale, and motivation.

In order for an organization to have an effective coaching or mentoring program, it is vital that the following tips are incorporated into the planning of a program:

- Strategy: aligning the program's goals with the organization's strategy, including the vision, mission, and values

- Coherence: establishing the program as part of the development plan means each participant is held accountable for engaging in the program

- Clarity: defining the objectives for all participants and the proposed outcomes so there is a full understanding of the goals

- Matching: pairing coaches/mentors with students/mentees based on a prescribed and structured method, including areas such as development needs, interests, and career path

- Support: providing simple resources and tools to support the program

By incorporating these tips into a coaching or mentoring program, an organization can work to have robust and effective programs that support learning and development at all levels. Additionally, it is also important to establish realistic expectations. It is vital to establish expectations about each participant's role, time commitment, and engagement, as well as what participants can expect to gain and when. Ensuring transparency of the expectations will encourage individuals to be a part of the program, which is especially important in voluntary mentoring programs. These tips are also appropriate to use as techniques when being a mentor. These tips can easily lead to effective techniques for a successful mentoring relationship and mentoring program when the tips are modified to reflect the relationship between the mentor and mentee or between the organization and program.

Employee Retention

Knowledge retention is one of the most important components of learning. If knowledge is not retained for future use, then the training is not successful. Retention is increased when information is processed and practiced at many levels. Repetition is also key to improving the retention of information learned in a training session. In order to determine the appropriate retention concepts to apply to a training, it is important to understand how individuals retain knowledge based on certain teaching methods.

There are two primary teaching styles: passive and participatory. Passive teaching includes giving lectures, reading to an audience or having participants read materials, watching videos, and providing demonstrations. Retention rates of knowledge achieved during a passive teaching method are relatively low, though. The average retention rates for passive teaching methods are: lectures: 5%; reading: 10%; audio-visual: 20%; and demonstration: 30%. These retention rates are extremely low, and a training program that contains only these elements could be seen as unsuccessful. Participatory teaching includes engaging groups in discussion, providing practice opportunities, and teaching others. Retention rates of knowledge achieved during a participatory teaching method are relatively high. The average retention rates for participatory teaching methods are: group discussion: 50%; practice: 75%; and teaching others: 90%. These retention rates are much higher than those seen with passive teaching methods. A training program that contains only these elements could be seen as moderately to extremely successful. It is important to note that these retention rates are averages. This means that individual retention rates could be higher or lower than the reported average.

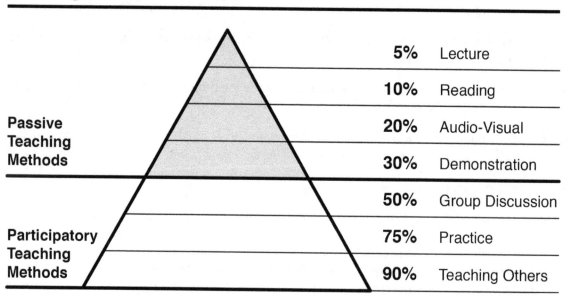

Average Retention Rates

Passive Teaching Methods
- 5% Lecture
- 10% Reading
- 20% Audio-Visual
- 30% Demonstration

Participatory Teaching Methods
- 50% Group Discussion
- 75% Practice
- 90% Teaching Others

Including various teaching methods can increase the retention rates of participants and maximize the learning opportunity. While some content should be trained with a passive teaching method, trainers should also incorporate participatory teaching methods to increase the knowledge retention. A training program may begin with a lecture on the subject matter, followed with a video, and then close with a practice exercise that results in a group discussion. By incorporating multiple teaching methods from both teaching methods, participant retention can be maximized, which will result in a successful training program.

Incorporating the above methods in training programs can increase participants' retention of the information as well as ensure a successful program. While it is important to ensure the actual training program is robust, with multiple teaching methods incorporated, it is also important to implement strategies outside and after the training program. Data has shown that after participating in a training program, individuals lose knowledge and information at a relatively quick pace unless the knowledge is immediately applied. Some research indicates that professionals could lose up to 80% of the training material learned within three to six months after the training is delivered. In order to maximize, enhance, and maintain knowledge retention, it is important to implement specific strategies before, during, and after the delivery of a training program. By having robust strategies in place, an organization can ensure that the information in maintained.

Before training is delivered, the program should be previewed to ensure that the training is complete, appropriate, and responding to a need. It is also appropriate to understand what the needs will be after the training program is delivered so that a plan can be put in place to address knowledge retention. Questions should be asked before the training is delivered to ensure that any concerns and issues can be resolved before the training is conducted. The program should then be communicated to all levels of the organization as appropriate. This communication should include the topic and subject matter, the goals and expectations of the training, and the learning objectives. This ensures buy-in at all levels of the organization, including supervisory support.

During the training, it is important that managers and leadership are visible and participating. Employees will respect and accept training at a higher level when it seen that there is a commitment from the leadership. If employees see leadership practicing principles of integrity, work ethic, honesty, and respect, they are generally more willing to exhibit these principles individually. This also is true for behaviors in the workplace. If employees see that management and leadership are not respectful of time, always arriving late to meetings or not being considerate of other's time and commitment, this will be reciprocated. Minimizing disruptions to a training is also important as it shows a clear commitment to the program and the importance of the subject matter, as well as the participation of individuals.

One important subject to include regarding disruptions is having participants turn off their phones. If this is not possible, then phones should be muted and only checked during breaks or other specific opportunities. Having a room of 25 participants all checking their phones for messages, emails, or other information can severely diminish the focus of the group. This is another example of how leadership can project an important message—if individuals see leadership focused on their phones, they will mirror this behavior and receive the message that the training is not that important. Individual commitment to a training program should not be taken lightly. It is only with the support of all levels of an organization that a training program can truly be successful.

After delivering a training program, it is important to communicate the expectations and commit to a follow-up plan. Participants should understand what is expected of them following a training program in both the short term and the long term. Participants should commit to a follow up plan to ensure the information and knowledge learned in the training program is retained and utilized in the course of their work. Additionally, it is important to ensure that the follow up plan include new resources, additional sessions, or other items as appropriate to continue engaging individuals in learning and growing.

One of the most vital components to ensuring a training program is successful with retained knowledge is to have the support and commitment of upper management and leadership. A training program can have the great resources, insightful information, engaging trainers, and amazing tools, but without support and commitment from the top of the organization, the program will not be nearly successful as it could be.

Techniques to Encourage Creativity and Innovation

Creativity and innovation are often what sets apart one organization from another. Encouraging employees to be creative and innovative can lead to developments and improvements that can change a company's course and lead to a path of success. Additionally, engaging employees in this manner can lead to improved satisfaction, morale, overall corporate success, and lower turnover. It is not always easy to engage employees creatively but research shows that many organizations believe a lack of innovative and creative ideas is a major roadblock to their potential success. By implementing specific techniques, an organization can promote a culture of creativity and innovation.

First and foremost, employees need to care. If employees do not feel connected to the company or its products and services, they have little reason to be creative and innovative. By including employees in discussions and affording an opportunity to provide feedback, an organization sets up a culture of caring. This can positively motivate employees to be engaged in coming up with new ideas and proposing new solutions. Additionally, organizations can further encourage creativity by empowering employees who propose new ideas and solutions to actually be a part of making them happen. This establishes a sense of trust for employees to eliminate fear or concern about taking chances with new and innovative ways of conducting business.

Another important technique used to encourage creativity and innovation is keeping the process as simple as possible. When appropriate and possible, eliminating cumbersome steps and bureaucratic red tape can help employees think more creatively. While it is not always possible to eliminate some parameters like legal requirements, government codes, or other rules and regulations, assistance in identifying these parameters and the related flexibility, if any, can encourage creativity. It also enables employees to gain an increased understanding as to why certain tasks or requests take longer than others.

Simple things such as an open-door policy, suggestion boxes, or brainstorming lunch sessions are excellent ways to create an environment that is conducive to creativity. Engaging in games and contests can also encourage creativity. Having a contest to win a gift card for the best idea is a great way to get employees excited about being creative and participate in the process. While most employees will be energized and excited about these events and the opportunity to be creative, others may not be. Some employees may be feeling overworked, and being creative is not something that is engaging to them. In this case it is important to reassure employees that work-life balance is important. Working together to potentially redistribute workload or provide additional resources may be appropriate and necessary. While this is not always feasible, when opportunities and new information arise to support employees it must be taken advantage of.

Another great technique to encourage creativity and innovation is to strategically identify diverse and uncommon teams to work together. People have a habit of always sitting at the lunch table with the people they know and work with the most. Encourage individuals to branch out and work with others who would not be part of a typical working relationship. By mixing multiple departments and levels of employees, the diversity in this new work group can bring about even more creativity. It also will provide an opportunity for individuals to get to know others and establish new relationships. Additionally, building teams in this manner will allow for learning more about each other's areas of expertise and how things get done. Employees can gain insights into other departments and how their work influences others directly and indirectly. Once the team has been established and expectations are provided, enable the members to work autonomously without being micromanaged. Creativity and innovation are not linear and usually do not occur within the confines of a set process. Instead, they flourish in brainstorming settings and flow with conversations, often building on other ideas or thoughts that are injected into the discussion. Allowing this freestyle dialogue and thought process to occur will substantially increase an employee's ability to be creative and innovative. Employees should be working toward the established goal that was provided but allowed to create the roadmap independently.

At the core of creativity and innovation is the ability to create new ideas. A commonly used technique to generate new ideas is the POINt technique.

- Pluses
- Opportunities
- Issues
- New Thinking

The POINt technique enables the individual to consider all the aspects of a new idea and then think through potential solutions to those aspects that could be a challenge to overcome. It is important to fully vet a new idea to ensure that any concerns or issues are considered. Brainstorming can assist with this process and encourage creativity at every level of the process.

As indicated earlier, it is vital for any program to have support and commitment from the highest levels of management in an organization. The leaders of the organization set the example for the entire workforce and when the leaders are engaged in creative and innovative thinking, it encourages the entire workforce to do the same. A great way to kick off a session that encourages creativity and innovation is to have individuals in leadership attend and share an example of how they implemented creativity and proposed a solution. Presenting cases of successes and failures can also be a great way to encourage employees to be open and willing to coming to the table with new ideas. If encouraging employee creativity is part of the culture, the organization is in a position to glean amazing results. From increased productivity, new ways of getting work done, streamlined procedures, elimination of costs and waste, employees will have a sense of pride having had a true impact.

Finally, when successes are a direct result of creative and innovative thinking, the individuals responsible must be recognized. Either informally or formally, an organization must ensure that recognition is given when due. Failing to do so could severely impact the willingness for employees to participate in the future.

Practice Questions

1. The tool that enables an employee to discuss future opportunities and the skills needed to achieve those opportunities is known as a(n) _____.
    a. Performance evaluation
    b. Individual development plan
    c. Training program
    d. Performance improvement plan

2. Which of the following are important pieces of data to incorporate into succession planning? (Select all that apply.)
    a. Job descriptions
    b. Compensation
    c. Exit interviews
    d. Organizational charts
    e. Attrition
    f. Benefits

3. Which of the following statements accurately characterize/s attrition? (Select all that apply.)
    a. Attrition is the process of visualizing current gaps in the organization.
    b. Attrition occurs when employees exit an organization, either voluntarily or involuntarily.
    c. Attrition is an organization's turnover rate.
    d. Attrition is an important metric that can enable an organization to make appropriate changes to retain employees.

4. What is the federal regulation that requires training in various safety and health areas?
    a. Fair Labor Standards Act (FLSA)
    b. Family Medical Leave Act (FMLA)
    c. Occupational Safety and Health Act (OSHA)
    d. Americans with Disabilities Act (ADA)

5. Match the learning theory with its primary focus:
    a. Behaviorism   1. How an individual interprets and applies new information
    b. Cognitivism   2. What an individual does
    c. Constructivism   3. An individual being self-directed in learning
    d. Experiential   4. How an individual processes information
    e. Connectivism   5. How an individual learns from their own experiences

6. Which of the following about a training program is true?
    a. When developing a training program, human resources does not need to ask anyone the needs of the organization.
    b. With regard to enrollment in training programs, all employees should attend every course offered.
    c. When creating a training program, increased structure results in increased participation and learning.
    d. It is not necessary for leadership to participate in or commit to training programs to ensure success.
    e. None of the above

7. Which element of adult learning refers to how participants apply the information to their job?
   a. Transference
   b. Reinforcement
   c. Orientation
   d. Motivation
   e. Retention

8. Match each step of the ADDIE process with its specific focus:
   a. Analyze   1. What should be included and the audience of the message
   b. Design   2. What the delivery of the training program will be
   c. Develop   3. How effective the training program was and validation for future use
   d. Implement   4. What is needed and the skills gaps in the organization
   e. Evaluate   5. What the actual content and materials will be

9. What is the correct progression in evaluating the effectiveness of a training program?
   a. Results; Behavior; Learning; Reaction
   b. Learning; Behavior, Results; Reaction
   c. Reaction; Learning; Behavior; Results
   d. Reaction; Results; Behavior; Learning

10. What do Key Performance Indicators (KPIs) of a training program show? (Select all that apply.)
    a. Progress toward a goal or objective
    b. Average training cost
    c. What matters and what needs attention
    d. A clear strategic picture
    e. Return on investment

11. Which of the following statements about Organizational Development (OD) are true? (Select all that apply.)
    a. OD focuses on changing organizational culture.
    b. OD is a series of methods and techniques that are used to facilitate long-term changes in an organization.
    c. Although they have individual impact and increase employee morale, OD models do not increase efficiency and productivity.
    d. OD is more effective when employees are engaged in the process.

12. What do the "5 Whys" reveal about a problem?
    a. Root cause
    b. Solution
    c. Impact
    d. Specific details

13. Drop and drag the following features to match them with the appropriate program, either Mentoring or Coaching.
    a. Informal program   Mentoring
    b. Formal program
    c. Structured time frame
    d. Ongoing relationship   Coaching
    e. Accomplish specific goals and objectives
    f. Offer insight, experience, and guidance

14. Which teaching method has the lowest retention rate?
    a. Demonstration
    b. Practice
    c. Lecture
    d. Reading
    e. Teaching others

15. Which of the following can create an environment that supports creativity and innovation? (Select all that apply.)
    a. Suggestion boxes
    b. Brainstorming
    c. Open-door policy
    d. Contests

Answer Explanations

1. B: An Individual Development Plan (IDP) is the tool used to engage employees in a discussion about future opportunities and skills need to accomplish their goals. While performance evaluations, training programs, and performance improvement plans are important and are aligned with the IDP, they are different tools that assess specific performance and needs during a set time frame as well as identify courses to provide learning opportunities.

2. A, B, D, E, & F: Job descriptions, compensation, organizational charts, attrition, and benefits are all important pieces of information that should be available and considered when working through a succession plan. Although exit interviews (Choice *C*) can contain important information that should be considered by an organization, the information is based on an individual's experience and issues should be address appropriately.

3. B, C, & D: Attrition occurs when employees leave an organization. Attrition can be broken down into voluntary and involuntary attrition; it is the data representation of an organization's turnover. Attrition is an important metric that can enable an organization to make appropriate changes to retain employees and minimize turnover. The process of visualizing gaps in an organization (Choice *A*) is called succession planning.

4. C: OSHA is the federal regulation that requires training in safety and health as well as all areas related to safety for their specific job. FLSA is the law that sets the standards to determine overtime compensation. FMLA is unpaid leave that employees can be eligible to take in the case of medical condition. ADA is the law protecting employees and applicants from discrimination due to having a disability.

5. A – 2; B – 4; C – 1; D – 5; E – 3: There are five common standard learning processes, each with a different focus. The focus of behaviorism is on what an individual does. Cognitivism focuses on how an individual processes information. The focus of constructivism is on how an individual interprets and applies new information. Experiential focuses on an individual's experiences and how they can learn from them. The focus of connectivism is on an individual being self-directed.

6. E: None of these statements are true. When developing a training program, many resources should be used to consider the needs of the organization. When delivering a training program, employees should be selected based on their individual needs and growth opportunities. The exception to this is that some training programs are mandatory and all employees must attend. When creating a training program, structure is important but flexibility should be added in where appropriate to encourage discussion and dynamic learning. It is vital for leadership to participate and commit to training programs to ensure success.

7. A: Transference is one of the most important elements of adult learning; it is how a participant understands the information learned in training and relates it to their job. Reinforcement, orientation, motivation, and retention are all important components of adult learning, but transference is the component that specifically correlates how an individual "transfers" the knowledge to their work.

8. A – 4; B – 1; C – 5; D – 2; & E – 3: The ADDIE model follows the steps Analyze, Design, Develop, Implement, and Evaluate. Analysis focuses on what is needed. Design focuses on what should be included and the audience of the message, Development focuses on the actual content and material, Implement focuses on the delivery of the program. Evaluation focuses on the effectiveness and validation of the training program.

9. C: The correct progression in evaluating the effectiveness of a training program is Reaction, Learning, Behavior, Results. Each level builds on the previous level. Some programs need only the two lower levels of evaluation, depending on the scope and impact of the training.

10. A, C, & D: KPIs add value by showing a clear picture of the implemented strategy, what matters and needs attention, and the progress towards goals. The average training costs and return on investment are examples of actual KPIs that can be calculated to show the effectiveness of training.

11. A, B, & D: OD focuses on changing organizational culture through a series of methods and techniques. OD is used to facilitate long-term change in and organization and is more effective when employees are involved in the process. OD has multiple positive effects which include individual impact and increasing employee morale, as well as increasing efficiency and productivity. Increasing efficiency and productivity are vital results that ensure an OD method was successful.

12. A: The "5 Whys" is a Six Sigma technique that enables discovery of a problem's root cause by asking and answering the question "Why?" five times. Although the solution, impact, and specific details of a problem are important pieces of information, the technique of "5 Whys" is used to specifically discover the root cause of a problem so that an effective solution can be put in place to address the true issue.

13. Mentoring – A, D, & F; Counseling – B, C, & E: Mentoring programs are informal and based on the goal of advising. They are an ongoing relationship that last an indefinite period of time and focus on personal growth and future opportunities. Coaching programs are formal and based on accomplishing a specific goal or objective. They are set for a certain period of time and focus on certain tasks.

14. C: The method with the lowest retention rate is Lecture at 5%, and the method with the highest retention rate is Teaching Others at 90% (Choice *E*). Demonstration (Choice *A*) has a 30% retention rate; Practice (Choice *B*) is 75%; Reading (Choice *D*) is 10%.

15. A, B, C, & D: Simple things can encourage a creative and innovative working environment. Suggestion boxes, brainstorming opportunities, an open-door policy, and contests can all engage employees to be creative and innovative.

Total Rewards

Compensation-Related Information and Payroll Issue Resolution

Human Resources professionals are responsible for managing information regarding compensation appropriately, responsibly, and accurately. Ensuring that employees are paid a fair, equitable, and appropriate wage for the work being performed is at the core of compensation-related work. There are numerous tools and resources available to ensure that compensation is being managed appropriately for an organization. Best practices and benchmarking can also be used to align an organization with standards that are practiced across a particular field or industry, business market, state, and beyond.

It is important to have robust practices relative to employee information that assure employees of the confidentiality and security of their information. With the ongoing threat of security breaches and identity theft, it is necessary to safeguard personal employee information, including compensation-related information. Data such as home addresses, dates of birth, social security numbers, direct deposit routing and account numbers, and other highly sensitive pieces of information should be held under lock and key, and when necessary and possible, encrypted.

Human Resources professionals are also responsible for assisting Payroll staff in resolving issues related to inaccuracies in payroll such as salary information, overtime calculations, hours to be paid, and retroactive changes including both overpayments and underpayments. Attention to detail in this area is vitally important as not only can this impact employees personally and financially, but noncompliance with federal and state regulations can cause fines, audits, and further scrutiny into an organization's policies and practices.

Another component that HR is responsible for is understanding and determining the Fair Labor Standards Act (FLSA) status of a position—whether the position is exempt or nonexempt in relation to overtime. Often referred to as "the wage and hour law," the FLSA law will determine if a position is eligible for overtime. Regular audits of this status for every position in an organization should be conducted to ensure compliance with this important law. Understanding that a position's roles and responsibilities evolve with time, it is important that positions are reviewed often to ensure that job descriptions are accurate. Job descriptions are the foundation of determining the FLSA status; if they are outdated or an inaccurate representation of the actual work being performed, the FLSA status could be inaccurate. The FLSA status for a position is an extremely important component to total compensation and how payroll will calculate an employee's salary. Without a robust knowledge of FLSA and how each position is impacted, Payroll could very well be compensating employees inaccurately. If an audit is conducted and errors and inconsistencies are discovered, an organization could face extreme penalties, fees, and retroactive payments to employees. This could have a huge negative impact to the business and the bottom line.

Human Resources is instrumental in ensuring that compensation is managed appropriately and conveyed to Payroll accurately. A strong working relationship that includes direct lines of communication and understanding of the roles and expectations between these two functions will only benefit an organization and the employees. Some organizations align Payroll within the Human Resources function, while others place Payroll within the Finance function. Regardless of where these two functions lie within an organizational reporting structure, Human Resources and Payroll are integral components to each other's success.

Awareness of Noncash Rewards

In recent years, a large focus has been directed toward noncash rewards and benefits that an organization offers to employees. It is becoming more important for organizations to focus on offering a wide array of these types of benefits to attract and retain top talent. While in previous years, the salary and take-home pay were the primary components of accepting a position with a company, times have changed. Employees want programs that allow for a more holistic approach to their lives versus just focusing on an hourly salary. Organizations have responded with programs that allow for more work/life balance, community-focused programs, and recognition. Employees now have options available to them such as:

- Telecommuting for a portion, or all, of their workweek,
- Adhering to an alternative work schedule such as a 9X80 or 4X10 schedule,
- Being paid for volunteering their time to a charity organization,
- On-site daycare and exercise facilities,
- Fresh, healthy, and affordable meal options,
- Tuition reimbursement and furthering education goals,
- Employee recognition programs, both informal and formal.

Each of the above noncash rewards is an option for an organization to consider. Some may be viable options, but others, based on the business model, organizational structure, customer needs, and staffing levels, may not be options that can be offered. It is important to assess each program individually to determine if it will have an impact for employees, both current and future. While some programs may offer a larger return on investment than others, each employee will value one or more at different levels. For a single mother with a young child, an on-site daycare facility may be the noncash reward that holds the largest, most significant impact. For an seasoned professional with over two decades of work experience, being offered the opportunity to be paid while working with Habitat for Humanity might hold a special value for this individual. Understanding an organization's employees and their needs allows for a proper assessment of which programs would be the best to offer for the biggest impact. It may be appropriate to survey current employees to discover what options would be most valued or to gather more creative and flexible ideas directly from them. Exit interviews are also an excellent tool for discovering from employees leaving the organization what impacted their decision to leave and if their new organization offers a specific noncash reward that attracted them.

In addition to creating and implementing these programs and options for employees, it is even more important to ensure that Human Resources communicates the programs with employees. A very common response from employees when asked if they knew about certain programs is "I had no idea we had that!" It is the responsibility of Human Resources to communicate frequently and regularly about such programs to make sure that employees are aware of them. Employees also appreciate the opportunity to regularly submit feedback on current programs as well as ideas for new programs. Having an online suggestion box or even soliciting random feedback from employees regarding new ideas is a fantastic way to engage employees so that they are part of the process.

Benefit Programs

Human Resources professionals are responsible for understanding the needs of the organization and of the employees who work for the organization. This includes having a robust knowledge of the best options in the areas of health insurance, retirement programs, employee assistance programs, life insurance, disability insurance, worker's compensation programs, flexible spending accounts, and voluntary insurance programs such as short-term and long-term disability programs.

It might be beneficial to conduct surveys with other agencies that provide similar services to ensure that an organization's offerings are appropriate for the employee population. It could also be beneficial to survey the current employees to determine which elements of the benefit package are meeting their needs and which elements should be reviewed or added.

Frequent review of costs and services should also be conducted to ensure that the return on investment of these programs is appropriate. It may be time to conduct an analysis to determine if another program or vendor would be suitable to provide better services at a lower cost.

Organizations can offer multiple choices to employees for health insurance coverage, including both preferred provider organization (PPO) and health maintenance organization (HMO) options, and sometimes, many choices of each type of plan to ensure the needs of employees can be met. Dental insurance, vision insurance, and prescription coverage are also options that employers offer to employees to ensure employees protect their health on all levels.

Employee assistance programs usually offer services related to a wide array of personal and professional counseling, including legal, financial, change management, stress management, marriage, divorce, and parental counseling, and on many other topics that individuals deal with in their personal and professional lives.

Communication of these plans is extremely important so that employees understand their options and have the information to make informed choices. Often, organizations conduct a health fair or benefits exposition with vendors from all their benefit providers to allow employees direct access.

Many organizations also allow a cafeteria style plan, which is a type of benefit plan dictated by Section 125 of the Internal Revenue Code. This type of plan allows employees to choose from two or more benefits consisting of cash or a qualified benefit plan. A Section 125 plan would identify a certain dollar amount that an employee is eligible for to assist them in paying for their benefits. If there are dollars remaining after their selections have been made, the employee can opt to take those dollars in another way. Employees could also "opt out" and receive the dollars provided as compensation. Usually an organization will structure their Section 125 plan to where the "opt out" amount is substantially less than the total amount given to assist with paying for benefits. This has become a huge matter in the State of California with a recent settled lawsuit *Flores v. City of San Gabriel*, in which the dollars received from the insurance "opt out" should have been considered when calculating overtime and other premium pay. As a general reminder, it is important for Human Resources professionals to know as much as possible regarding federal and state laws—as well as current case law—as they might change the way an organization needs to implement benefit programs.

Federally-Compliant Compensation and Benefit Programs

Regardless of the programs offered concerning total rewards, each program must be federally compliant with all laws. It is important to remember that some states have their own individual laws and versions of compliance. In some cases, the state law does not align with the federal law. In these situations, it is important to remember that, in general, the law that is the most generous to the employee is the law that should be followed. From the Fair Labor Standards Act (FLSA), the Family and Medical Leave Act (FMLA), Americans with Disabilities Act (ADA), Affordable Care Act (ACA), and other state leave programs providing benefits such as paid family leave, additional leave rights, disability, and worker's compensation, Human Resources professionals must ensure that every benefit and program aligns with the most generous level of benefit provided.

An organization's policies should ensure that employees receive compensation and benefits in alignment with these federal laws. Policies should clearly communicate to employees their rights as well as the responsibilities of the employer and employee. While an employer may offer FMLA because the company employs more than fifty employees, it should be clearly communicated that employees must be employed for twelve months and have worked at least 1,250 hours in that twelve-month time period to be eligible under the FMLA law. The policy should also clearly communicate the procedure for applying for this benefit, what the benefit is (including how compensation is handled), and what is expected of both parties throughout the process. In the same manner, employees should know the process for working with their employer if they have a disability under the ADA. This process should be clearly outlined in the policy and include the rights and responsibilities of the employer and employee, the complete process, including how to request reasonable accommodations and work restrictions, and how independent medical evaluations will be handled.

Additionally, it is important to understand the Equal Pay Act (EPA) of 1963. Gender equality in pay is a major topic of discussion today, and organizations must ensure that their practices regarding compensation and benefits are compliant with these laws. The EPA amended the FLSA law relative to gender inequality to ensure that men and women are paid the same wage for the same work. The Equal Pay Act of 2010 was passed to help correct the disparity that many women faced regarding their pay when doing similar jobs that their male counterparts were doing. This law helped to ensure that a woman's contract terms for a position were the same as a man's contract terms. Continued legislation has been seen to correct these disparities as well. Recently, the state of California passed a law in that an organization cannot request historical salary information from a candidate to use in preparing an offer of employment. The reasoning for this is that if a woman has experienced discrimination in her job history relative to pay and that information is used to determine her new salary, the disparity of pay will most likely continue and never be corrected.

Federal Laws and Regulations Regarding Total Rewards

The Department of Labor (DOL) administers and enforces over 180 federal laws, many of which govern the areas of Wages and Hours, Workplace Safety and Health, Workers' Compensation, Employee Benefit Safety, Unions and Their Members, and Garnishment of Wages. While all federal laws and regulations are important and must be incorporated into an organization's policies and practices, the focus of this section is on the following: the Fair Labor Standards Act (FLSA) and the Family and Medical Leave Act (FMLA). These two laws focus on the total rewards components of compensation and leave related to illness or injury.

The FLSA federal statute was passed to ensure workers are protected from abuses related to compensation. The FLSA ensures workers are paid a living wage and mandates how workers are paid for overtime work. Often referred to as the "wage and hour law," the FLSA controls minimum wage, overtime, equal pay, recordkeeping, and child labor. Private sector and public sector employers are subject to following the FLSA and understanding which guidelines apply. In addition to the above list of compensation-related items, government agencies must also be familiar with other labor laws such as the Davis-Bacon Act, which requires the agency to pay a prevailing wage rate and fringe benefits to certain contractors for certain work.

The overtime rule under the FLSA requires that employees be paid an annual salary of $47,476 or more in order to qualify as an exempt employee. This salary threshold is in addition to a duties test that would qualify a position as exempt or nonexempt. In general, executive, administrative, professional, outside sales, and certain computer-related employees are exempt from the FLSA. There are other exemptions; each position should be evaluated to ensure its specific FLSA status based on the most recent law and current duties of the position.

An exempt employee is an employee who is not subject to the FLSA requirements, and as such is not eligible for overtime. Exempt employees are considered to be salaried employees and are paid a fixed salary regardless of the total number of hours they work. They are paid for a body of work regardless of how long it takes to complete the work. Per the FLSA, there is no limit on the number of hours an exempt employee may work. A nonexempt employee is an employee who is subject to the FLSA requirements and is eligible for overtime. Nonexempt employees are considered hourly employees and are to be paid at least the minimum wage of the state as well as all overtime due. Overtime must be paid at time-and-a-half for all hours worked over forty hours in any one week. Some agencies have practices put in place to pay overtime based on a daily basis for all hours worked over eight hours in any one day. However, it is up to the Human Resources and Payroll professionals to ensure that all criteria are met based on the state requirements for paying overtime and the policies, procedures, and practices that align.

The Family and Medical Leave Act (FMLA) of 1993 requires covered employers to provide employees with job protection and unpaid leave for qualifying medical and family reasons. FMLA entitles eligible employees to take up to twelve weeks of unpaid, job-protected leave each year for the following reasons:

- The birth or care of a child
- The placement of a child for adoption or foster care
- The care of a child, spouse, or parent with a serious health condition
- The employee's own serious health condition

Additionally, covered servicemembers with a serious injury or illness may take up to twenty-six weeks of FMLA leave. Organizations must be covered under the FMLA law to be able to offer their employees FMLA—this requires employing more than fifty employees within a seventy-five mile radius of the primary workplace. Additionally, employees must have been employed with this employer at least twelve months and have worked a minimum of 1,250 hours within that time period to be eligible for FMLA.

While FMLA is unpaid, employees can take their accrued leave to cover this time and ensure they remain in a paid status while on FMLA. Depending on the organization's policies, employees most generally can take sick leave, vacation leave, personal leave, and other forms of leave to receive a paycheck during the time being on FMLA. Many states such as California have programs such as disability insurance and paid family leave that employees can apply for to assist with compensation while out on FMLA. Organizations can then coordinate benefits with these state programs so that employees receive the maximum amount of benefits while on FMLA. Human Resources and Payroll will work with the employee and the state agencies to provide accurate compensation and leave information to coordinate benefits and determine how to best assist the employee during their leave. In many cases, depending on the salary, leave balances and state benefits, an employee may be able to collect one hundred percent of their salary between all the available benefits during their FMLA leave.

It is also important to understand that certain states may have their own regulations allowing additional unpaid leave relating to specific qualifying events. For example, in the state of California, the California Family Rights Act (CFRA) allows for eligible employees to take additional unpaid time off for qualified leave requests. These additional state laws require a robust partnership between Human Resources and Payroll to ensure that employees receive the maximum benefits allowable under federal and state laws. Understanding how each regulation works and how they interconnect or differ from each other is vital to ensuring that policies are written to reflect all benefits afforded to employees. These policies should be reviewed periodically to ensure they are in compliance with the current regulations. As lawmakers frequently pass new bills to add, change, or update benefits, it is vital to ensure the organization is in compliance with managing an employee's FMLA and other leave benefits. And as previously indicated, if there are differences between the federal and state laws, the law that is the most generous to the employee is the law that should be followed.

Compensation Policies, Processes, and Analysis

Above all, compensation policies should ensure fairness, equity, and competitiveness while following all federal and state regulations. One function of Human Resources professionals is to orient new employees to the culture and policies of the organization. Compensation policies are at the core of these orientations and should also be made available to employees who have worked for the organization for a period of time. Organizations can offer refresher training opportunities to ensure that all employees have an understanding of the current policies. With changes to laws and company policy, there may have been some changes since an employee was first hired. It is important to ensure that employees have knowledge of and understand the current policy.

Policies should be written to ensure employees understand how an organization pays employees. From overtime payments and options, shift differentials, and merit increases to vacation and leave accruals, all policies should be clear, concise, and understandable. Employees should also understand what the standard work week structure is as well as the core service hours for customers. If employees have options related to their work week structure, these should be outlined in a policy that includes how employees can take advantage of these other options.

Policies should communicate when employees will receive their paycheck and the options they have regarding how to receive their paycheck. Options such as a paper check or direct deposit should be communicated along with how to request and set up each. Overtime policies should dictate how and when overtime is earned, how it is paid based on a time-and-a-half rate, and if compensatory time can be selected as an option. Compensatory time, commonly known as "comp time," is an option that employees can select instead of receiving overtime pay. In lieu of receiving the overtime pay, employees receive the time-and-a-half, or one and a half hours, of leave instead of pay. Compensation policies should also address holiday pay with a defined list of approved holidays. Vacation leave policies should be communicated to employees and include accrual rates, maximum accrual balance, carryover year to year, and cash out options.

Employees should clearly understand what they will earn in vacation leave and when they will earn it. An organization can determine when it will provide employees with their vacation leave. Two options would be to provide the vacation leave annually in January, based on service from the previous year, or to have employees earn their leave on a bi-weekly or monthly basis. While employees should be held responsible for managing their own leave appropriately, it is the responsibility of Human Resources to ensure that employees understand their rights and options regarding vacation leave.

Human Resources professionals are responsible for ensuring that the compensation policies are reflective of actual process. In other words, the policies should accurately capture how the organization operates on a daily basis. If a policy needs to be updated because it would be in the organization's or employees' best interest, a thorough review should be conducted and, if appropriate, the policy updated accordingly. It is important to understand that any change, regardless of size, may have unintended consequences to both parties. Conducting a thorough review and involving stakeholders for both the organization and the employees before changes are implemented can assist in more options for consideration, opportunities to communicate thoroughly, and making the change easier for all.

Policies should continually be audited for accuracy and legal compliance. Many organizations will put all of their policies on a standard schedule so that every policy is reviewed at a specific time. If a change in the law occurs outside of this schedule, then an ad hoc review and audit would be conducted to ensure the policy is compliant. Human Resources professionals should be proactive in reviewing their policies. One component of these reviews is to conduct benchmarking and best practices research in an effort to provide employees the best options regarding total rewards. If an organization is a market leader in total rewards, it is important to stay on top of the latest and greatest options in total rewards, whereas a market follower will just do what everyone else is doing without being more creative or going above and beyond in the area of total rewards.

Another important component to compensation policy and review is the evaluation of a salary to ensure employees are being paid appropriately for their work. Work will evolve and new tasks and responsibilities may be added to an employee's workload. It is important to make sure that these new tasks are taken into account regarding compensation. Human Resources professionals should ensure the policy for requesting an evaluation is robust and clear, including forms and information for employees to complete and review. Timelines should also be included regarding the length of time it will most likely take to complete a review and how changes to salary will be handled. Supervisors and employees should have the option to submit a request to evaluate a salary and upper management should be involved in the overall process and decision making. If there is not sufficient budget to account for an increase in salary due to the added work, it may be appropriate to reassign the new work to another employee to resolve the issue, or to remove other elements of work to ensure the workload is balanced.

A market review of an organization's compensation may also be pertinent to ensure that employees are being paid a competitive wage. A market review is an analysis of other organizations in the same or similar industry with similar demographics such as staffing levels, budget, and other components. A market review assesses how an organization aligns with other agencies in the areas of total rewards to ensure compensation and benefits are appropriate. If an organization is seeing a higher than normal rate of attrition, a market review might assist in determining if they are paying a wage that would encourage employees to stay with or join the organization.

Prior to conducting a market review, Human Resources professionals should work with executive management to ensure that the organization's priorities regarding compensation and total rewards are understood and align with current policies and practices. In general, market leaders set the bar; market followers do what everyone else is doing; market laggers offer less to employees. An organization's priorities regarding compensation must be clear so that the market data can be interpreted accurately and recommendations made that align with the priorities. If an organization is a market lagger, then recommendations that are out of the box, creative, and more than what competitors are offering will not align with the priorities set.

Budgeting, Payroll, and Accounting Practices Regarding Compensation and Benefits

Budgeting is one of the most important functions that an organization is responsible for developing, maintaining, and updating. Budgeting and following healthy financial practices ensure that the organization can maintain its core services to customers as well as the personnel staffing to deliver those services. Human Resources plays an instrumental role in the budgeting process by providing accurate information related to compensation and benefits for all employees. The budget planning process can be positively impacted by understanding benefits increases, foreseeing salary increases (such as cost of living adjustments, merit increases, and training), and knowing when certain events such as salary reviews and market assessments will occur.

Planning a budget with inaccurate or incomplete information can have a significant impact and could cause ramifications such as poor customer products, or even layoffs and hiring freezes. The collaborative efforts of Payroll and Human Resources to deliver worksheets or other tools that outline personnel costs is a convenient and effective way to assist department managers with their budgets. Personnel costs should include any increases that could be seen in the next budget year that the department manager should consider when planning the budget. Salary, taxes, pension, training, education, shift differential, benefit increases, vacation leave payouts, and any other personnel costs should be reported to ensure a full and complete view of the staffing budget. Human Resources can also assist departments in understanding the cost savings when a position has been vacant for a period of time. Having a full understanding of personnel costs is instrumental in the budgeting process.

Just as it is important for department managers to understand personnel costs in the budgeting process, it is equally important for employees to understand their paychecks and how they are paid. Beginning with new hire orientation, Human Resources professionals should strive to ensure that employees understand their paychecks. Determining an hourly rate is only one component. In addition to communicating to employees how often they will be paid, employers should also explain how that pay will be distributed. Some organizations allow their employees to be paid with a paper check, a direct deposit, or even a transfer to a debit card. While some organizations allow this flexibility in how to receive the pay, other organizations streamline their payroll by requiring employees to adhere to their pay policy with only one form of payment. The most common form of payment is direct deposit, which can be requested by employees with the submission of a voided check.

Each organization prepares paychecks differently; therefore, it is important to communicate to employees the layout of the paychecks so there is understanding of each line item. Salary, including overtime, payouts, differentials, and other forms of payment should be clearly itemized. Deductions such as federal and state taxes, social security, disability, and worker's compensation insurance should each have their own line item and be clearly identified. Contributions to pensions and medical premiums, additional compensation such as car or phone allowances, and any other special premium pay should be clearly communicated on employees' paychecks. It is important for each type of compensation, deduction, and contribution to be specifically identified for many reasons: employees may need to separate out certain pay for tax purposes, wage garnishments may need to be made based on base pay only, pension contributions need to be calculated based on certain types of pay, and it is easier to identify certain types of compensation or benefits when auditing. An additional item that many organizations include on paychecks is the leave balance status including vacation, sick, personal, short-term disability, holiday, or other types of leave. This ensures that employees are receiving this information on a regular basis so that they can manage their time appropriately.

There may be times when an error is made on a paycheck, so that there is an overpayment or an underpayment. There could be multiple reasons for an error, but it is important for Human Resources and Payroll to work together in a consistent practice to correct the mistake for the employees as well as to conduct an audit to ensure the mistake did not occur in other cases. If the mistake was a one-time event, the issue can be resolved quickly; however, if it is discovered during the audit that the mistake was ongoing and occurred on multiple occasions, potentially with multiple employees, it would be prudent to review policy and practice to ensure that the mistake is fully understood and corrected so that it does not occur again in the future.

Every employee must complete the appropriate paperwork when beginning their employment with an organization. This includes paperwork to set up their employee profile in the system. Employees should expect to complete several forms specific to just their pay. W-4 forms for federal and state tax withholdings, direct deposit forms, benefit enrollment forms, deferred compensation forms, and retirement forms are some of the most common forms that new employees can expect to complete. After new hire orientation, it is important for Human Resources to communicate to all employees where they can find these forms to update their information in the future. Tax withholdings may need to change due to a divorce or marriage, banking information may change, benefits may need to be updated due to the birth of a child, or employees may want to increase their voluntary contribution to their deferred compensation account. Employees will have different needs at different times, and it is important to ensure that they know where to find the forms and information needed when they need it.

Additionally, open enrollment for benefits selection is a process that Human Resources and/or Payroll is responsible for on an annual basis. Working with employees to understand their benefits, the costs associated with the benefits, and the changes they can expect in the next year is extremely important. This allows employees to plan for their family's needs relative to their medical needs. Employees may only change their medical benefit selections on an annual basis during a defined period of time, usually in September and/or October. It is important to ensure employees understand this, as open enrollment is the only time employees can make changes to their selections unless they experience a qualifying event during the year. Qualifying events are marriage, divorce, birth or adoption of a child, and the loss or gain of a spouse's job.

Job Analysis and Evaluation Concepts and Methods

An organization will need positions to be analyzed and evaluated for many reasons. From changing the process of how work is to be done, removing ineffective processes, managing attrition and turnover, or setting new pay practices and incentives, jobs can be analyzed to ensure an organization is effectively and efficiently performing work. There are numerous ways of reviewing a job to evaluate the position. A job can be evaluated at various times, including when it is created, when the job is open and being recruited, and if the job changes and responsibilities are added, deleted, or changed based on the organizational needs.

To ensure that the results are accurate and appropriate when performing a job analysis, it is important to fully understand the tools being applied to evaluate the position. Using multiple tools can also ensure that a holistic review is conducted and no pieces are missing from the analysis. It is vital to ensure that a consistent method is used when reviewing a position. Regardless of the tool(s) used to conduct a job analysis, the core components of a position to be reviewed should include the following:

- Scope of work: exact job duties including an idea of daily, weekly, monthly, and annual assignments and responsibilities

- Impact of work on other positions and the organization

- Working conditions: equipment, hazards

- Supervisory role, if any

- Reporting relationships

- Relationships, internal and external

- Leadership role, formal or informal

- Minimum requirements to perform the job: knowledge, skills, abilities

- Minimum qualifications, training, and experience required

Job Analysis

Job Description

Job Title

Job Location

Job Summary

Reporting to

Working Conditions

Job Duties

Machines to be Used

Hazards

Job Specification

Qualifications

Experience

Training

Skills

Responsibilities

Emotional Characteristics

Sensory Demands

Gaining an understanding of these components can be achieved by having the individual complete a questionnaire and providing information and answers to many questions about what they do. Following up to this questionnaire, interviewing the individual can lead to a deeper understanding of the role. It may also be beneficial to interview other employees who may be impacted by this work, to ensure an understanding of how the position impacts others. Finally, it is helpful to observe the actual work being done. Just as on-the-job training can prove to be more beneficial than classroom training, so can actually seeing the work being done when analyzing a job. A deeper understanding can be gained by learning about the actual ins and outs of a position.

Job Analysis Method

Observation Method

Interview Method

Questionnaire Method

Once the information has been received from the various analysis tools being used, all pertinent data and information should be thoroughly reviewed to determine if the employee is performing work outside of their current job description. If the information from the job analysis does not align with the job description, the Human Resources professional should first work to update the job description with the accurate description of the work being done. Once the new job description is finalized, then the salary reviews can be conducted based on the work described. Two salary assessments should be conducted: one to determine if the salary is appropriate based on the internal review methods of the organization, and one to determine if the salary is appropriate based on an external market review. The salary may be determined to be too high, too low, or set at a rate appropriate with the work being performed. Regardless of the determination, it is important to maintain open and accurate communication with the parties involved in the analysis and the eventual recommendation(s). If there are additional questions that come up during the process, it is important to ask these to add to the information being used in the analysis.

In general, there are five primary methods of analyzing a job. While each may have variations, the core features of each method remain the same. The following table summarizes these five methods, their features, and the pros and cons for implementing each. In looking at this chart, it is easier to understand why using multiple methods may be beneficial for an organization.

Method	Features	Pros	Cons
Ranking Method	Ranks jobs in order based on the value in relationship to each other and to the organization	Easy to implement	Does not consider market rates or specific, individual factors of certain jobs
Classification/Grading Method	Groups jobs to reflect levels of skill at preset grade classifications	Straightforward, quick to implement	Jobs may end up being forced into a grade and not truly reflective of the work being done
Point Factor Method	Identifies factors, then adds value and weight to each with the individual factor scores, adding up to an overall score	Individual factors are considered, allows for more objectivity	Does not consider market rates and some specialized positions may not receive credit for certain factors
Factor Comparison Method	Identifies factors, then groups them with each factor being assigned a dollar amount	Systematic and analytical process	Complex system, difficult to communicate, and can contain some subjectivity
Competitive Market Analysis Method	Reviews external data and compares jobs to like positions	Considers the organization's priorities, examines job value against market rates	Difficulty in gaining access to information and organizations may not be comparable in scope and other factors

Human Resources professionals can use various methods of evaluating a job. While there are multiple available, methods should be selected based on the organization's needs and used consistently. Having multiple methods available can be a benefit for an organization that has widely different positions, such as administrative, construction, maintenance, executive, or engineering. One particular analysis may not work as well with all of the different positions. Having multiple tools may be necessary to ensure that jobs can be assessed properly and accurately. A position should be viewed objectively, and the selected method should fairly assess the responsibilities and ultimately, the salary. It may be prudent to hire an outside consultant to establish the process and method(s) for the organization to implement. It may also be wise to routinely have an external review conducted every few years to ensure that the organization's analysis is objective and aligned with current methods and practices.

Job Pricing and Pay Structures

Job pricing is the process by which an organization determines the salary of positions. Job pricing utilizes information from job descriptions, job analyses, and evaluations, and any other pertinent information available to make a recommendation. Human Resources professionals will often include internal equity, external equity, and market information in the evaluation to ensure a holistic approach to setting a salary. Additional factors such as attrition and difficulty in attracting qualified candidates may also be considered when establishing a salary.

Internal equity refers to the parity of salary between positions within the same organization. Factors such as minimum qualifications, effort and responsibility, working conditions, education and training, supervisory responsibilities, scope of responsibility, and impact to the organization should be reviewed to determine similarities between positions to ensure that there is equity. It is important that employees understand how internal equity is utilized when setting a salary. If an employee believes they are not being paid a fair salary comparatively to another employee, then the organization could face scrutiny for this disparity. This could include complaints, grievances, and/or lawsuits that may result in back pay, penalties, fines, and attorney's fees. Having a robust compensation policy regarding how internal equity will be used in setting salary assists in explaining and defending salary decisions.

External equity and market pricing information are commonly used by organizations to establish salary for positions. This information can be found in salary surveys established either by a third-party organization or through individual survey information at the request of the organization. This information is important to review and can help to ensure that the organization is able to attract qualified candidates during the recruitment process and retain employees once hired. If a competitor is paying a much higher salary, they may easily be able to poach candidates by attracting them with the higher salary. If an organization is experiencing a high attrition rate for certain positions or difficulty in attracting qualified candidates in the recruitment process, it may be beneficial to conduct a market review to determine if competitive wages are a factor and make appropriate changes to job pricing and salary structures if necessary.

Organizations should ensure a robust compensation philosophy and strategy to attract and retain qualified candidates and employees. A common strategy is to compensate positions within five percent of the average market salary. If a position's salary falls within a range of five percent above or below the average market salary of a comparable organization's position, the salary would be accepted as appropriate, fair, and equitable. If the salary is outside of the five percent range, Human Resources professionals should assess the reasons this is occurring and make appropriate recommendations to address the disparity.

The salary structure is also an important component within the scope of job pricing. Salary structures generally reflect a salary range that compensates for various levels of experience. Positions have a job description that reflects minimum qualifications, specifically the experience and education required for being able to do the job. The salary range should align with these minimum qualifications in that more experienced candidates could earn more within the salary range than less experienced candidates. This type of salary structure also allows for an employee to grow within the salary structure based on their specific work with the organization. There is flexibility for organizations to determine how broad a salary range should be. Some organizations have a practice of keeping a salary range within a ten to twenty percent range, whereas others establish salary ranges with a forty to sixty percent range. The following chart shows two sample ranges with a twenty percent and sixty percent salary range and how different these ranges can be. Note that an employee who is hired under a salary range with a larger range percentage between the minimum and maximum salary has a bigger opportunity for growth within the range.

Sample Range	Minimum Salary	Midpoint Salary	Maximum Salary	Range %
001	$50,000	$55,000	$60,000	20%
002	$50,000	$65,000	$80,000	60%

An organization can also incorporate various range percentages for different groups of positions. Entry level positions that do not require education or many years of experience may have a lower range percentage, whereas executives and professionals who do require extensive, specific experience may have ranges with a much higher percentage.

Regardless of how an organization establishes the minimum and maximum amounts of a salary range, the compensation policy should clearly establish the parameters in which new hires are offered a starting salary, when employees are eligible for increases, and how employees can be eligible for increases. Organizations should also establish the number of individual steps within a salary range to show the progression opportunities that employees are able to achieve. Below is a chart showing a sample five-step range plan that indicates how the above sample ranges could be broken down in five opportunities for increases throughout an employee's history within a specific position.

Salary Range	Step 1	Step 2	Step 3	Step 4	Step 5
001	$50,000	$52,500	$55,000	$57,500	$60,000
002	$50,000	$57,500	$65,000	$75,500	$80,000

Having multiple steps within a salary range allows an organization flexibility in hiring at different steps based on a candidate's experience and qualifications. Having multiple steps also allows an organization to provide additional compensation for outstanding performance attached to a stellar year of performance. These are items that should be clearly written as policy and practiced within the organization to ensure that all individuals are treated fairly and provided with the same opportunities for advancement. An example of this would be a policy that dictates all new employees will be hired at Step 1 except in the circumstance that they provide salary information indicating that this would be a lesser compensation amount than they are currently earning. The policy can also dictate when to offer a higher step based on the experience the candidate is bringing to the organization. Additionally, the policy can provide direction for requesting additional steps due to performance and the process to initiate this action. Many organizations tie salary increases within a salary range to the employee's service date, on an annual basis, and to their annual performance review. Compensation policies should not only discuss movement within a range, but also movement between ranges and how the appropriate step should be selected.

Finally, incentives such as pay for performance, bonus pay, and special monetary awards due to performing work that has substantial impact to the organization, such as cost savings, should be considered in alignment with the base compensation for a position. Reviewing all of the information available for each position in the context of special incentive programs should be consistently applied to each position being considered.

Noncash Compensation

As mentioned previously, noncash compensation can be a powerful incentive and motivator for employees. Organizations have seen a shift in the importance of these programs relative to the recruitment and retention of employees. Previously, the base salary was the primary factor in accepting a position or staying with an organization. In the last several years, this has shifted to an overall review of all compensation variables, including base salary and noncash compensation. Employees are looking for options, flexibility, and programs that allow for self-care, family time, community involvement, recognition, development, and overall flexibility.

Human Resources professionals are responsible for researching, implementing, and managing noncash compensation programs. These programs can be extensive and require heavy involvement, or they can be simple and easily facilitated. Regardless of the complexity of noncash programs, overall, employees appreciate options that allow for a more balanced and healthier lifestyle. These programs can include alternative work schedules, on-site facilities such as daycare, tuition reimbursement, professional development, community involvement programs, and recognition programs.

Many organizations have begun to implement a flexible and alternative work schedule. These work schedules deviate from the standard weekly work schedule of 9:00 a.m. to 5:00 p.m., Monday through Friday. Depending on the customer service needs and standard business operating hours, organizations are implementing different work schedules such a 4X10 or 9X80 schedule. On a 4X10 work schedule, employees work four days a week for ten hours each day. Some organizations may be able to close for the fifth work day, so all employees are off work, or allow employees to select their day off each week. On a 9X80 work schedule, in a two-week period, employees work a full eighty hours in only nine days. For eight of these days, employees work nine hours and for day, employees work eight hours. These types of flexible work schedules can allow employees to have a more balanced work and home life. The table below provides some examples of flexible work schedules:

Work Schedule	Monday	Tuesday	Wednesday	Thursday	Friday
5X8	8 hours	8 hours	8 hours	8 hours	8 hours
4X10	10 hours	10 hours	10 hours	10 hours	OFF
9X80 week 1	9 hours	9 hours	9 hours	9 hours	8 hours
9X80 week 2	9 hours	9 hours	9 hours	9 hours	OFF

More organizations are offering employees on-site facilities such as daycare, exercise facilities, and meal service. Rising daycare costs are a huge issue that parents face in addition to allocating time in the day for drop off and pick up. While there are many things to consider with having a daycare facility on-site including liability, insurance, proper facilities, and trained staff, it is an option that more organizations are considering, as it can increase employee morale and performance as well as retention for the organization. Exercise facilities are also being incorporated into the facility plans to allow employees an opportunity to exercise on breaks and lunch, or before and after work. Having this convenient option available is one that many employees appreciate as it can help maximize the time during the day and help enforce a healthy lifestyle. In the same vein of healthy living, having convenient, affordable, and healthy meal options available to employees is another noncash program that can have a dramatic impact with employees, both future and current. If the facility is unable to have a cafeteria and healthy, fresh food available, organizations can work with local restaurants and grocery stores to provide discounts or incentives to employees.

Tuition reimbursement and professional development are more common programs that have been in place for some time with some organizations. Encouraging education by supporting employees with reimbursement for tuition costs is an excellent way for an organization to support and motivate their employees. This further education can positively impact the organization by having a more educated workforce that is well trained and knowledgeable, and, by applying this new education, can be more proactive and productive in their work. Policies should be developed that provide an understanding of the expectations of employees and the organization, including terms to pay back the reimbursement if an employee leaves the organization within a certain time period. Professional development—through training programs offered by the organization, as well as through outside agencies and professional organizations—is an excellent opportunity for employees to continue progressing on their professional career path. When an organization shows their employees that education, knowledge, training, and development are important, employees will generally be energized, motivated, and passionate about what they do.

Community involvement programs are an excellent way to engage employees in their passions and show support. Some organizations will provide employees with additional leave time that is to be used specifically for community involvement. Whether working at a local food bank or building homes with Habitat for Humanity, employees have the flexibility and ability to use a certain amount of time—without having to use their personal vacation leave time—to give back to their communities.

Recognition programs, both formal and informal, should be a common and frequent practice that organizations engage. Recognizing employees informally at department meetings, issuing a monthly write up in a newsletter to highlight a job well done, or scheduling a formal annual event to recognize service and special contributions to the organization are all important aspects to recognizing employees and the work they do on a daily, weekly, monthly, and annual basis. Special awards such as "Employee of the Year" are important to employees and should not be minimized. Organizations can align special awards with their corporate values and engage their employees by encouraging everyone, regardless of their title and level, to nominate those who display specific traits in their work or went above and beyond for customers or the team.

Employee suggestion programs are great ways to receive feedback from employees regarding current programs and new, future programs. Having employees involved in the review of current programs and outlining new programs is an excellent way to engage and involve employees. Engaged employees are generally more involved in these programs and can engage other employees by communicating the information during everyday interactions.

An important aspect of noncash compensation is creativity. While policies are necessary for the administration of each program, it is important to understand what employees want and what they value. What may seem like a great idea on paper may not be an incentive that employees actually appreciate or need. Engaging employees in the process of creating these programs is essential to ensuring their success.

As with all programs, it is necessary for Human Resources to fully communicate to employees the benefits available. While most employees are very aware of medical insurance benefits due to having to complete annual enrollment forms and getting insurance cards, many employees can be unaware of other programs available. Communicating clearly and frequently is vital to the success of any program.

Methods of Aligning and Benchmarking Compensation and Benefits

Employees are typically fairly knowledgeable about market rates for compensation and benefits. Information is readily available in various formats and employees use every piece of information available to make an informed decision. Organizations must know how they compare to other competitors in order to attract and retain qualified employees.

First, organizations must select the sources that will be used to gather current and relevant market salary information. Organizations should ensure these sources are providing data from competitors in similar industries, location, and size. While it is not necessary to benchmark every single position, it is beneficial to review at least fifty to seventy-five percent of positions, assuming the information is available. This is why it is important to select a comparable organization: to ensure that the positions that need to be compared are available. Data sources can include 1) published surveys that are provided by a third-party organization and include information that is self-reported by employers, 2) online data that are located on various websites and include information that is self-reported by employees, or 3) custom surveys utilizing relationships with other Human Resources professionals within the competitor's organization to access the information. While custom surveys may take longer to complete, they would be specific to the organization's informational needs and in a format that would allow comparisons to be viewed in an easier way. Published surveys may not present a full picture of an organization's total rewards, specifically around the noncash compensation programs. It is wise for a company to utilize at least two to three different data sources to ensure accuracy. Regardless of the data source selected, it is vital to understand the information and how it is represented so that it can be analyzed accurately.

Second, organizations must itemize the information they wish to analyze and understand how to ensure different pieces of data are put into terms that can be compared appropriately, or an "apples to apples" comparison. Information should be broken down and include as much detail as possible to ensure that dollar amounts can be assigned when appropriate. Breaking down an annual salary to an hourly rate will allow a total dollar amount to be calculated for leave balances. This will allow a total compensation to be calculated. Below is a sample list that an organization can begin with to gather data:

- Agency Name
- Job Title
- Supervisory Responsibilities: yes or no
- Supervisor
- Minimum Annual and Hourly Salary
- Maximum Annual and Hourly Salary
- Employer Retirement Contribution
- Social Security Contribution
- Employer Medical, Dental and Vision Contribution
- Employer Long Term Disability and Life Insurance Contribution
- Specialty Pay: Bilingual Pay, Incentive Pay
- Employer Deferred Compensation Contribution
- Holidays (Total Number and Hours)
- Administrative Leave
- Personal Leave
- Vacation Leave and Cash Out Option
- Sick Leave
- Noncash Benefits: Programs offered that stand out

It is important to add items as necessary to ensure that a complete picture is presented. Completing the survey and compiling the data may provide ideas for additional programs and benefits to offer. Additionally, it may be beneficial to indicate future negotiated increases, such as cost of living adjustments, to ensure that the analysis is holistic, accurate, and accounts for how the data will change within the next year or two.

Third, organizations must select the positions to be compared. It is key to understand the work being performed so that appropriate comparable positions can be selected. Job titles should not be the only factor that is used to select comparable positions. It is also important to select various positions at many levels of responsibility. Selections should be across departments and experience levels. Management and administrative positions should be evenly selected to ensure that individual, as well as supervisory, benchmarking can be reviewed. Reviewing the salary differences between a manager and subordinates is an additional benefit to having all of the information available and can assist with internal equity reviews.

Taking into account the salary differences between a supervisor and subordinate is important to ensure that the supervisory responsibilities are being properly compensated and there is no allowance for wage compression. Wage compression between supervisors and subordinates can create poor morale and allow for ineffective working relationships. **Wage compression,** in this example, would be that a supervisor is making a small amount more—or even the same, in certain circumstances—than the subordinate, potentially compromising their effectiveness in the role. Wage compression can also refer to new employees being paid a higher salary than long-term employees. Fortunately, with new legislation, it is becoming more difficult, if not illegal, for organizations to justify different pay rates for multiple individuals doing the same job.

Organizations may want to benchmark specific programs as well, to ensure they are offering an appropriate program. The best example for this regards medical insurance coverage. Some organizations offer one plan to their employees, whereas other organizations offer many plans. There may be an industry standard for certain organizations to offer a specific plan based on the employee needs; employees, however, want flexibility and options. Giving them various options for medical insurance coverage is an additional advantage because each employee has different needs relative to their benefits, especially medical insurance coverage.

Finally, once all of the information has been collected and organized into a working document, Human Resources professionals should begin to analyze the data. It is important to look for trends, disparities, concerns, and possible areas for improvement. Averages should be calculated to determine where the organization falls in the market. If a policy dictates that an organization will be within five percent of either side of the market average, this information should be used to determine recommendations. There may be extenuating factors, though, that justify the disparity, and these should be considered.

Any recommendations presented should be supported by the data and represented in a final report that is clear, concise, and easy to follow. It is important or Human Resources professionals to remember that when presenting this information and recommendations, the message should be kept simple, focused, clear, and specific. The data should be pointed to when necessary and the presented should ensure that the audience is following along. Questions and dialogue within the group should be encouraged. This will require a full and complete understanding of the organization's information, the data, the analysis, and recommendations. Being able to justify the recommendations with the data is important, as is being able to answer questions about any of the information.

Benefits Programs' Policies, Processes, and Analysis

As with all programs offered by an organization, having a robust and clear policy is vital to ensure employees understand their rights and entitlements as well as their responsibilities. Benefits programs can be complex, and it is the best interest of the both the organization and employees to provide as much information as possible. It is common for organizations to provide an overview of the total rewards package during the hiring and recruitment process to attract candidates. Additional information should be provided to candidates during the offer process to ensure that a complete view is available to make a decision in joining an organization. One an employee is hired, a thorough new hire orientation should be offered to review each benefit—from insurance programs available, vacation leave time accruals, employee assistance programs, and other noncash rewards. During the new hire orientation, employees should be afforded the opportunity to complete necessary paperwork or to take the paperwork with them to review options if they are not prepared to make benefit selections at that time.

Benefits programs policies should be inclusive of details such as how premiums are paid and when, if opt out options are provided or if participation is mandatory, eligibility terms and waiting periods, and contact information for the specific service providers. Employees should also understand enrollment periods, how changes to a benefit can be made outside of an enrollment period, and any other pertinent information that is helpful to understand how benefits work.

Human Resources professionals are responsible for ensuring that employees understand how to make benefit selections and coverage changes, and how to sign up for a new program. An important component with benefits is having an understanding of timeframes. New employees should understand how long they are required to wait before they are eligible for coverage. Some organizations may have a waiting of period of thirty days with coverage starting the first of the month following that timeframe. Some organizations may offer immediate eligibility for coverage. Regardless of when benefits eligibility starts, employees must understand this important piece of information so that they can make informed decisions. Generally, employees are provided with an open enrollment period each year during which they may make changes to their benefits for the next calendar year.

Open enrollment is the only time that an employee can make changes to their medical insurance unless a qualifying event occurs during the year. A qualifying event is an event such as marriage, divorce, birth of a child, adopting a child, a spouse gaining a job, or a spouse losing or a job and the coverage tied to that job. Qualifying events should be clearly outlined and defined in the policy, as well as the timeframe required for employees to complete paperwork to change their coverage if one of the events occurs outside of open enrollment. Employees have a window of time to make changes and if an employee does not abide by the timeframe, they will not be allowed to make a change until the open enrollment period for the following year. An example of this would be providing employees a window of thirty days after the birth of a child to provide paperwork and supporting documentation to add the new child to the medical insurance. If the paperwork is submitted outside of this window, the employee will need to wait until the next open enrollment period to add the child for the next year.

An additional element that should be detailed in a benefits policy regarding medical insurance coverage is when this coverage ends upon an employee leaving the organization. Some organizations will end coverage effective immediately, on an employee's last day with the organization. Other organizations will provide coverage through the end of the month that the employee leaves. Regardless of when coverage ends, it is important to ensure that employees understand this component, as it will assist them in making decisions about retirement or changing employers.

Benefits policies should also be put in place regarding leave programs. Vacation and sick leave should be fully explained and cover terms such as accrual rates, caps for maximum balances, usage and how to request leave, requesting leave donations, and payout information. Many organizations are changing over to a Paid time Off (PTO) program, which allows employees to accrue PTO to cover any types of absence regardless of the reason. PTO would cover vacation requests, sick leave, and any other kind of leave request. The same terms should be explained regarding PTO just as if the leave is broken down into separate balances. Many organizations with a PTO program find it easier to implement and manage for employees.

It is important for Human Resources professionals to continuously review and analyze benefits programs and their corresponding policies. Programs should be reviewed to ensure they are appropriate and provide employees with the necessary benefits for their health and well-being. Policy reviews should also include a look into costs and effectiveness. New programs are being created frequently in the competitive market and incorporating new and fresh programs to a total rewards package can be invigorating to employees. Even if programs are not replaced, the corresponding policy should be reviewed on a regular basis to provide updates that may be implemented by either the vendor providing the service or the organization.

When analyzing a benefits program, many different variables should be looked at to ensure a robust analysis. Items to be examined should include a review of costs for both the employer and employee, deductible and out-of-pocket maximum amount changes, network reviews, covered services, copays, prescription drug coverage and costs, and other items specific to coverages such as maternity, mental health, substance abuse, and other commonly used services through insurance plans. Benchmarking these benefit terms with other available options, like benchmarking salary discussed earlier, will allow Human Resources professionals to understand how their benefits align with those of competitors. This analysis can then be used to support recommendations made for changes to benefits.

Total rewards should be reviewed often to ensure employees are provided with a package inclusive of compensation and benefits that is competitive, fair, equitable, and appropriate for the work that will be done. Whether this is performed annually, every five years, or just as needed based on changes to the workforce (such as attrition), these assessments should be thorough and done with updated information.

Practice Questions

1. What law is commonly referred to as the "wage and hour" law?
    a. Department of Labor
    b. Fair Labor Standards Act
    c. Affordable Care Act
    d. Family and Medical Leave Act

2. The FLSA law determines whether a position is eligible for which of the following?
    a. Bilingual pay
    b. Overtime
    c. Merit increases
    d. All of the above

3. Human Resources professionals interact frequently with the _____ department regarding compensation practices.
    a. Legal
    b. Information Technology
    c. Payroll
    d. None of the above

4. Which of the following programs are considered noncash rewards? (Select all that apply.)
    a. Alternative work schedules
    b. Recognition programs
    c. Overtime
    d. Professional development
    e. On-site facilities

5. Employee feedback gathered by _____ is a beneficial way to engage employees and enhances communication between the employer and employees.
    a. Exit interviews
    b. Surveys
    c. Ad hoc emails
    d. All of the above

6. Why is communication with employees regarding benefits is extremely important? (Select all that apply.)
    a. So that employees understand their options
    b. So that employees can train new employees
    c. So that employees have information to make informed choices
    d. So that employees realize the costs and obligations of the organization

7. Employees must be employed for _____ months and work a minimum of _____ hours in the past year to be eligible for the Family and Medical Leave Act.
    a. 6/2,000
    b. 9/1,500
    c. 1/1,250

8. Employers can offer _____ benefits than the federal or state statutes require, as long as a policy is written to support it. (Select all that apply.)
   a. the same benefits
   b. greater benefits
   c. lesser benefits

9. _____ employees are not covered under the Fair Labor Standards Act, and therefore not eligible for overtime.
   a. Exempt
   b. Nonexempt
   c. Nonsupervisory
   d. Administrative

10. Which of the following statements is TRUE regarding the Family and Medical Leave Act? (Select all that apply.)
   a. The FMLA is paid leave and does not require vacation or sick leave to be taken.
   b. The FMLA is unpaid leave.
   c. Employees can use vacation or sick leave to receive pay during a protected FMLA leave.
   d. Because FMLA is a federal program, organizations do not need a policy regarding this program.

11. A _____ is an analysis of other organizations in the same or similar industry with similar demographics.
   a. Policy review
   b. Process audit
   c. Market review
   d. Classification audit

12. Which of the following items should be included on an employee's paycheck?
   a. All forms of salary including overtime, specialty pay, etc.
   b. Benefits deductions and contributions
   c. Retirement deductions and contributions
   d. All of the above

13. Which of the below statements is TRUE regarding medical benefits?
   a. Employees can change their medical benefits at any time they wish.
   b. Employees can only change their medical benefits if they experience a qualifying event.
   c. Employees can only change their medical benefits during the annual open enrollment.
   d. None of the above

14. Which of the following components of a position should be reviewed and assessed while conducting a job analysis? (Select all that apply.)
   a. Impact of work
   b. Salary
   c. Work schedule
   d. Job title
   e. Minimum experience required
   f. Scope of work

15. Match the job analysis tool with its definition:

    a. Employee survey
    b. Employee interview
    c. Job description
    d. On-the-job observation

    1. A complete list of duties, responsibilities, and required skills
    2. A visual review of the actual work being performed
    3. A series of written questions to be completed by the individual
    4. A conversation to discuss the work to be performed

16. Match the job analysis ranking method with its main feature:

    a. Ranking
    b. Classification/Grading
    c. Point Factor
    d. Factor Comparison
    e. Competitive market analysis

    1. Groups jobs to reflect levels of skill
    2. Reviews external data to compare jobs
    3. Identifies factors then groups them
    4. Ranks jobs in order based on value to each other
    5. Identifies factors and then adds value and weight

17. Which of the following statements is INACCURATE regarding job analysis ranking methods?

    a. Human Resources professionals must be familiar with and completely understand a ranking method prior to applying it to analyze a job.
    b. Only one ranking method should be used when evaluating a job.
    c. Various ranking methods may be useful when analyzing different jobs.

18. _____ equity refers to the parity of salary between positions within the same organization; _____ equity refers to the parity of salary between positions in different organizations.

    a. External/Market review
    b. Aligned/External
    c. Internal/Eternal
    d. Internal/Aligned

19. What factors should organizations take into account when setting a salary for a position? (Select all that apply.)

    a. Minimum experience required
    b. The actual work being performed
    c. Internal equity
    d. Appropriateness
    e. Salary Range

20. Which of the following are flexible work schedules often offered under an alternate work schedule program? (Select all that apply.)

    a. 4X10
    b. 9X80
    c. 5X8
    d. None of the above

21. Which of the following statements are TRUE regarding recognition programs? (Select all that apply.)

    a. Recognition programs should formal and structured.
    b. Recognition programs do not have an impact on employee morale.
    c. Recognition programs are unnecessary.
    d. Recognition programs should be informal and unplanned.

22. Benchmarking is important to ensure that an organization knows which of the following:
    a. How an organization compares to competitors
    b. Potential reasons for employees leaving the organization
    c. A full perspective and understanding of the organization's total rewards
    d. All of the above

23. Which of the following is NOT a qualifying event that allows an employee to make changes to their medical insurance coverage outside of open enrollment?
    a. Marriage
    b. Birth of a child
    c. Divorce
    d. Adoption
    e. Change of mind

Answer Explanations

1. B: The Fair Labor Standards Act (FLSA) law determines whether a position is eligible for overtime compensation. The Department of Labor administers and enforces many laws, including the FLSA, while the Affordable Care Act and the Family and Medical Leave Act laws determine rights relative to medical insurance and protected leave.

2. B: The FLSA law sets the standards to determine if a position is eligible for overtime compensation. An organization determines within their policies if bilingual pay is offered as well as if and when merit increases will be awarded to an employee.

3. C: Human Resources professionals frequently interact with Payroll in numerous ways and working together is integral to an organization and the compensation practices and policies. Human Resources will work closely with Legal and Information Technology related to many matters but not on a daily basis regarding compensation practices.

4. A, B, D, & E: Alternative work schedules, recognition programs, professional development, and on-site facilities are all noncash rewards that an organization can offer to employees. Overtime is a cash payment for hours worked over forty hours per week or eight hours per day based on the organization's policy.

5. D: All of the above. Exit interviews, surveys, and ad hoc emails are all different and great ways to engage employees, gain feedback on programs, and enhance the communication between employers and employees.

6. A & C: Communication regarding benefits is vital between employers and employees so there is an understanding of all benefits and options when making decisions. This allows employees to have information to make informed choices. It is not the responsibility of employees to train new employees in benefits, but rather the responsibility of Human Resources. And while it is beneficial for employees to understand costs and how the organization operates, it is not a requirement that employees realize the costs and obligations of the organization regarding benefits.

7. C: Employees must work for an organization for 12 months and work a minimum of 1,250 hours in the past year to be eligible for the benefits of the Family and Medical Leave Act.

8. A, B: Employers can offer the same or greater benefits than what the federal or state statutes require, as long as a policy is written to support it. Employers cannot offer programs and benefits that are less generous than those afforded to them via federal and state law.

9. A: Exempt employees are not covered under the FLSA and not eligible for overtime. Non-exempt employees are covered under the FLSA and eligible for overtime compensation. Non-supervisory and administrative employees are descriptions of the work an employees does within a certain position but alone do not determine the FLSA status.

10. B & C: The FMLA is unpaid leave (so Choice *A* is incorrect), but employees can take vacation and sick leave to receive pay during a protected FMLA leave; thus, Choices *B* and *C* are correct. The FMLA is not a paid leave and organizations should have a policy regarding this leave that includes the responsibilities of the employer and employee, the entitlements afforded to taking this leave, and the process to request FMLA.

11. C: A market review is the analysis of competitor's compensation and benefits to ensure an organization is paying employees a competitive salary. Choices *A, B,* and *D* are incorrect as a policy review is an in-depth review of current policies and practices to determine updates and changes, a process audit is a look into a particular procedure, and a classification audit is a review of a particular job and its corresponding job description.

12. D: As much information as possible regarding compensation should be included on an employee's paycheck and communicated to them so there is an understanding of how the paycheck is arranged. Information such as all forms of salary including overtime, specialty pay, etc., benefits deductions and contributions, and retirement deductions and contributions should all be include on an employee's paycheck.

13. D: Changes to medical benefits can only occur during open enrollment for the upcoming year or within a certain time frame during the year following a qualifying event. While Choices *B* and *C* are somewhat true, it is not true that they are the only times that medical benefits can be changed. Additionally, employees cannot change their medical benefits simply because they change their mind.

14. A, E, & F: An effective job analysis should include impact of work, scope of work, working conditions, supervisory roles, reporting relationships, internal and external relationships, leadership role, minimum experience requirements, and minimum qualifications. While salary, work schedule, and job title are important pieces of information, they are not used for a job analysis.

15. A – 3, B – 4, C – 1, & D – 2. An employee survey is a series of written questions to be completed by the individual performing the work that is being analyzed. An employee interview is a conversation to discuss the work being performed and ask additional follow-up questions that may arise after reviewing the survey. A job description is the complete list of duties, responsibilities, and required skills that may need to be updated to reflect an accurate picture of the work being performed. An on-the-job observation is a visual review of the actual being performed. All of the above job analysis tools should be used together to complete a thorough assessment.

16. A – 3, B – 1, C – 4, D – 2, & E– 2: There are various ranking methods to use in conducting a job analysis, each having pros and cons. The ranking method ranks jobs in order based on value to each other. The classification/grading method groups jobs to reflect levels of skill. The point factor method ranks jobs in order based on value to each other. The factor comparison identifies factors and then groups them. The competitive market analysis reviews external data to compare jobs.

17. B: The inaccurate component of this statement is related to using only one ranking method. Human Resources professionals should be completely familiar with the tools being used before applying them to analyze a job and various rankings methods should be used to fully understand a job and different jobs within an organization. This allows a holistic view of positions and in using multiple tools, will allow various different perspectives to come through.

18. C: Internal equity refers to the parity of salary between positions within the same organization; External equity refers to the parity of salary between positions between different organizations. While it is important to take into account market review information and ensure that the salary is aligned on various levels, internal and external equity refers to the parity of salary within the same organization and between different organizations. Both are important to utilize when referring salary and pay structures.

19. A, B, C, D, & E: Salary structures should consider the minimum experience required, the actual work being performed, internal equity, appropriateness, and salary range. All of these should be taken into account when setting a salary range.

20. A & B: Alternate work schedules offered to employees can allow flexibility for employees. The 4X10 schedule allows employees to only work 4 days a week, 10 hours a day. The 9X80 schedule allows employees to work 9 out of 10 days within a two week period, 9 hours a day for 8 days and 8 hours a day for 1 day. The 5X8 schedule is a standard schedule working five days a week, 8 hours a day; therefore it is not considered an alternate work schedule.

21. A & D: Recognition programs should be common and frequent, and can be formal or informal, structured or unplanned. Formal programs are important but informal programs are just as important and may even have a bigger impact with employee morale. Recognition programs definitely have an impact on employee morale and are necessary for an organization to offer.

22. D: Benchmarking allows an organization to understand how they compare to other organizations, reasons for attrition, and an understanding of the current total rewards programs, which can allow for focused changes to certain programs.

23. A, B, C, & D: Only a qualifying event allows an employee to make changes outside of open enrollment. Qualifying events include marriage, divorce, birth or adoption of a child, or a spouse's loss or gain of a job. A change of mind is not a qualifying event.

Employee and Labor Relations

Functional Effectiveness in the Employee Lifecycle

The **employee lifecycle** is the roadmap that an organization uses to create a collaborative and engaged workforce. It consists of various stages that include attracting qualified applicants; recruiting the best and brightest candidates; onboarding new employees; developing and managing employees, their careers, and professional growth; retaining employees; and transitioning employees out of the organization when the time is appropriate. Human Resources professionals are responsible for ensuring that each stage of the employee lifecycle is robust, appropriate, and meets the needs of both the organization and the employee. When opportunities to enhance a lifecycle stage are identified, recommendations should be made, and changes implemented. The employee lifecycle should encourage and deliver a strong employee experience throughout an entire career or working experience with an organization.

The employee lifecycle can be assessed for effectiveness based on the level of employee engagement at each lifecycle stage. Additionally, each stage should be adaptable, relevant, sustainable, and executable. The first stage of the lifecycle is attracting qualified applicants. Employees should take an active role in representing the organization. Engaged employees can serve as ambassadors to the organization and attract applicants to apply for open positions. The second stage of the lifecycle is recruiting the best and brightest candidates to work for the organization. Engaged employees who like the job, team, coworkers, and organization are more likely to recommend friends and professionals to apply for open positions. The third stage of the lifecycle is onboarding new employees. Engaged employees are excited about joining a new organization and are generally more likely to help others transition into the new organization and role. The fourth stage of the lifecycle is developing and managing employees, their careers, and professional growth.

Engaged employees seek out and request learning opportunities to increase their knowledge, and skill sets to enhance their productivity in their current role and to provide future opportunities for promotion. Organizations that encourage employees to be innovative and creative allow for an even more engaged workforce that quickly translates to efficiency and productivity. The fifth stage of the lifecycle is retaining employees. Retention can be encouraged through recognition and acknowledgement as well as ensuring appropriate and necessary compensation and benefits. The sixth and final stage of the lifecycle is transitioning employees out of the organization. While this can occur voluntarily or involuntarily, employees must be separated from the organization in an appropriate and respectful manner. If an employee is retiring, the organization should ensure knowledge is retained and as much information can be transferred to new employees or the team to ensure continuity. Engaged employees who leave an organization in good standing, whether through retirement or resignation, will generally stay in contact with their coworkers.

Each stage is vital to the overall employee experience. While the development and retention stages will last the longest in terms of time, every stage is necessary and dependent on the other stages. Assessing the effectiveness of each can be determined by establishing key metrics that measure the success of programs within each stage. Additionally, initiating employee surveys to provide direct feedback in each of these areas is an excellent best practice. This feedback should be considered when determining to continue programs or establish new programs to revitalize an initiative.

Employee Engagement Data

Gathering employee engagement data through a survey is an excellent best practice to implement within an organization; however, it is just as important to ensure that the results are communicated, and action is taken. Without communication and action, positive changes will not be seen from the survey alone.

The first step to initiate an employee engagement survey is to plan the survey. Planning the survey involves determining the data that should be collected, how the data will be collected, setting up the method to analyze the information gathered, writing the questions, and setting up the survey. Once the survey is initiated, it cannot be changed. It is important to ensure the survey is appropriate during the planning phase and will yield the information needed.

The second step is to establish a communications plan. The communications plan should include who will be responsible for each message, what will be communicated, timeframes, and directions. The communications should be written for the employees who will be taking the survey. Ensuring that all messages are clear, concise, and specific is vital for all communications and will lead to better participation rates and responses. Additionally, employees should fully understand how the survey was planned and prepared, how the data will be analyzed and used, and that all responses will be kept confidential. While it may be necessary for employees to identify the department and area they work in, employees should be confident that their responses will not be used inappropriately.

The third step is to run the survey and allow employees adequate time to complete and turn in the survey. Employees should know how and where to ask for assistance, when and where surveys are to be submitted, and how to complete the survey. Surveys may be available online or in paper format, and employees should understand how to complete either format based on their comfort level with each. While the survey is being conducted, it is important to continue communications with employees, to send reminders and requests to complete the survey.

Once the survey has been completed, the fourth step is to analyze the results. Computing a response rate is one of the first measurements that should be calculated, as this will show how effective the survey was in receiving feedback from employees. The response rate may even be a standard benchmark metric for the department to use to track success in the future. After calculating and analyzing the results, recommendations should be proposed to address key areas of improvement. Additionally, it is also important to recognize areas that are successful. Focusing on the areas that are done well is just as important as focusing on the areas that need improvement.

Once the recommendations have been approved for implementation, it is vitally important to communicate the results and the action plans to employees. Employees need to know how the information will be used and what they can expect in the future. If there is ultimately no action or change implemented, employees will be less engaged in the future to participate and provide feedback. Conducting surveys frequently is a great way to determine if employees are responding to new programs. If an organization is taking proactive steps to communicate, implement change, and keep employees engaged and motivated, momentum and innovation will continue to grow and become part of the culture of the overall organization.

Organizational Culture, Theories, and Practices

Organizational culture is defined as the shared beliefs, values, philosophies, and assumptions within an organization. There can be various cultures within an organization—division, department, workgroup, and teams—but in general, all separate cultures should align with the higher-level cultures. There are four primary culture types: clan, adhocracy, hierarchy, and market. Each culture has different benefits to an organization relative to flexibility, stability, control, focus, and strategy. The **clan culture** focuses on collaboration with leaders that are facilitators, mentors, and team builders. The clan culture is built on a foundation of employee development and participation at all levels of the organization. The **adhocracy culture** focuses on creativity with leaders who are innovators, entrepreneurs, and visionaries. The adhocracy culture is built on a foundation of innovation, vision, and new resources. The **hierarchy culture** focuses on control and process with leaders that are organizers, coordinators, and monitors. The hierarchy culture is built on a foundation of control and efficiency through the use of stable and consistent processes. The **market culture** focuses on competition with leaders that are hard driven, competitors, and producers. The market culture is built on a foundation of aggressive competitiveness and customer focus.

When Human Resources professionals identify, or are made aware of, concerns and issues within an organization's culture, it is important to fully understand the issues and provide recommendations to leadership that fully address these issues. It may be a good idea to incorporate elements from different organizational cultures into an organization's holistic philosophy. Each organization, department, and team will naturally create and maintain a culture within the individual work groups. It is important to ensure that the overall culture and philosophies flow downward and upward to each level, allowing smaller groups to nurture a culture that aligns within the overall organizational culture. To change or strengthen the culture of an organization, Human Resources professionals should follow a standard process to ensure effective and productive results.

First, it is important to understand the values and personalities of the leadership. Transformational leadership can reshape and change a culture but must take ownership and be held accountable for initiating change at the highest levels of the organization. Once the leadership style is understood, it is important to align the facts and information to determine the changes needed to initiate a cultural change at each level of the organization. Once the recommendations have been proposed and accepted for implementation, it is important to align these recommendations with rewards and incentives that support the changes. Employees who understand how and when their behavior will be rewarded and incentivized will be more likely to embrace and support the changes being implemented. Strengthening organizational culture will occur when leadership supports workforce stability and communicates to employees regularly and frequently. Communication is key to any initiative and communication plans can determine success or failure of a program. Finally, Human Resources professionals should incorporate the culture and cultural initiatives into the recruitment process. Newly hired employees should understand the organization and the culture prior to accepting an offer of employment. Ensuring that there is a cultural fit for both the organization and employee is vital to the employment experience and retaining the most qualified individuals.

Creating cultural change is difficult and does not happen quickly. When Human Resources professionals implement a strong, well-thought-out process that is supported by leadership and communicated clearly and frequently, employees will feel empowered to incorporate these changes at an individual level and within the workgroups and teams.

Diversity and Inclusion

Human Resources professionals are responsible for understanding Equal Employment Opportunity, Affirmative Action, and Diversity and Inclusion when assessing and implementing employee programs. **Equal Employment Opportunity** refers to the enforcement of statutes, laws, and regulations to prevent employment discrimination. **Affirmative Action** refers to the effort to achieve equity and equality in the workforce through outreach to eliminate barriers in the recruitment process. **Diversity and Inclusion** refs to leveraging differences within the workforce to achieve better results and higher levels of productivity and efficiency. By creating and maintaining an inclusive work environment where all employees are respected, an organization can effectively improve performance and enhance the customer and employee experience. By incorporating programs that align with the diversity and inclusion vision, an organization is able to support employee performance successfully, recruit the best talent, develop talent and expand skills, strengthen the employer brand, motivate employees with a positive employment experience, and strengthen the organization's market position.

Organizations that align a robust and holistic diversity and inclusion strategy to the workforce focus on the following areas:

- Effective leadership
- Employee engagement
- Inclusive culture
- Competitive talent

Effective leadership is achieved by ensuring consistency, commitment, and initiative. Building leaders at all levels of the organization allows for a deep and diverse leadership talent pipeline. Additionally, ensuring a strong succession planning program can identify talent for development in key leadership roles.

Employee engagement is achieved by implementing and facilitating programs that allow employees to have a shared purpose and community within the organization. By providing training and resources to every leader, the organization can build and sustain a diverse internal talent pool. **Inclusive culture** is achieved by aligning the business strategy and high-level goals and leveraging the knowledge of employees with the diversity and inclusion strategy. Expanding engagement encourages recruitment efforts and ensures leadership capabilities within employees, resulting in a culture of transparency and openness for new ideas and innovation. *Competitive talent* is achieved by developing a diversity recruiting strategy that addresses skills gaps within the current workforce. By making targeted and specific decisions relative to recruiting and hiring, an organization can optimize the workforce, innovation, and overall effectiveness.

Employee resource groups (ERGs) are groups of individuals who participate in initiatives, programs, and activities with others of a shared background, common interest, or other similarity. ERGs foster diversity and inclusiveness within the organization and provide an opportunity for employees to discuss valuable viewpoints regarding programs, concerns, and other issues. ERGs are an excellent way to engage the community as well. By inviting community members to participate in an ERG, new viewpoints and perspectives can be gained and discussed. New ideas can be shared through brainstorming sessions and potentially implemented as new programs. Additionally, by engaging community members within an ERG, corporate responsibility can be enhanced by ensuring an understanding from all sides. Employees who have the opportunity to hear directly from the community can incorporate this feedback into their work and recommendations. Similarly, community members who have the opportunity to hear directly from the employees can have a deeper understanding of the daily work and responsibilities of the organization.

Programs Relative to Health, Safety, Security, and Privacy

A **health and safety workplace program** is a defined plan of action designed to prevent injuries and illnesses, promote a healthy workplace environment, and reinforce a culture of health and wellness. Effective programs have been shown to reduce injuries and illnesses as well as increase employee wellness and ultimately satisfaction. Health and safety workplace programs are master plans that identify and control the risks that employees could face, and also cover how to respond to emergencies. All workplace programs should align with federal and state legal and regulatory requirements. In general, programs should be available to all employees and be nondiscriminatory, to ensure that all individuals have the same opportunities and benefits available. Additionally, organizations should take a proactive and robust effort to ensure that employees operate in a safe manner, so as to prevent injury. Workplace programs that incorporate frequent training and refresher programs in worker's compensation, health and safety, emergency response, and workplace violence are vital to ensure a healthy and safe work environment. Programs should outline the company's commitment to a safe workplace and how each program aligns with this goal.

Effective workplace programs engage leadership throughout the entire process from creation to implementation, evaluation, and review. Engaging employees at all levels of an organization allows for maximum participation and support of programs. Additionally, workplace programs should have an efficient and clear communication plan throughout the entire process. As regulations are updated, programs should also be updated to ensure compliance. Any changes should be clearly communicated to employees to ensure understanding. Programs should clearly communicate the responsibilities and accountabilities for all employees, including management and leadership. Workplace programs that are strategically created with various stakeholders are more likely to succeed. Stakeholders should include management, leadership, wellness committees, and employees at various levels within the organization. Creating a mission statement and a strategic plan that incorporates short-term and long-term goals is important to ensure that individual programs align with the overall goals. Workplace programs should address the needs of the organization and employees that are discovered through workplace assessments, evaluations of current programs, employee surveys, health risk assessments, and data analysis. If appropriate and resources are available, incentives are an excellent practice to incorporate to increase participation and support. Workplace programs should be evaluated on a regular basis to ensure effectiveness and legal compliance. Programs can be evaluated in various ways, such as participation and utilization rates, satisfaction levels, absenteeism and presenteeism, productivity, employee morale and retention, and return on investment. It is important to communicate these results to employees to continue support and usage of the programs.

Effective health and safety workplace programs provide multiple benefits, including reductions in healthcare costs and sick leave usage, increases in productivity and efficiency, better employee morale, greater job satisfaction, and greater retention of employees. Additionally, these programs provide for increased leadership opportunities, connectivity, better communication, increased creativity, and empathy. Empowering employees, providing growth opportunities, building internal connections, and encouraging innovation lead to a culture of teamwork and collaboration with employees understanding how their roles, skills, and contributions support the organization.

Organizational Policies and Procedures

Policies and procedures are significant, as they communicate the values and expectations of an organization. They ensure accountability, implement best practices, and facilitate decision making. **Policies** are the standards or guides to the organizational philosophy, mission, and values. **Procedures** are targeted and specific action plans to achieve the organization's goals. Most organizations implement various procedures to ensure consistency, equity, and fairness, including standard operating procedures, employee handbooks, and time/attendance rules.

Standard operating procedures (SOPs) ensure that processes are completed accurately and efficiently every time. SOPs are documents that describe specific details of a task or operation to ensure the quality of work completed. They provide a set of instructions, steps, and guidelines for individuals to follow to ensure safety, compliance, and accuracy each time the process is completed. Additionally, SOPs maximize efficiency and productivity by minimizing errors and rework while maximizing resources and continuous improvement. SOPs can also protect the organization and employees when questions of legality or compliance arise.

Employee handbooks are structured manuals that communicate expectations regarding the employment experience. Provided with a handbook, employees can take ownership of locating answers to commonly asked questions or understanding a specific program. Employee handbooks should strive to achieve the following:

- Introduce employees to the organizational culture, including the mission, values, and goals

- Communicate expectations for employees and management

- Ensure key policies are clearly understood

- Showcase the benefits offered to employees such as wellness programs, employee assistance programs, discounts, recognition programs, training opportunities, and more

- Ensure compliance with federal and state laws

- Provide employees with their rights, responsibilities, and where to go for help

- Defend against employment claims

Employee handbooks should also define the standard work schedule, the performance evaluation process, the dress code, and emergency procedures. Employee handbooks serve many purposes, specifically being a reference guide, a communication tool, and an enforcement of company policies. A common best practice is to require all new employees to read the handbook and return a notification that the handbook has been read and understood, to protect the organization from frivolous claims pertaining to not knowing about a particular program or policy.

Time and attendance procedures establish the requirements and expectations of employees regarding reliability and punctuality. Ensuring employees are available, on time, and at work maintains a productive and fair work environment for all employees. These procedures should communicate the process for requesting and scheduling time off from work, including vacation and illness leave, as appropriate. Procedures for requesting medical leaves, such as the Family Medical Leave Act (FMLA), should also be detailed in the time and attendance procedures. Employees should have a clear understanding of their responsibilities when it comes to not being at work. Excessive absenteeism and tardiness create a burden on the company and other employees. When an employee will be late or absent at the last minute, it is important to have an established procedure in which they can call in to report being late or absent due to an emergency or unforeseen circumstance. Time and attendance procedures should also stipulate the consequences for failing to adhere to the expectations of being on time and at work. These consequences could include disciplinary action—up to and including termination—depending on the severity and frequency of the absences and tardiness.

Complaints Involving Employment Practices, Behavior, and Working Conditions

Managing complaints or concerns should always be addressed in a fair and consistent manner regardless of the subject of the complaint. While specific complaints may require different processes due to complexity or legal issues, it is important to have standardized processes and practices. It is also important to understand when to inform leadership of issues and concerns. It may be appropriate to communicate a synopsis, including resolutions, at the end of a process for informational purposes only; however, based on the issue, severity, risks, and impacts, it may be necessary to communicate to leadership immediately after the complaint is received. Leadership may need to be involved in the investigation and process, including the recommendations and action plan to resolve the concerns. It is important to understand the level of communication needed based on the issue.

Handling complaints, either informal or formal, should follow a structured process. Employees should have a full understanding of how and to whom a complaint can be submitted as well as an understanding of how the process will unfold and an estimate of time needed. Seeking to understand as much as possible about the issue should be at the core of the process. This is accomplished by investigating that involves asking questions, researching practices, analyzing data, and following up on additional pieces of information gained throughout process. Being respectful, responsive, attentive, empathetic, and available will assist in ensuring an effective complaint handling process.

The goal of handling any complaint is to resolve the issue at the lowest level possible. To be successful, employees, especially supervisors, should be trained in conflict resolution methods. **Conflict resolution** involves the following:

- Identify the problem that is causing the issue
- Identify the feelings, perceptions, and opinions regarding the issue
- Identify the potential impacts of the issue as well as the impacts of any resolution implemented
- Identify the recommendation and actions to implement to resolve the issue
- Work toward resolution of the issue
- Communicate the resolution with all parties as appropriate

If conflict resolution methods do not resolve the issue, then more formal approaches should be taken to escalate the issue. Ensuring that the issue is resolved in the most effective and efficient way possible is the goal of any process. Filing a grievance, submitting a formal complaint, or reaching out to other oversight organizations that investigate matters such as safety issues (Occupational Safety and Health Administration) or employment practices (Equal Employment Opportunity Commission) may be appropriate as a next step. However, it is important to note that depending on the issue, it may be appropriate to begin the complaint handling process at a more formal level. Examples of these issues would be sexual harassment, workplace violence, discriminatory practices regarding promotions, unsafe working conditions, or other concerns that deserve an escalated response. In each of these examples, leadership should be notified immediately to ensure that the issues are addressed promptly and appropriately. Once a case has been resolved, it may be appropriate to review applicable policies and procedures to ensure that necessary changes are made so that future incidents may be avoided.

Positive Employee and Labor Relations

Employee and labor relations refers to the maintenance of an effective working relationship with employees and the labor unions that represent them. By working together in various settings, organizations can establish positive working relationships with both labor unions and individual employees. Generally, Human Resources professionals are responsible for maintaining and nurturing the relationship with the labor unions that represent employees; however, it is also the responsibility of management and leadership to ensure strong relationships with employees on a day-to-day basis.

Organizations can implement many best practices to ensure strong and effective partnerships. Most of these best practices fall under the overarching theme of frequent and open communication. Implementing a strong communications plan includes incorporating an open-door policy, meeting regularly, establishing joint committees, providing accurate information and reports, inviting various management and leadership levels to employee meetings, and demonstrating a genuine concern for the employees and their well-being. Open-door policies are an excellent practice that can be implemented at all levels of an organization. Open-door policies encourage and nurture open communication between employees and managers, resulting in a healthier workplace.

Meeting regularly is important to ensure that all parties are informed and educated on pending issues, the status of project works such as policy development, and employee matters. Providing a standing meeting date and time that occurs regularly is an excellent way to ensure that meetings occur. A best practice to incorporate to ensure meetings are effective and efficient is to have both parties submit items to for an agenda that will be published before the meeting. This allows for all parties to be prepared for discussions and status updates.

Establishing joint committees is also a best practice to incorporate into meeting regularly. Often, certain subjects are not appropriate or necessary to bring into a standing meeting until certain research has been conducted. In these cases, creating a joint committee to discuss, research, and analyze the issue is an excellent way to involve individual employees in the process prior to making a decision. Employees are generally more satisfied and supportive with programs and actions when they have been involved in the process.

Providing accurate information and reports is also important to ensure that all parties have the same data and are working from the same playbook. Reports may be requested on an as-needed basis or may be part of a standard and regular process and run at a certain time each month or quarter. Having a complete understanding of employee demographics is an important piece of information when working to establish positive employee and labor relations.

Another best practice is to engage employees and management or leadership during standing meetings. Inviting employees to have lunch with leadership to discuss concerns or issues is a great way to connect individuals; however, some employees may not feel comfortable in this setting, so it is important to incorporate other opportunities as well. These may include having leadership attend union or employee meetings to provide information or field questions. Ensuring multiple ways of connection and communication is vital to engaging as many employees as possible. In doing so, leadership also conveys a message that the organization has a genuine concern for employees and their overall well-being. All of these best practices support the idea of honest concern for employees, which is the cornerstone of positive employee and labor relations.

Performance Management Process

Performance management is the continuous process of planning, coaching, evaluating, and rewarding the performance of individual employees, workgroups or teams, and departments with the goal of aligning performance and achievements with the overall strategic goals and mission of the organization.

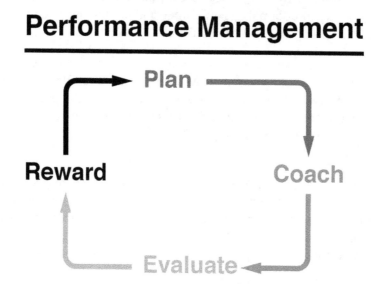

A typical performance management process begins with executive leadership planning and finalizing overall organizational goals for a given year. These goals are then translated to specific objectives and achievements for departments and management and then further defined to align with programs and performance targets for individual employees. Once the goals and objectives have been planned at all levels of the organization, supervisors can then begin to coach employees on the best way to be successful in achieving the goals within the context of the job.

Utilizing a formal performance review process that includes performance appraisals and development plans is an excellent resource to engage employees in discussions about performance, achievements, training, resources, and development. Informal reviews are also a helpful tool to provide employees insight as to their progress in achieving the goals outlined for the year. Providing status updates throughout the year ensures that employees are on track to reach their goals and also provides an opportunity to reassess the objectives or the position, if needed. If the position needs to be reviewed to ensure the job description and responsibilities are an accurate representation of the work being done, tools such as a job analysis can be used. It is important to conduct these conversations within the performance management process, but not at the end during the evaluation process. This could lead to unsatisfactory performance evaluations that are not technically warranted and have other further reaching consequences such as poor employee morale, higher turnover, decreased productivity, and negative customer satisfaction. Evaluations should be fair, clear, accurate, and succinct. They should present a picture of the work that the employee has completed throughout the year, showing how the achieved objectives assist in the organization achieving its overall goals and objectives.

Finally, employees should be rewarded as appropriate and available. Recognition should be given for a job well done and if budgetary resources available, merit increases, bonus awards, or other pay for performance programs should be enacted. If budgetary resources are not available for a monetary award, other awards should be considered to continue to incentivize employees to exceed their goals and objectives. Top performers can be recognized in employee newsletters with specific examples of the accomplishments achieved. Recognition programs that acknowledge employee accomplishments quarterly and annually—even resulting in a highly coveted "Employee of the Year" award—can be implemented to continue to recognize employees' achievements.

A vitally important tool to utilize throughout the entire performance management process is communication and feedback in both directions—up and down. It is a common occurrence for communication to only flow down: leadership to management to supervision to individual employees. Employees should be encouraged to speak with peers, supervisors, management, and leadership as appropriate regarding concerns, questions, or needs such as resources or training. Ensuring this flow of communication promotes engagement throughout the process, increasing the success of the overall process and ultimately meeting the achievements at all levels.

Performance Activities and Employment Activities by Corresponding Legal Risks

Organizations are often faced with employees who are not performing to the standards required of the position or the company. In these cases, there are various performance activities that can be initiated to improve performance. Informal and formal coaching, performance improvement plans, demotions, and increased training requirements are all actions that an organization can initiate to communicate deficient performance and work with the employee to improve. In the case that an employee does not or cannot make the improvements necessary to perform the job at the level required, an organization may need to discipline the employee up to and including termination, or an involuntary separation.

To mitigate legal risks in these cases, it is important to begin documenting conversations, expectations, and poor performance. Having the documentation that justifies the corrective actions being implemented is vital to decreasing the risks that an organization may face through a claim or lawsuit. Employees should also be fully aware of the deficiencies in their performance so that there are no surprises. By providing employees with the information and opportunities to improve, the organization can better protect itself in the case of litigation. If an employee is not aware of what needs to be improved upon or the expectations of these improvements, such as timing, the employee can make the claim that there was not sufficient opportunity provided to change the behavior or improve the performance. It is vital to ensure clear, concise, and specific details when dealing with poor performance as these processes are often scrutinized in cases of discrimination or termination.

In the cases of job eliminations or reductions in force, many organizations attempt to adjust headcount and personnel through attrition. When an employee retires or resigns, the organization will not backfill the open position and instead reallocate or eliminate the work that was done. Once the target headcount is reached, then the final workflow process will be determined with positions reformatted and adjusted to align with the new workflow. In the case that job eliminations or reductions in force are required, the organization should always look to incorporate voluntary separation programs to attempt to reduce headcount in this manner. Oftentimes, there are no other options and involuntary separations must occur. In these cases, Human Resources is responsible for understanding the employee demographics and working with the department managers to recommend the positions that will be eliminated.

It is important to remember that reductions should be recommended based on the position, not the individual. Reductions in force or job eliminations should not be determined based on the individual employees. These actions are not intended to deal with poor performers. Remaining focused on the job duties and determining the need for the position should be the core basis of selecting a position for elimination. In doing so, the organization will be in a better position legally if a reduction in force or job elimination is challenged. If employees can be transferred or reassigned to other positions, even if additional training is required, every effort should be made to accomplish this. Organizations that have no choice but to end the employment relationship often work to create an affordable severance package for employees. Offering severance in the form of compensation, benefit extension, career transition services, employee assistance programs, and other services is an excellent option that can help employees transition out of the organization smoothly.

Employee Relations Activities and Analysis

Employee relations is defined as the intended strategy of an organization about what needs to be changed relative to the relationships with employees and, if applicable, their representative unions. Additionally, employee relations is a study of the rules, policies, procedures, and agreements that employees are managed against as individuals and as departments. Employee relations management is about ensuring that any organizational changes recommended are accepted and successfully implemented. To establish a best-class employee relations program, Human Resources professionals should understand the individual components within employee relations and work to align these components with the overall strategy and vision of the employee relations program. Employee relations includes the following components, which lend to establishing a strong employee relations program:

- Employee involvement
- Employee communication
- Employee counseling
- Employee discipline
- Employee rights

These components build the organizational culture that employees work within. The ultimate goal of the organizational culture and employee relations strategy is to create an environment in which employees feel they are being treated fairly. Positive and successful employee relations can have significant impacts to the organization such as improving productivity, ensuring implementation of key initiatives, reducing employee costs, and helping employees to grow and develop. Employees are more likely to have a willingness to perform their job well, maintain a positive attitude, stay motivated and motivate others, and have a high level of satisfaction and commitment to the organization. Additionally, employees are more likely to understand their roles and goals within the organization, with their concerns and needs being addressed quickly and efficiently. Finally, employees have the ability to align their personal goals with the department and organizational goals, which can improve morale, loyalty, and productivity.

Employee involvement refers to creating an environment where employees have an impact on decisions and actions that directly affect their jobs. Every employee is regarded as unique and a contributor to the organization, and therefore, directly involved in assisting the organization in meeting its goals. Employees' input is sought out and valued by management, even if not implemented. Employee involvement is most effective when individuals are trained in team effectiveness, communication, and problem solving. Additionally, organizations that have robust reward and recognition programs along with effective communication plans are more likely to have strong employee involvement and effective employee relations.

Employee communication refers specifically to two main styles of communication: 1) vertical, and 2) horizontal. Employees should receive and provide communications in a vertical style. **Vertical communications** include upward and downward messaging. **Upward communications** are the messages that flow from the lower levels to the higher levels of an organization. Upward communications include suggestion boxes, employee surveys, open-door policies and procedures, face-to-face conversations, and department meetings to provide insights. **Downward communications** are the messages that flow from the upper levels to the lower levels of an organization. Downward communications include directives from executive leadership, policies and procedures, performance feedback, official memos and instructions, annual reports, and handbooks. Each type of communication is vital to the success of an organization's employee relations program. Additionally, horizontal communication is also important to the communications within an organization. **Horizontal communications** are the messages that flow laterally between employees within the same rank. These communications often include problem solving, coordination, and sharing or learning between positions. Horizontal communication is generally informal but is powerful in its impact within the organization.

Employee counseling refers to the process used when a performance problem cannot be addressed with training or coaching methods. Employee counseling is vital to uncovering the reasons for poor performance and focuses on performance-related behaviors to ensure a positive outcome. Ensuring the employee understands and accepts the problem is the first goal of employee counseling. Once this has occurred, solutions can be explored to manage the expectations and resolve the issue. Sometimes, the root cause of a performance concern is a personal issue that the employee is dealing with. In these circumstances, once this has been discovered, Human Resources professionals can direct the employee to resources available to assist. **Employee Assistance Programs (EAPs)** are excellent programs to have available to employees to help them work through personal issues so that the employees can focus on work at work.

Employee discipline refers to the tool used by management to improve poor performance and enforce appropriate behavior to ensure a productive and safe workplace. It is vital to ensure that employee discipline is fair and equitable and that employees clearly understand the rules and regulations being enforced, the process to raise concerns and issues, the investigation process, and the penalties involved. If progressive discipline is utilized, employees should understand the intention and when it is appropriate to be used. **Progressive discipline** is a discipline system that imposes progressively greater disciplinary measures based on the conduct of an employee. An example of this would be an employee receiving a written warning for attendance issues. If the attendance issues do not change after a stipulated period of time, the employee would receive a day of discipline imposed. Additional future incidents may then be given increased discipline time off until either the behavior is changed permanently, or other corrective action is needed. Similarly, it is important that employees understand some behavior may not warrant progressive discipline and the corrective action may be immediate termination. An example of this would be engaging in a physical altercation with or sexually harassing a fellow employee. Both of these examples would be appropriate to progress to discipline beyond a written warning after the first offense, including immediate termination after conducting a full investigation. Employees should have clearly defined expectations regarding their behavior and performance as well as what will occur if there are issues with either.

Employee rights refers to the rights that all employees have, including fair and equitable treatment, representation, privacy, grievances, and appeals processes. Employees have the right to know that any investigation conducted was fair and thorough, with sufficient opportunities provided to convey all sides of the situation. Employees should be afforded the right to representation, if applicable. If employees are represented by a union, representation should be offered, especially during disciplinary procedures and investigations. If an employee is not afforded this right, it could interfere with the integrity of the investigation and subsequent discipline. Employees should be afforded the right of privacy. Any disciplinary action, corrective counseling, investigation information, or other details specific to an employee should be held with an appropriate level of confidentiality. Additionally, employees should understand the rights associated with filing a grievance or appeal to resolve an issue or argue a decision such as a disciplinary action.

Ensuring that each of the above components is strong, transparent, and understood will allow an organization to have an effective and productive employee relations program. Employees will more likely be fully engaged, involved, productive, and efficient in their work.

Federal Laws and Procedures Affecting Employment, Labor Relations, Safety, and Security

The first major labor statute passed in the United States was the Norris-LaGuardia Act of 1932. The **Norris-LaGuardia Act** endorsed collective bargaining as public policy and established government recognition that the job to a worker is more important than a worker to a corporation. Establishing this relationship was vital in showing that the only real power an employee has is in impacting employers through concerted activity. While this act did not create new rights, it curbed the power of courts to intervene in labor disputes and declared that unions could operate free from corporate control and interference.

The **National Labor Relations Act (NLRA)** is the basic law governing relations between labor unions and employees, giving employees the right to organize and bargain collectively. The NLRA is also known as the **Wagner Act** and was passed in 1935. The NLRA prohibits both employers and unions from violating the basic rights of employees, which include the following:

- The right to self-organize a union to negotiate with the employer
- The right to form, join, or assist labor organizations
- The right to bargain collectively about wages, working conditions, and other subjects
- The right to discuss employment terms and conditions of employment
- The right to choose representatives to bargain
- The right to take action to improve working conditions by raising work-related complaints
- The right to strike and picket, as appropriate
- The right to engage in protected activities
- The right to refrain from any of the above

Additionally, the NLRA stipulates that employers cannot prohibit employees from soliciting for a union during nonwork time or from distributing union literature or communications during nonwork time. The NLRA also prohibits the union from threatening employees with termination or other unjust actions unless union support is given. Finally, the NLRA established the **National Labor Relations Board (NLRB).** The NLRB certifies organized labor unions, supervises elections, and has the power to act against unfair business practices.

The NLRA establishes that both parties must negotiate and bargain in "good faith." **Good faith bargaining** refers to the honest attempt made by both the employer and union to reach an agreement. Good faith bargaining does not obligate either the employer or union to specific concessions or proposals. The basic requirements for bargaining in good faith include approaching negotiations with sincere resolve to reach an agreement, meeting regularly and at reasonable times, putting agreements in writing if requested, and having authorized representatives available and present at the scheduled times. The NLRA also establishes that mandatory subjects of bargaining must be negotiated between labor and management. **Mandatory subjects of bargaining** include wages, benefits, time off, hours, seniority, safety conditions, working conditions, employee testing protocols, disciplinary procedures, and recruitment issues such as promotion and demotion.

In 1947, the **Taft-Hartley Act**, or the **Labor-Management Relations Act,** was passed to amend the NLRA and limit employee labor rights. The Taft-Hartley Act provided that employers also have the right to go to the NLRB and allows for protections to the employers. This act prohibited unions from engaging in the following behavior:

- Forcing employees to support and join the union
- Refusing to bargain in good faith with employers
- Carrying out certain kinds of strikes
- Charging excessive union fees
- Going on strike during certain periods of time

It also provides for a cooling-off period in negotiation. Additionally, this act allowed states to pass "right-to-work laws," banned union contributions to political campaigns, required that union leaders swear they were not communists, and allowed for government intervention in certain circumstances. Finally, the Taft-Hartley Act established the **Federal Mediation and Conciliation Service (FMCS)** to help resolve negotiating disputes.

In 1959, the **Landrum-Griffin Act,** or the **Labor-Management Reporting and Disclosure Act,** was passed to again amend the NLRA. The Landrum-Griffin Act increased reporting requirements, regulated union affairs, and protected union members from improper union leadership to safeguard union member rights and prevent inappropriate practices by employers and union officers. This act is a bill of rights for union members, providing election procedures, accounting practices, and leadership oversight. This act was intended to protect the interests of the individual union members. This act provides union members the right to:

- Identify and propose candidates for office
- Vote in elections to select a board of representatives
- Attend and participate in union meetings
- Vote on union business
- Review and audit union accounts and records for transparency and accountability
- File grievances against union officers as appropriate to protect the integrity of the union

The history of unions in the United States goes back to ensuring a fair wage for a fair day's work, with employers providing a safe workplace. Employees should leave work in the same physical condition that they arrived. While there are various federal laws enacted to protect worker's rights as discussed above, as well as laws that protect wages, working conditions, safety and wellness, and other areas of concern, some individuals still want unions to represent their interest with employers. While there are many misperceptions about why employees might consider and want a union, the following are the most common reasons for unionizing a workforce:

- Poor communications
- Poor leadership and management
- Supervisors and employee treatment
- Stagnate wages and benefits
- Healthcare and retirement plans
- Safety and working conditions
- Workload and stress
- Job security
- Employee morale
- Lack of employee recognition and appreciation

There is usually not one specific reason that a group of employees may look to unionize, but rather a culmination of multiple factors that lead to a disengaged, unmotivated, and dissatisfied group of employees.

Human Relations, Culture, and Values Concepts

Human relations refers to the process by which an organization understands the needs of individuals both separate from and within the workplace, specifically the relationships and connections that individuals have with others. Human relations looks at how individuals interact and cooperate with each other when working together within a group setting to achieve common goals. Additionally, human relations recognizes, respects, and safeguards the dignity of each individual along with their specific efforts and contributions toward achieving the goals of the group and organization. Furthermore, it is vital to understand the following five basic fundamental principles regarding human relations:

- Individuals are emotional, intelligent, psychological, and social beings.
- Emotions are natural and can cause mild or strong feelings.
- Situations cannot be completely controlled, and uncertainty exists.
- People don't change simply because someone else wants them to.
- Individuals can change and evolve to new situations and circumstances when ready.

A major focus of human relations is the hierarchy of needs. The **hierarchy of needs,** as defined by Abraham Maslow, considers various levels of motivating requirements that individuals need both outside and within the workplace to achieve full potential and stability. The hierarchy of needs establishes the theory of human motivation within the professional working environment. The following pyramid outlines the fundamental levels of individual needs that must be met in order to achieve maximum potential. Each level must be achieved and maintained prior to achieving the next higher level of needs.

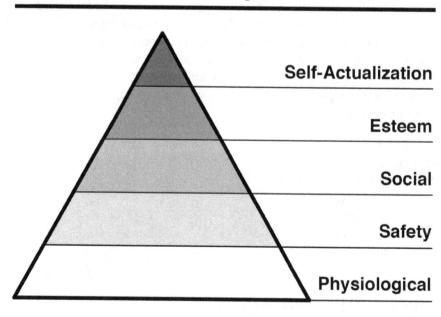

Physiological needs, often referred to as **life needs,** include food, water, shelter, and sleep. They are the basic human needs that an individual must have to sustain life. These physiological needs are the base and foundation of human needs. **Safety needs,** often referred to as **security needs,** include the security and safety specific to the individual's body, employment, resources, family, health, and property. The physiological and safety needs form the basic needs of an individual within the hierarchy of needs, but these two levels alone do not establish motivation for an individual; rather, they can serve as demotivators if an individual only achieves these two levels. **Social needs,** often referred to as **belonging needs,** include intimate relationships, friendships, and family. **Esteem needs,** often referred to as **respect needs,** include self-esteem, confidence, achievement, self-respect, prestige, and feelings of accomplishment. The social and esteem needs form the psychological needs of an individual and it is within these two levels that an individual can be motivated to achieve higher levels of success. The highest level of motivation is self-actualization and includes achieving one's full potential at all levels within their life. **Self-actualization** is the self-fulfillment need and includes complete understanding and personal growth in morality, creativity, spontaneity, and problem solving. Self-actualization and full motivation can only be achieved when all levels of needs are met and realized. Individuals who have achieved all levels of this hierarchy are highly engaged, extremely productive and efficient, and, in general, completely satisfied with the organization.

Applying Maslow's hierarchy of needs to the organizational culture can be done by understanding and ensuring appropriate and specific applications for each need level. Physiological needs can be met by paying a competitive salary, offering overtime opportunities, providing an appropriate working environment that includes necessary tools and resources, and delivering a fair benefits package that includes paid time off such as holidays, vacation, and sick leave. Safety needs can be met by ensuring safe and healthy working conditions, job security, and programs put in place to assist employees through periods of transition. Social needs can be met by offering positive and encouraging team environments, friendly yet professional supervisory relationships, and approachable executive leadership. Esteem needs can be met by providing employees job titles that accurately reflect the job being performed while also allowing for an appropriate level of authority, recognizing employees formally and informally for achievements and contributions, and providing employees opportunities for growth and development. Self-actualization needs can be met by providing employees with opportunities to be innovative and creative, allowing for mentoring opportunities to and from other employees, and affording opportunities to promote within the organization.

Incorporating the hierarchy of needs and appropriate applications to achieve each level can establish and support the defined core values within an organization. Ensuring that employees are fully engaged and operating at a highly productive level adds value to the organization on many levels, such as excellent customer service, organizational agility and flexibility, innovative thinking, learning and development, and social responsibility. Human relations is at the center of these concepts and practices by treating employees with dignity and respect while understanding and recognizing the work, achievements, and contributions being accomplished on a daily basis. When all of these concepts are applied consistently and effectively within an organization, a culture is established that includes ethical behaviors, transparency, valued employees, respect, and achieving success on all levels.

Assessing Employee Attitudes, Opinions, and Satisfaction

Employee surveys are an efficient and effective method to measure employee attitudes, opinions, and overall satisfaction. Surveys can provide perspectives at various levels of the organization, including the satisfaction of individuals with their specific position, supervisor, executive leadership, and the entire organization and company culture. Surveys allow an organization to monitor trends in specific areas, assess impacts of policy changes, compare employee satisfaction with other organizations and competitors, and provide insight on the areas of improvement that are important to employees. Additionally, surveys can offer the opportunity to review employee perspectives regarding compensation, benefits, time off, recognition, training opportunities, communication, culture, leadership, and any other area that may need to be assessed. The survey results can then be used to determine and support necessary actions to implement for improvement.

Surveys evaluate attitudes and satisfaction in various categories. It is important to periodically survey employees to gain insight on how the culture is changing, for better or for worse. It is also important to involve and engage employees in the survey early on in the process. When employees are involved in the planning, coordination, and implementation of any program, including surveys, the organization usually sees increased participation, fair and honest feedback, and increased motivation to participate in the actions that result from the survey. It is extremely important to note that it is vital that an organization communicate with employees before, during, and after the survey. Post-survey communication should include the results, actions, and goals that will be implemented from the information received. If an organization does not intend to act based on the survey results, then a survey should not be conducted. In cases where organizations do not communicate or take action from employee surveys, employees generally become disengaged, lose motivation, and are less likely to participate in future surveys.

Surveys can take various forms. Organizations may want an overall, holistic view of employee satisfaction and opinions to fully delve into changing culture and process as necessary. Organizations also may want to conduct a short and specific survey that provides an opportunity for employees to respond to one focused topic. Regardless of the depth or topics of a survey, it is important to follow best practices:

- Conduct a survey only when a committed leadership team is supporting the entire process

- If appropriate and feasible, partner with an expert who will conduct the actual survey and provide the results; if this is not an option, ensure that the Human Resources professional conducting the survey is educated and trained on conducting employee surveys

- Establish a strong and thorough communication plan

- Establish a task team to review the results and determine an action plan; identify champions for specific topics

- Share data consistently at all levels of the organization

- Keep the survey simple and execute the process flawlessly

- Identify resources to implement the survey and the resulting action plan

- Plan for a follow-up opportunity to provide additional and new information based on the action plan for leadership to adjust a course of action if necessary

- Do not commit to another survey for a minimum of eighteen to twenty-four months

- Invest in post survey results and action plan, including time, budget, training, and other resources

When creating the survey, an organization may want to provide a voluntary opportunity for employees to identify demographic information. Demographic information such as department, age, years of service, gender, and supervisory responsibilities can serve to provide the organization with specific concerns and areas of focus within certain departments or for certain segments of the employee population. An example of this would be a survey question regarding safe working conditions. An overall satisfaction rate may yield a satisfactory score; however, if the data are broken down further by department, a lower satisfaction rate may be seen for particular departments, which could indicate there is an issue that should be reviewed and resolved. Without having the ability to sort and separate the data, concerns may be missed as the overall satisfaction rates are an average of all responses. An employee concern, however, with providing any identifying information is the chance to be recognized and connected with the responses provided.

Confidentiality is an important component to surveys and employees should feel comfortable in providing honest feedback without the fear of repercussions. This is one positive aspect of using a third-party provider to conduct the survey, as the external vendor can compute the information provided on the survey, including the demographic information, and then produce requested reports to show the results.

Conducting employee surveys is driven by the desire to understand the organization and implement change that will positively impact the culture, engagement, motivation, and progress on an individual level as well as an organizational level. If surveys are conducted professionally, results are communicated, and action plans are implemented with full commitment from executive leadership, organizations will see positive changes. These positive changes can include loyalty and higher retention rates, satisfaction and motivation, innovation and creativity, and ultimately, higher customer satisfaction. Satisfied employees provide excellent customer service, resulting in satisfied customers.

Diversity and Inclusion

Diversity is defined as the similarities, differences, and opportunities inherent in the individual and organizational characteristics that form the workplace. **Inclusion** is defined as respecting and valuing diversity. A simple and extremely accurate definition provided by Andres Tapia states that, "Diversity is the mix. Inclusion is making the mix work." Verna Myers provided the description "Diversity is being invited to the party; inclusion is being asked to dance." Both of these specific definitions provide the basis of how diversity is integral to inclusion, but inclusion is the actual end result and goal.

The impacts of a strong diversity and inclusion strategy are far reaching, beyond the internal employees and organization. The culture and core values of the organization are the foundation for the framework of an organization's mission and align with achieving the overall objectives. There are four main areas that an organization's diversity and inclusion strategy will impact:

- Workplace
- Workforce
- Marketplace
- Community

Diversity and inclusion within the workplace foster an inclusive environment in which different backgrounds, perspectives, behaviors, and experiences are valued and respected. Diversity and inclusion within the workforce build a diverse talent pipeline and provide high impact engagement, innovation, involvement, and development programs. Diversity and inclusion within the marketplace serve the diverse needs of customers, shareholders, and executive leadership through the products and services provided. Additionally, diversity within and among suppliers and vendors, as well as marketing efforts, is recognized with preference given to the brand and organization. Diversity and inclusion within the community shows the organization as a good corporate citizen with demonstrated social responsibility through community leadership, involvement, philanthropy, and volunteering. Overall, the organization is able to build and sustain a culture and environment where all employees are embraced and valued for who they are. This allows each employee to reach their full potential and enable the organization to meet and exceed the goals and achievements identified.

Historically, diversity initiatives were incorporated into organizations based on a moral imperative to have the workforce reflect the external labor market and community population. Recruitment programs and methods were incorporated to attract and hire individuals from various backgrounds. The issue that has become apparent over the years, however, is that simply hiring more diverse individuals is not enough and should not be the ending point for establishing a diverse working environment. Currently, organizations are focusing on inclusion and establishing an inclusive working environment for all employees. Organizations establish inclusion by:

- Utilizing diverse perspectives and opinions to broaden problem solving, innovation, and creativity
- Encouraging collaboration and learning from differences, flexibility, and fairness
- Embedding inclusive values in organizational structures, policies, and practices

Each individual has a distinct and unique set of skills, values, goals, and motivations for both their professional and personal life. For an organization to attract a diverse, talented, and best-in-class workforce, an inclusive environment and culture must be present.

To establish an inclusive workplace, four pillars must be created, supported, and functional: awareness, mobilization, action, and alignment. **Awareness** is the pillar that raises the understanding and mindfulness of the organization and employees toward the diversity and inclusion initiatives. Awareness prepares employees for the acceptance of the culture and the willingness to accept changes that increase inclusion. Activities that encourage awareness include education, bias training, cultural immersion, and job training. **Mobilization** is the pillar that sets up the policies, processes, procedures, and systems that allow for accountability for all employees at all levels. **Action** is the pillar that implements the strategies through specific efforts and tactics. Activities within the action pillar include working with diverse suppliers and vendors, actively engaging employees to build an inclusive workplace, and structuring programs that align with inclusion. **Alignment** is the pillar that essential to ensuring a successful implementation of all diversity and inclusion strategies. Alignment focuses on analyzing, reviewing, and revising strategies, policies, and ways of conducting business to meet employee and customer expectations. Additionally, alignment strengthens innovation, engagement, and loyalty from both employees and customers.

For diversity and inclusion strategies to be successful, organizations must have leaders who understand and value a diverse workforce, as well as recognize the learning and challenges that different perspectives can provide. The organizational culture must create a high standard of performance for all employees at all levels and the culture must encourage openness, honesty, and transparency. The culture must stimulate personal development, make employees feel valued, and be clear in the commitment to employees. Finally, the organization must have a clear vision and define success related to diversity and inclusion. Organizations that have a culture that values and is committed to diversity and inclusion see real and high-impact benefits. Diverse thinking and bringing in different opinions and perspectives leads to an almost seventy percent increase in innovation. Inclusive leadership and management increases the likelihood of new customers and employees, leading to an almost fifty percent increase in the likelihood to grow market share and market presence. Motivated teams lead to employees being twice as engaged and motivated to provide input and affect change. Overall, performance at all levels within the organization is stronger when diverse leadership and different experiences are available.

Recordkeeping Requirements

Effective records and information management is extremely important. Human Resources professionals should familiarize themselves with all federal and state regulations regarding recordkeeping. Different pieces of information have different retention periods to maintain compliance. Ensuring compliance is extremely important because if an organization is outside of compliance, the ramifications could be far reaching and expensive. From paying hefty fines to losing data critical for lawsuits or other legal matters, ensuring a robust recordkeeping process should be a high priority to limit exposure and liability for an organization.

Personnel files are one of the most important and fundamental recordkeeping functions within Human Resources. When an employee is hired, a file should be created that is the primary storage location for all matters relating to the individual employees. The personnel file should include, but is not limited to:

- Recruitment flyer for position hired into

- Application

- Offer letter and Acceptance

- New hire checklist

- New hire documents, including the employee's employment eligibility form (I-9), federal and state tax forms, direct deposit form, benefits enrollment paperwork, and copies of all corresponding documentation such driver's license, passport, social security card, marriage license, birth certificate(s), and voided check(s)

As an employee continues employment with the organization, new forms and documents should be added to the personnel file. This could include promotional offers of employment, benefits change forms, performance evaluations, medical leave requests and documentation, disciplinary records, training records, and letters of resignation or termination. It is important to understand the retention rules regarding the personnel file as well as the items contained within the personnel file when applying the organization's policies to files. As with any other policy, it is necessary to review recordkeeping policies and practices frequently. If updates are needed, they should be vetted and fully understood before implementation. As retention schedules are changed, organizations should see that updates to the policies are implemented swiftly to ensure compliance at the new required timeframe.

An organization may choose to standardize a filing system in which all records for an employee are maintained within the personnel file; a common best practice is to separate specific documents and maintain a separate filing system. This type of filing practice can be easier to use in cases of audits or file destruction. Reviewing all employee files could be cumbersome and time-consuming; however, if an organization must review all of the I-9 forms to ensure those that require destruction per the retention period are completed, it would be much easier to have a specified binder or file with all employee I-9 documents available. Similarly, training documents would also be another file to maintain separately to ensure easier access when reviewing statistics and ensuring compliance for mandatory training.

When establishing methods for recordkeeping, organizations should ensure that records are maintained to meet the internal needs of the business as well as the department that is managing them. Records should be maintained in such a way that can assist in defending actions and providing justifications and history. Organizations must remain in compliance regarding records and are also responsible for ensuring that resources are available and used in the most efficient and effective manner possible.

All records should be kept in a manner that ensures privacy and confidentiality. From locking cabinets to establishing a locking mechanism on the doors to rooms that house personnel files, Human Resources should make every attempt and effort to safeguard employee personnel files. Information contained within these files is sensitive and includes everything from social security numbers, dates of birth, and other information for not only the employee but their spouse and children. If a data breach does occur, organizations should do everything to ensure that their employees and families are protected in the case of identity theft.

In addition to employee personnel files, organizations are also required to keep thorough and detailed records specific to areas within the organization. Each department is responsible for maintaining compliance regarding records specific to their areas of expertise. The **Occupational Safety Hazard Act (OSHA)** requires detailed reporting regarding work-related injuries and illnesses as well as frequent posting of information. Federal statutes concerning sexual harassment require detailed reporting of annual mandatory supervisory training. The **Fair Labor Standards Act (FLSA)** requires detailed reporting regarding timecards, time entry, compensation earned and calculated, and other wages and benefits paid to employees. From regulations relating to purchasing and accounting to historical documentation regarding contract negotiations, each type of record should have a policy and retention schedule that indicates how long an organization is required to keep the record. It may be necessary to keep records beyond the retention schedule, though, for historical knowledge purposes or to establish patterns. Many organizations have shifted to electronic platforms to manage employee records, documents, and information; however, efforts still must be taken to ensure confidentiality and privacy to protect the data. Cybersecurity has escalated with the increase of hacking, phishing, and malware, and provides a different level of protection.

Occupational Injury and Illness Prevention Techniques

Occupational injuries and illnesses can be expensive. Not only is an employee's health and personal well-being impacted, but an organization can experience costly impacts such as medical costs, reduced productivity, overtime costs, training replacements, legal fees, or fines for noncompliance. Developing, implementing, updating, and maintaining an effective workplace safety program requires the following:

- Engage and involve management and employees
- Analyze the workplace, employees, and operations
- Mitigate hazards and safety issues
- Implement frequent training
- Review, respond, and improve the plan based on actual day-to-day experiences

When employees are engaged in a process and management is committed to the process, employees at all levels of the organization are more likely to support the process. Safety is everyone's responsibility.

In order for an organization to identify and implement effective prevention techniques to minimize and eliminate occupational injuries and illness, it must first fully understand the injuries and illness that occur. An effective method to use to gain this understanding is the 5 W method. By answering the five questions—Who? What? Where? When? And Why?—an organization can gain the information necessary to incorporate prevention techniques that will make an impact.

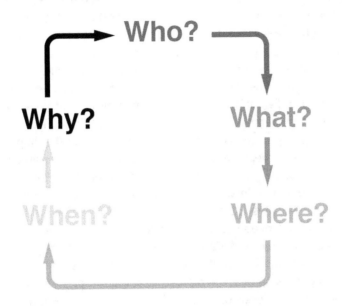

Who is being injured? What types of injuries are occurring? Where are the injuries occurring? When are the injuries occurring? Why or how are the injuries occurring? By answering these questions, specific and targeted actions can be incorporated into the safety policies, everyday work practices, and organizational culture. Once an organization has reviewed the information regarding specific injuries and illness, a focused and targeted plan can be implemented to address the specific concerns. Employees can be provided with informational tools and resources regarding these specific injuries and prevention techniques to educate and inform while ideally minimizing injuries. Additionally, employees can be provided with instruction sheets regarding other common injuries and prevention techniques.

While many positions have specific injury or illness concerns, there are some injuries and illnesses that can occur regardless of the position or organization. Some of these common injuries can include carpal tunnel syndrome, airborne allergies, back pain, eye strain, and work-related stress. By offering information to employees to reduce or eliminate common injuries, organizations can establish the safety culture for employees. When employees understand their role and responsibilities regarding the health and safety within an organization, prevention techniques will be more accepted and practiced on a daily basis. Incorporating safe practices in daily life, such as wearing a seatbelt when driving in a car or using a handrail when climbing stairs, often permeates to safe practices in the workplace, such as wearing safety glasses or paying attention to slip and fall hazards.

When possible, employers should address any safety hazards and concerns identified. Safe practices are necessary to ensure employees are protected from injuries and illnesses; however, when safety hazards can be addressed or removed, organizations should take steps to mitigate the issues. Additionally, employers should incorporate training programs that frequently refresh information for employees, including how to report an injury, how to report a safety concern, and how to prevent injuries.

Both employees and employers have responsibilities when it comes to preventing workplace injuries and illnesses. Understanding these responsibilities is another overarching and more general technique to prevent injuries and illness. Employees have the right to know about any workplace hazards. Employees also have the right to participate in problem solving to address health and safety problems, as well as to refuse to do work that is unsafe. Employees, however, must follow the laws and workplace policies and procedures regarding health, safety, and work practices. Employees must wear and use all **personal protective equipment (PPE)** as assigned and work in a manner that is safe and will not hurt any employees, including themselves. PPE is the required gear provided to an employee to perform their job safely and effectively; it includes clothing, footwear, tools, and vehicles. PPE can range from safety glasses or steel-toed boots to coveralls or Kevlar gloves. PPE can also include specific tools or items necessary to perform the job. Additionally, employees are responsible for reporting any hazards or injuries to the supervisor or other responsible individuals as identified in the policies. Employers must make sure employees know about and understand all hazards and dangers within the workplace and specific jobs by providing instructions, training, and supervision. Employers must ensure that supervisors are trained in the requirements to protect employee's health and safety. Employers are responsible for creating the policies and procedures regarding workplace health and safety and ensuring that all employees understand and follow each one. Supervisors should understand how to hold employees accountable for wearing any required PPE as well as train employees in safe work practices specific to their job. Organizations are also responsible for updating policies, procedures, and practices when new issues and concerns arise. As employees work to be more innovative and identify creative solutions for being more productive and effective, new safety concerns or hazards could be identified. In this case, it is important to fully understand the concerns, engage employees in discussing solutions, and update policies and procedures as appropriate. Overall, leaders at all levels of an organization should do everything reasonable to protect employees from being injured or acquiring a work-related illness.

Workplace Safety and Security Risks

Workplace security is defined as managing all personnel, equipment, and facilities in order to protect each and is concerned with mitigating and managing risks such as violence, bomb threats, natural or manmade disasters, cyberthreats, or data breaches. To have a safe workplace, risk assessments should be conducted frequently to determine and evaluate potential weaknesses. Employers are required to identify hazards and remove them, evaluate risks, reduce or control risks, and record the issues discovered in the assessment. Employees are required to cooperate with the employer regarding health and safety matters, inform supervisors about potential safety matters, and adhere to all work and safety policies and procedures. A safer workplace for everyone should always be the goal.

A safe working environment is one of the biggest concerns for employers and employees. Organizations can instigate the following practices regarding workplace safety:

- Each employee is responsible for their own safety AND the safety of their fellow employees
- All accidents are preventable
- Follow all organizational rules, regulations, policies, and procedures
- Assess any risk by stopping and thinking BEFORE acting
- Be proactive about safety
- Obey all safety signs
- Use the right tool for the job
- Wear all protective equipment
- Avoid any unnecessary hazards
- Do not engage in activities if not properly trained

- Manage lifting appropriately and safely
- Do not take shortcuts or skip steps in a process
- Incorporate good housekeeping by maintaining a clean and orderly work area
- Always be prepared

By incorporating these rules and encouraging employees to consistently follow and practice each, an organization can inspire a safety-focused culture that is employee driven. It is not enough to have great policies on paper. Safety must be practiced in every action by employees and supported by a committed leadership.

In addition to following the above rules, employees should also be engaged regarding maintaining a safe workspace. Employees should be informed, trained, and regularly updated regarding evacuation routes and appropriate responses to fire, tornadoes, floods, tsunamis, and other natural disasters. Depending on the location of the facility, employees should know proper procedures to deal with the applicable natural disasters. Additionally, employees should also be trained in the appropriate responses to active shooter situations, bomb threats, or suspicious mail and packages. Employees need to know where to find the fire extinguisher, AED, and first aid kit, as well as know the protocol regarding communication plans and contact information. It is far better to have the knowledge and not need it than to need the knowledge and not have it. Being prepared is a far better situation to be in than not being prepared.

A common catchphrase used recently is "if you see something, say something." While cliché, it is also incredibly accurate and appropriate in the workplace regarding safety and security. Employees should be encouraged and supported to report concerns and issues, even if it seems unimportant or insignificant. While one employee may not see significance in an event, there may be a history they are unaware of. Additionally, another employee may have a different perspective that offers insight and potentially changes a course of action for the better. If someone feels that something is not quite right, it is better to report the issue for further review by experts and trained professionals, rather of remaining silent and having something happen.

Ultimately, safety and security are the responsibility of all employees. Regardless of the specific situation, a technique that can be applied to any circumstance is the STAR technique:

S Stop

T Think

A Act

R Review

Following each of these steps when faced with a safety or security concern, employees are able to protect themselves and others by making the best decisions and taking the appropriate actions. By providing information on as many safety issues and concerns as possible, an organization can help facilitate learning with employees. A best practice is to have regular safety meetings that provide tips and techniques that can be used on a daily basis. Office safety basics can include how to: select, wear, and clean safety glasses; lift boxes safely; effectively use a fire extinguisher; climb and use a ladder; walk in winter climates; clean and organize a workspace; and wear and clean appropriate work attire such as personal protection equipment.

A final thought regarding workplace safety concerns ergonomics. **Ergonomics** is defined as fitting an employee's workplace conditions to the job demands and the specific needs of the individual. Ergonomics can include a proper chair with specific back support. Ergonomics needs can be addressed with simple or complex solutions depending on the physical need. Ensuring employee safety is the goal and minimizing injuries in the workplace is the goal. Carpal tunnel syndrome is a real and costly issue that many employees face. Identifying different keyboard options to minimize discomfort and resolve the physical issue for employees is a great example of how ergonomics can be applied. From standing desks to monitor arms for computer screens, there are numerous options for employees to resolve physical issues and ensure their safety and well-being.

Emergency Response, Business Continuity, and Disaster Recovery

Emergency response, disaster management, emergency management, and emergency planning are all forms of the same principle: organizations must be prepared in the case of an emergency, with all employees understanding the plan and the individual roles played within the plan. Emergency action plans should be developed and implemented to ensure the safe evacuation of employees. These plans should address as many situations as possible and the circumstances in which specific actions should be deployed. They should also address the methods and resources available to protect employees, as well as the responsibilities of all employees, including champions or team leaders.

Emergency management focuses on four key areas: preparedness, response, recovery, and mitigation. Each of these four areas is vital to the overall success of handling an emergency.

Emergency Management

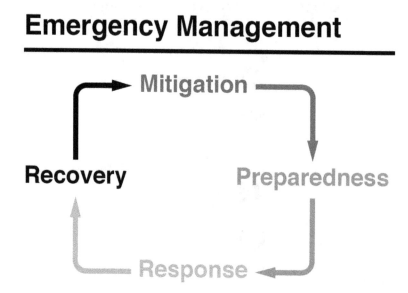

Preparedness focuses on any and all activities that an organization engages in prior to a disaster occurring. Drafting plans and action items, initiating evacuation drills, training employees, and providing opportunities to assess the effectiveness of the plan are all key initiatives to address when preparing for emergency and the responses necessary.

Response focuses on any and all activities that occur during a disaster. Issuing public warnings, engaging emergency operations and centers of operations, evacuating facilities, and communicating to employees are vital to managing a disaster effectively and efficiently. Additionally, working in real time and with live data and information can assist in redirecting resources to meet new and changing needs during the disaster.

Recovery focuses on any and all activities following a disaster. Establishing temporary workspaces, initiating and processing injury reports and claims, providing counseling services, and approving time off are essential to ensuring the work operations return to business as usual as quickly as possible. Many organizations have a special policy regarding additional paid time off to attend to personal business as a result of an emergency or disaster. Depending on the circumstances and requests, organizations may approve additional time from vacation or sick leave time for employees to attend to personal needs.

Mitigation focuses on any and all activities that reduce the effects of a disaster. At the conclusion of a disaster, reviewing the response and corresponding outcomes can provide additional insight as to what went right and what went wrong. This analysis allows an organization to effectively update and revise plans to address future occurrences. Actions such as updating zoning and building codes, providing additional training and education, or scheduling additional evacuation drills could be warranted based on the outcomes of the incident. The goal of any disaster management plan is to ensure that employees are prepared for various emergencies that could occur and have the knowledge and understanding to follow the appropriate procedures and protocols that provide for their safety and the safety of others.

When developing an emergency response plan, it is important to understand the three primary levels of responses: operational, communications, and management. Each is critical to ensuring a fully developed and effective response plan. **Operational responses** should focus on implementing the protocols and procedures when responding to an emergency with the ultimate goal to first protect all employees and second protect the business operations. Operational responses should assess the situation, determine the level of action appropriate and necessary, and brief leadership with the details. **Communications responses** should focus on ensuring that all employees, regardless of location or level, receive the messages and information necessary to follow the appropriate emergency response protocol. Additionally, Human Resources should ensure that data are available to contact employees and their families in the case of an emergency. Other elements of the communication plan should include messaging and information to the public, news media, government officials, and other appropriate parties as identified in the emergency action plan. Finally, **management responses** should include mobilizing and initiating crisis teams to assess the situation and determine the safety of employees. Management is responsible for engaging and advising senior leadership regarding the situation, response, and outcomes. If necessary, management should also begin assessing the action plans for future events and prepare for any additional external communications. Employees will need to know how to receive information if not at work due to particular emergencies. Many organizations use a phone tree or a local AM radio station to communicate information on a wide scale.

Once the disaster has concluded, it is necessary to assess the damage. First and foremost, all employees should be accounted for and an assessment of any injuries reviewed. Second, a review of the business operations should be conducted. Secondary operational locations may need to be set up and engaged to ensure that business operations and continuity of service can be continued. If a secondary location is not necessary, a full review of the facility should be conducted prior to returning employees to the facility. It is also important to understand that all individuals process emergencies differently. Having empathy and patience with employees as they process the disaster is important and a best practice that many organizations employ is the utilization of counselors through an **Employee Assistance Program (EAP).**

Internal Investigation, Monitoring, and Surveillance

Internal investigations are conducted when issues arise or complaints are submitted. Regardless of how an issue comes to the attention of Human Resources, an investigation should be conducted to ensure that any concerns or potential policy violations are corrected, and appropriate responses and actions are delivered. Employees should understand how to submit a complaint regardless of who it is against or what the subject matter. Internal investigations can be both informal and formal, but both should be conducted with good-faith efforts that result in a rational and supported conclusion. Informal investigations could result in a formal investigation to ensure the issues are fully reviewed and understood. Additionally, a formal investigation could result in an external third-party investigation to ensure impartiality and a full vetting of the issues from an outside perspective. While it is a best practice to attempt to resolve issues and concerns at the lowest level possible, there will always be a need to investigate claims and concerns. Human Resources professionals should be properly and formally trained to investigate complaints.

Internal investigations should always include interviews with the employee making the complaint, the employee who the complaint is against (if any), all witnesses to the incident, and any other party that may have firsthand information and knowledge of the incident. While it is a good practice to have prepared questions for all interviews, it is also appropriate to ask additional questions if new information is presented during the interview to ensure that a full understanding of the incident is gathered. It may be necessary to schedule follow-up interviews based on the information that is gathered or new evidence that is gained. At the conclusion of gathering all of the information, interviewing all of the appropriate parties, and assessing the credibility of the investigation, Human Resources professionals should prepare a conclusion and recommendation to resolve the initial complaint. Investigation conclusions should be rational, specific, and legally defensible based solely on the information gathered during the investigation. Resolution could be conflict resolution between two employees, changing policy or procedure to address a workplace issue, creating training programs for employees to work better together in a team dynamic, and/or discipline if appropriate. Multiple resolutions may be necessary to ensure that the issue is fully addressed and potential future occurrences are eliminated.

When conducting an internal investigation, there are various best practices to incorporate into the process to ensure a thorough and fair investigation. First, it is important to be proactive and not reactive. Investigators should take a proactive approach when gathering information from employees and researching data and details. Being proactive allows the organization to gather the most recent and current information available. Witnesses are more likely to remember details and specifics when the incident is fresh and recent, versus trying to recount information regarding something that happened a while ago. Being proactive also includes being broad and open to identifying new resources that would have information pertinent to the case versus only relying on one individual's account of an incident. A common quote used to describe this is to "follow the leads." If an investigator follows the leads and goes where the evidence leads, the investigation is more likely to yield an accurate assessment and conclusion of the incident.

Second, it is important to agree to the purpose and specific issue being investigated. When employees understand what the investigation is attempting to define or discover, they are more likely to be able to provide specifics to the incidents being claimed. While during the investigation, information may arise that is outside of the original scope; it is important to ensure that either the initial investigation is expanded, or a secondary investigation is conducted to review the new information.

Third, investigations should always be independent and impartial. Investigations should be conducted by individuals who can review the evidence and conduct interviews that are not biased or looking for only one perspective. Depending on the professional relationship between the employee complaining and the Human Resources professional conducting the investigation, it may be appropriate to bring in an external investigator who can maintain impartiality. Not only does this allow for a fair and accurate investigation, conclusion, and proposed recommendation, but also avoids allegations or the perception of conflicts of interest.

Fourth, completed investigations and recommendations should align with the organization's policies, procedures, and goals. If there is not alignment based on the behavior of employees, the investigation may prompt a review and evaluation of the policies, procedures, and goals of the organization. Regularly reviewing these items against the behaviors of employees allows the organization to implement programs that can affect cultural change and promote appropriate and respectful behavior.

Finally, investigations should always consider the consequences and repercussions of the issues being brought forward and the effects of not handling and resolving the issues quickly and completely. Many states have laws that hold supervisors responsible for their behavior, as well as the organization, if appropriate actions are not taken to correct behavior or hold employees responsible. Society today is holding individuals to a higher standard regarding sexual harassment and many federal statutes are being passed to ensure accountability, transparency, understanding, and consequences. In addition to this, many states are mandating frequent training and requirements regarding training for specific levels of employees. Supervisors may be required to frequently attend expanded training sessions to ensure a thorough knowledge and understanding of the responsibilities when supervising others. However, organizations, are responsible for ensuring training requirements are met and that actions are taken to address issues. By conducting fair, impartial, thorough, and proactive investigations, Human Resources professionals can protect employees and the organization.

Data Security and Privacy

Data security is defined as the security relating to the confidentiality, availability, and integrity of data. Data security focuses on the physical security of a premises as well as the logical security of data and digital information. Data security includes issues such as the confidentiality, integrity, and availability of data, network protection, and the physical security of facilities, equipment, transport, and employees. **Data privacy** is defined as the appropriate use and control of the data. Data privacy focuses on protocols that employees have over their personal and work-related data and how to protect it from unwanted or harmful uses. Data privacy includes issues such as how data are processed, where data are held, and how long data will be retained. Data security and privacy are vitally important and while separate concepts, both relate to the protection of data and ensuring that information is safe and secure.

Data security and privacy are critically important to protect through robust policies and procedures, knowledge and training, and continued vigilance on an everyday basis. New efforts are constantly being identified to undermine and hack organizational systems to gain access to personal information such as social security numbers, dates of birth, health information, and banking information. Additionally, organizational information such as account information and access, credit cards, and sensitive and proprietary information is also at risk with these security breaches. Security breaches can allow unauthorized individuals access to private information. Not only can this have an impact to the employees and the organization, but it can have a negative impact regarding publicity and social media, which can result in decreased customer loyalty and business. It is crucial for organizations to manage privacy and security issues effectively and as a core competency. Employees should have a feeling of security and not worry that their personal information could be stolen through a data breach.

Organizations can implement many best practices to ensure that data are safe and secure. First, organizations can fully evaluate, approve, and protect data. A great example is the compliance and procedures set in place for the **Health Insurance Portability and Accountability Act (HIPAA)** data, or medical information. A data breach of HIPAA data could be cause for serious concern as well as violate the legal statutes. This violation could include fees and fines for violating the law. Second, organizations can control and limit access to data and the networks, ensuring that only authorized individuals can gain access. Encryption is an excellent practice that many organizations utilize. **Encryption** for emails ensures that only the sender and authorized recipient can access the email and information included. If a recipient does not have the proper encryption software, the information cannot be accessed. Third, organizations can secure devices and install privacy and control mechanisms such as compliance proof and identification software to ensure that only the authorized employee can gain access. Many organizations require a double authentication, or two-factor verification, to ensure the identity of the individual accessing the information. Employees' access to information can be aligned with their position and role within the organization to ensure access is only granted to the information necessary for the work being conducted. Finally, organizations can ensure that all employees receive regular and frequent compliance training.

Training programs should be included for all employees to understand how to create and update an appropriate password to ensure that if their computers are stolen, information is protected. Additionally, employees should be trained in how to identify malware, suspicious emails and requests, and viruses sent through emails. Reports should not include social security numbers, dates of birth, or other confidential information. In the case that this information is required to report, the report should be monitored to ensure that the hard copies are controlled and maintained. While most data and security breaches are unintentional, there are very real consequences that can impact the employees and the organization. For example, consider that a full employee roster that includes social security numbers, home addresses, and dates of birth is printed and then disposed of in a regular trash receptacle. This report could easily be discovered in a garbage bin and identities stolen for illegal purposes. While this may have been a simple oversight, the consequences could be tremendous. Employees could now face having to monitor their credit and identity, and the organization could need to arrange to provide and fund credit monitoring for a period of time to ensure that the impact to employees is minimal. Procedures should be put in place to ensure that data are secure. Personnel files should be kept under lock and key, printed reports and documents should be disposed of in a confidential and private manner, and passwords should be strong.

If a data breach does occur, it is important to report the incident immediately so that appropriate responses and necessary actions can be deployed as soon as possible. Initiating immediate action can limit the exposure and liability of the organization. Executive leadership should be informed of the issue and corrective action taken. Additionally, a communication plan should be created and deployed to ensure that employees understand the breach and what it means on a professional, work-related basis and, if applicable, a personal basis. A best practice would be to incorporate an emergency management and action plan specific to a data breach that ensures appropriate actions are taken to address the issue.

Collective Bargaining Process, Terms, and Concepts

Collective bargaining refers to the process of negotiation between management and union representatives regarding issues such as compensation, benefits, working hours, disciplinary processes, layoffs and terminations, grievance and arbitration processes, union activities, and employee rights. Furthermore, collective bargaining is the continued relationship between management and union representatives that involves the exchange of commitments to resolve conflicts and issues. While collective bargaining is required by law for both parties to negotiate in good faith, success is only achieved when both parties are willing to listen, understand, and compromise. **Good faith bargaining** refers to the duty of both parties to demonstrate a sincere and honest intent to reach agreement, be reasonable, communicate honestly, and negotiate in the best interest of the employees. It is important to note that collective bargaining is a group action that many refer to as an art form. Collective bargaining should not be a competitive process, but rather a continuous and logical process that involves strategy and understanding.

Collective bargaining is the formal process to negotiate contracts and agreements between an employer and union representative. There are various objectives that collective bargaining seeks to achieve:

- Settle disputes or conflicts regarding wages, benefits, working conditions, or safety concerns

- Protect employees' interests

- Resolve differences over difficult and stressful issues

- Negotiate voluntarily and as needed, without the influence or interference of an outside third party who is not as familiar with the organization and employees

- Agree to amicable terms and conditions through a give-and-take strategy

- Co-exist and work together peacefully for the mutual benefit and morale of all employees

- Maintain employee and employer relationships

A best practice that many negotiators utilize at the bargaining table is to establish ground rules at the beginning of the process. **Ground rules** refers to a set of items agreed upon by both parties to assist the negotiations process. Ground rules establish respect for both parties, the time and efforts each puts forth, and other specific areas that may arise during negotiations. Ground rules should establish the following:

- Who speaks for the parties and the individuals representing each party

- When subject matter experts will be called in and the specific purpose

- Where, when, and how long the parties will meet

- A cut-off date for submitting new proposals

- How formal proposals and responses will be made

- Communications plans regarding media or external communications

- What form of agreement will be acceptable: full and complete document or an itemized list of changes agreed to

- Any other specific details pertinent to the negotiations

There are five basic steps to the collective bargaining process: prepare, discuss, propose, bargain, and settlement. While this process is shown below as a linear process, there can be multiple twists and turns when bargaining in real life. Negotiators should be prepared for surprises and unexpected events that could derail negotiations.

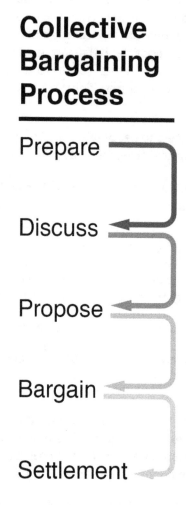

Collective Bargaining Process

Prepare

Discuss

Propose

Bargain

Settlement

Prior to beginning the negotiation process, it is vital for both sides to begin preparation and determining what needs to be changed, added, updated, deleted, or remain status quo. Each side should come to the negotiation table well prepared and ready to begin discussions. During discussions, new ideas may be presented from the opposing side that require additional preparation before they can be conducted. This should be discussed, and a plan agreed on to engage in further discussions. Proposals should be given that are thoughtful and based on the needs of the party. They should be clear, concise, and fully communicate the intent of the suggestion as well as provide an understanding of the effects of the change. The employer usually bears the responsibility of costing out a contract and determining the expenses related to new proposals. As each new proposal is discussed, the open dialogue should include transparency regarding the costs associated with each. If an organization only has authorization to spend a certain amount of money to settle a contract, there will need to be negotiations conducted in how to spend that money. If every proposal has a cost attached, the sides may have to agree to the proposals that will be agreed upon that will meet the cost allocation provided and have the most positive impact to the organization and employees.

An example of this is proposing a five percent increase in wages and additional time off that would equate to an additional two percent increase in cost. If the organization is only approved to negotiate an increase of four percent, the parties may want to negotiate a smaller increase to both wages and time so that both areas are receiving an increase, but the overall cost is within the approved cost threshold. When situations like this arise, a vital piece of information is understanding the needs and wants of the employees so that the best decision can be made. When all of the proposals have been discussed and bargaining has occurred for each, the parties can agree to the terms and conditions through a formal settlement. Each side should have the opportunity to review the final documents before signing. Once the official settlement has occurred, the union representatives must then begin the education and communication process with the membership for ratification of the proposal. **Ratification** is the process in which represented employees vote to approve or deny the proposed settlement. If the settlement is ratified, then the organization will move forward to receiving final approval through a board or executive authority and then finally implementing the terms of the settlement.

Once a final settlement is achieved and ready for implementation, it is important to roll out a communication plan so that employees will understand what will happen and when. Employees should clearly understand what changed, what stayed the same, and, if appropriate, why.

Performance Management Process, Procedures, and Analysis

Performance management is the strategic process that creates a work environment where employees are enabled and engaged to perform to the best of their abilities and achieve their goals. The performance management process includes setting goals, gathering information on performance, reviewing and evaluating performance against the goals, providing feedback to employees, and offering learning opportunities. This process allows employees to have clarity regarding roles, responsibilities, and expectations, while offering opportunities to discuss achievements and accomplishments. There are two primary purposes of performance management: strategic and administrative. The strategic purpose of a performance management process is to align employee performance and actions with the overarching organizational goals. Employees should understand how these achievements and accomplishments tie into the broader organizational strategy and objectives, and the discussions within the performance management process provide these opportunities. The administrative purpose of a performance management process is to identify strong-performing and high-producing employees. Identifying the strong performers within an organization allows for better decision making regarding administrative decisions such position changes, salary increases, and future special assignments and opportunities.

There are four phases known as the "four Ds" of performance management: define, document, discuss, and develop. The **define phase** refers to the step in which managers define what should be achieved and accomplished through the performance review. Defining these goals allows for specific metrics to be developed that can measure performance. The **document phase** refers to the step in which managers evaluate individual performance and maintain a record to provide specific feedback to employees during the performance review. By keeping an ongoing record of performance, information will be readily available when preparing formal review documents. Performance can then be more accurately measured and assessed. The **discuss phase** refers to the step in which managers have a regularly scheduled conversation with employees to openly discuss performance over a specific period of time. Many organizations require annual performance reviews, with additional reviews added based on probation periods, poor performance, or other factors. It is a best practice for managers to meet more frequently than once a year to discuss performance. This allows employees to quickly identify when performance is not meeting expectations and take corrective actions instead of waiting for an annual review. The **develop phase** refers to the step in which managers take the information available through the performance review process and provide learning opportunities to employees. Employees who are not meeting expectations or are struggling in their position should be offered learning opportunities to improve their performance. Likewise, employees who are meeting and exceeding expectations should be offered learning opportunities to expand their knowledge base and further professional growth.

Human Resources professionals are responsible for ensuring that the performance management system, process, methods, tools, and forms are designed to accurately reflect an employee's performance in a fair and objective manner. Managers should be trained in how to use the tools and forms as well as how to deliver the review. Human Resources professionals are also responsible for tracking the performance reviews that are completed and providing managers with updates and reminders when reviews are due. Additionally, the performance reviews should be maintained in the employee's individual personnel file. If a negative review is warranted, managers should work with Human Resources to ensure that training opportunities or corrective actions are identified and deployed. If more frequent reviews are necessary, a schedule should be developed to ensure that the employee is given all of the necessary information and tools.

Managers are responsible for evaluating the performance of the employees who directly report to them. Managers should complete the forms as accurately as possible and provide as much details as possible to ensure that employees have a full understanding of the performance and achievements accomplished. Likewise, if an employee is not performing to the standards required, details should be provided to ensure a full understanding of the concerns and issues as well as the plan moving forward to address these concerns. Managers should deliver performance reviews face-to-face and provide employees with the opportunity to read and comment on the review. Employees should also be provided the opportunity to comment on, and provide responses to, the information within the performance review.

It is important to understand that the performance management process is only as good as the information provided by managers and supervisors within the process. If an organization has a "check the box" culture regarding performance reviews, then employees most likely are not getting good information regarding their performance. Organizations should institute a culture of learning, achievement, recognition, and promotion. Managers and employees should feel valued and integral to the success of the organization. When performance management is done well, this process can lend to a strong culture that supports employees and ultimately succeeds in meeting the organizational achievements. Tools should be created to support these efforts and allow for a robust dialogue with employees regarding performance; however, even the best tools will not change a culture that does not value recognizing employee performance and achievements.

Termination Approaches, Concepts, and Terms

Employees can be terminated from an organization for many reasons. **Involuntary terminations** are the separation of an employee that are warranted due to poor performance, failure of probation, disciplinary actions due to inappropriate conduct or policy violations, or layoffs. **Voluntary terminations** are the separations of an employee due a decision made solely by the employee. Generally, voluntary terminations are resignations due to taking a position with another organization, retirement, or leaving the workforce due to personal reasons such as relocation, choosing to have a family and stay home with the children, or health concerns.

Employees who are involuntarily terminated should be provided with due process based on the reasoning for the separation. If an employee is being terminated for poor performance or failure of probation, the manager should work with Human Resources prior to the termination to ensure that the employee is aware of this issue and allowed to have an appropriate amount of time to correct the issues. If sufficient progress is not made within a specified period of time, Human Resources should then work through the appropriate process to terminate employment. In the case of terminating an employee due to inappropriate conduct or policy violations, again, due process should be afforded. Conducting a proper investigation and determining the appropriate level of discipline should be standard procedure. Depending on the violation, immediate termination may be appropriate; however, if progressive discipline is appropriate, the employee will need to progress through the levels of disciplinary action prior to being terminated. When an employee is terminated in these circumstances, Human Resources should ensure that a safe and secure environment is provided to deliver the message. A common practice is to terminate an employee at the end of their scheduled shift and/or at the end of the workweek. Efforts should be taken to ensure the safety of all employees and may include having a security guard or a police officer on-site and available in the case of emergencies. Employees being terminated should be afforded the opportunity to collect their belongings; however, in some circumstances, it may be more appropriate to mail personal belongings to the individual to expedite leaving the premises. The information technology department should be notified to immediately disable all access to systems, change passwords, and set up out-of-office messages and auto-forwarding of emails.

In the event that an employee is being laid off, Human Resources should ensure that the employee is provided with as much notice as possible and any resources are made available to the employee. On-site counselors may be appropriate to ensure employees receive the message in a safe environment with readily available resources. When an employee is laid off, it is important to remember that each individual will handle this news differently. Reactions from crying or yelling to no reaction at all are normal. Human Resources professional should be trained and prepared to handle any situation.

When an employee voluntarily resigns, a common practice is to provide a two-week notice to the employer to make arrangements and transition the employee out of the organization. An exit interview is a best practice that many organizations utilize to provide the employee an opportunity to communicate what the organization does well and what the organization could do better. Additionally, questions regarding compensation, benefits, programs, training, opportunities, supervision, and other topics are appropriate to learn more about the impact these items may have had in the decision to leave. Some organizations use this opportunity to ask questions about policy violations, harassment, discrimination, or other inappropriate behaviors that the employee may have witnessed or been subjected to during their employment. This information allows the organization to respond accordingly and take corrective action if necessary. Understanding the reasons why employees voluntarily exit an organization can help determine ways to retain current and future employees and address the gaps and needs to increase retention.

Regardless of the type of termination, all employees should receive exit paperwork that documents information such as the following:

- Final paycheck details, including if a special check will be issued and when
- Leave balance payouts
- Insurance information including when coverage will end
- COBRA and insurance extension information
- Contact information for Human Resources
- Unemployment information

Human Resources professionals should be familiar with state requirements regarding when final paychecks are to be processed. For instance, in the state of California, all private organizations must issue the final paycheck, including all leave balance payouts and any compensation owed, within specific timeframes. If the employer has terminated the employee involuntarily, the final paycheck must be processed and provided to the employee at the time of termination. If an employee resigns and provides no notice, the employer must process the paycheck and provide it to the former employee within three working days. And if an employee resigns with a period of notice, the final paycheck must be processed and provided to the employee on their last working day. It is vital to understand these legal requirements as the organization can face penalties and fines if they are not followed accurately.

Practice Questions

1. Which of the following statements is/are TRUE regarding the employee lifecycle? (Select all that apply.)
    a. The employee lifecycle encourages a strong employee experience.
    b. The employee lifecycle refers to the recruitment and selection of employees.
    c. The employee lifecycle is the roadmap used to create an engaged workforce.
    d. The employee lifecycle should be revitalized and updated as necessary.

2. Which stage(s) of the employee lifecycle is/are the most important to the process and overall employee experience? (Select all that apply.)
    a. Attracting qualified applicants
    b. Recruiting the best and brightest candidates
    c. Onboarding new employees
    d. Developing and managing employees
    e. Retaining employees
    f. Transitioning employees out of the organization

3. The survey measurement calculating the _____ shows how effective a survey was in receiving feedback from employees.
    a. Satisfaction rate
    b. Response rate
    c. Communication plan
    d. Action items

4. Which of the following statements is FALSE regarding employee engagement surveys?
    a. Surveys that focus on employee engagement are a best practice to implement.
    b. Conducting surveys often allows an organization to determine if employees are responding to new programs.
    c. Surveys that focus solely on gathering information are just as effective and productive as surveys that focus on actions and making changes.
    d. Survey messages should be clear, concise, and specific.

5. Match the culture type with the primary focus and foundation of each.
    a. Clan   1. Competition, built on a foundation of competitiveness and customer focus
    b. Adhocracy   2. Collaboration, built on a foundation of participation at all levels
    c. Hierarchy   3. Control and process, built on a foundation of control and efficiency
    d. Market   4. Creativity, built on a foundation of innovation, vision, and resources

6. _____ is key to any initiative and can determine the ultimate success or failure of a program.
    a. Transformational leadership
    b. Organizational culture
    c. Cultural fit
    d. Communication

7. Match the key term with the proper definition.
   a. Diversity and Inclusion
   b. Equal Employment Opportunity
   c. Affirmative Action

   1. Enforce statutes and laws that prevent discrimination
   2. Leverage differences within the workforce for better results
   3. Efforts to achieve equity and equality in the workforce

8. Which of the following statements are TRUE regarding employee resource groups (ERGs)? (Select all that apply.)
   a. ERGs are excellent ways to engage the community.
   b. ERGs foster diversity and inclusiveness, providing opportunities to discuss valuable viewpoints.
   c. ERGs are groups of organizations who work together to better understand the market within a particular community.
   d. ERGs allow for a deeper understanding of the work being done by an organization and the employees.

9. Which of the following are objectives of a health and safety workplace program? (Select all that apply.)
   a. Reinforce a culture of health and wellness
   b. Promote a healthy home environment
   c. Promote a healthy workplace environment
   d. Prevent injuries and illnesses
   e. Engage leadership

10. Match the key term with the proper definition.
    a. Policies
    b. Procedures
    c. Employee handbook
    d. Standard operating procedures

    1. Structured manuals that communicate employee expectations
    2. Documents describing details to complete a task
    3. Standards or guides to the philosophy, mission, and values
    4. Targeted and specific action plans to meet established goals

11. Which of the following should an employee handbook strive to achieve? (Select all that apply.)
    a. Ensure compliance with laws
    b. Provide employees with their rights and responsibilities
    c. Provide forms and documents to complete for onboarding
    d. Introduce key senior leadership
    e. Define work schedules

12. _____ establish(es) the requirements and expectations of employees regarding reliability as well as stipulate the consequences for not adhering to these requirements.
    a. Family Medical Leave Act (FMLA)
    b. Time and Attendance Procedures
    c. Disciplinary actions
    d. Employee handbooks

13. What is the ultimate goal of handling any complaint?
    a. Following a structure process to resolve the issues
    b. Informing leadership immediately of the issues
    c. Resolving the issue at the lowest level possible
    d. Being respectful and responsive

14. Conflict resolution identifies which of the following? (Select all that apply.)
    a. Feelings, perceptions, and opinions regarding an issue
    b. Recommendations and actions to resolve the issue
    c. Communication techniques to deliver the plan
    d. Problems that are causing an issue
    e. Potential impacts of the issue

15. _____ encourage and nurture open communication between employees and managers.
    a. Strong and effective partnerships
    b. Multiple ways of communications
    c. Best practices
    d. Open door policies

16. Which of the following statements is TRUE regarding employee and labor relations?
    a. Employee and labor relations is the sole responsibility of Human Resources.
    b. Employee and labor relations is the maintenance of effective working relationships with employees and the labor unions that represent them.
    c. Employee and labor relations manage themselves and require attention only as needed.
    d. The cornerstone of positive employee and labor relations is joint committees.

17. The performance management process begins with _____ and concludes with employee _____.
    a. planning, recognition.
    b. coaching, evaluation.
    c. planning, evaluation.
    d. recognition, coaching.

18. Why is communication in both an upward and downward direction important? (Select all that apply.)
    a. Increases success of a process
    b. Ensures achievements are met
    c. Places the responsibility on employees
    d. Allows for maximum engagement

19. Which of the following should be the core basis in selecting a position for job elimination?
    a. Employee information such as age, years of service, and retirement eligibility
    b. Employee performance
    c. Employee disciplinary history
    d. Job duties and organizational need

20. _____ can assist employees with their transition out of an organization and can include compensation, extension of benefits, transition services, and other services.
    a. Employee Assistance Programs
    b. Severance packages
    c. Reductions in force
    d. Performance management

21. Match the key term with the appropriate description.
    a. Employee relations
    b. Employee involvement
    c. Employee communication
    d. Employee counseling
    e. Employee discipline
    f. Employee rights

    1. Process used to address a performance problem when training or coaching methods do not resolve the issue
    2. Study of the rules, policies, procedures, and agreements that employees are held accountable to
    3. Vertical and horizontal lines of messages
    4. Tools used by management to improve poor performance and enforce appropriate behavior
    5. Environment that values employees and seeks out input
    6. Privileges that all employees are afforded, including fair and equitable treatment

22. Drop and drag the types of message that align with each style of communication:
    a. Suggestion boxes
    b. Formal   Vertical
    c. Coordination
    d. Face-to-face
    e. Problem solving   Horizontal
    f. Informal
    g. Learning
    h. Department meetings
    i. Peer-to-peer

23. Which of the following benefits are realized when an organization practices and maintains strong employee relations? (Select all that apply.)
    a. Engaged employees
    b. Increased budgets
    c. Enhanced employee rights
    d. Increased productivity

24. _____ refers to the honest attempt made by both an employer and union to reach an agreement.
    a. Mandatory subjects of bargaining
    b. Good faith bargaining
    c. Collective bargaining
    d. Labor relations

25. Match the Act to the proper regulation that was enacted with its passing.
    a. Norris-LaGuardia Act
    b. National Labor Relations Act
    c. Taft-Hartley Act
    d. Landrum-Griffin Act

    1. Increased reporting requirements, regulated union affairs, and protected union members from
       inappropriate practices
    2. Governs relations between unions and employees, allowing the right to organize and bargain
    3. Endorses collective bargaining as public policy
    4. Provides employers with the additional rights and protections

26. Which of the following statements are TRUE regarding human relations? (Select all that apply.)
    a. Human relations focuses on how individuals interact and cooperate with each other.
    b. Human relations is the process by which an organization understands the needs of the customer.
    c. Human relations recognizes and respects each individual.
    d. Human relations focuses on the hierarchy of needs.

27. Place the needs identified within Maslow's hierarchy of needs in the proper order.
    a. Social
    b. Esteem
    c. Safety
    d. Self-Actualization
    e. Physiological

28. When conducting a survey to assess employee satisfaction, it is important to communicate
    _____ with employees. (Select all that apply.)
    a. Before
    b. During
    c. After
    d. Action plans

29. Which of the following is a best practice regarding employee surveys?
    a. Committed leadership is not necessary for an effective survey.
    b. Surveys should require employees to identify themselves to ensure appropriate actions are taken.
    c. Commit to surveying employees every six to twelve months.
    d. Share data consistently at all levels of the organization.

30. Which statements below are TRUE regarding diversity and inclusion? (Select all that apply.)
    a. Diversity and inclusion foster an inclusive environment in which differences are valued and
    respected.
    b. Diversity and inclusion strategies have an impact solely in the workplace.
    c. Diversity is the mixture and inclusion is making the mixture work.
    d. The impacts of a strong diversity and inclusion strategy are seen within the organization but do not
    have an external impact.

31. Match the inclusive workplace pillar with its description.
    a. Awareness   1. Set up the policies and procedures that allow for accountability
    b. Mobilization   2. Analyze, review, and revise policies and procedures
    c. Action   3. Implement strategies through specific actions and plans
    d. Alignment   4. Raise the understanding of employees toward diversity initiatives

32. Which of the following are benefits resulting from establishing a commitment to diversity and inclusion? (Select all that apply.)
    a. Increased innovation
    b. Stronger performance
    c. Expansion in market share
    d. Enhanced engagement
    e. Greater motivation

33. _____ are one of the most important and fundamental recordkeeping functions within Human Resources.
    a. New hire documents
    b. Offer letters
    c. Personnel files
    d. Timecards

34. Which of the following statements regarding recordkeeping requirements are TRUE? (Select all that apply.)
    a. It is not necessary for recordkeeping to meet the needs of the business.
    b. Records should be kept in a manner that ensures privacy and confidentiality.
    c. Each type of record should have a policy and retention schedule.
    d. Training documents are not necessary to retain.

35. Which of the following liabilities could occur if an organization does NOT maintain compliance regarding recordkeeping?
    a. Expensive fines
    b. Unorganized information
    c. Losing data
    d. There are no liabilities

36. _____ is the required gear provided to employees to perform their job safely and effectively.
    a. Work boots
    b. A uniform
    c. A tool belt
    d. Personal protective equipment

37. Which of the following statements regarding safety and safety programs is FALSE?
    a. The 5 W method is a technique that can be used to understand why injuries and illness are occurring.
    b. Safety is the responsibility of leadership and management.
    c. Safety programs require the organization to implement frequent training.
    d. Safety programs analyze the workplace, employees, and operations.

38. Which of the following is the accurate step sequence for the STAR technique?
    a. Stop, Think, Act, Review
    b. Safety, Think, Act, Review
    c. Safety, Think, Avoid, Risk
    d. Stop, Train, Assess, Review

39. Which of the following responsibilities are required by employers regarding workplace security? (Select all that apply.)
    a. Identify hazards and recommend alternate work processes as "workarounds"
    b. Evaluate, reduce, and control risks
    c. Work together with employees
    d. Inform supervisors about potential safety matters
    e. Handle issues informally and without creating a record

40. _____ is defined as fitting an employee's workplace conditions to the job demands and specific individual needs.
    a. Workplace security
    b. STAR technique
    c. Safety
    d. Ergonomics

41. Match the key emergency management area to the specific activities within each.
    a. Preparedness   1. Establishing temporary workplaces, initiating claims, and providing counseling
    b. Response   2. Issuing public warnings, engaging emergency operations, and evacuations
    c. Recovery   3. Drafting plans, initiating evacuation drills, and training employees
    d. Mitigation   4. Reviewing the response, analyzing actions, and updating plans

42. Which of the following statements is TRUE regarding the goal of any disaster management plan?
    a. To ensure that employees are prepared for emergencies and have the knowledge to follow appropriate protocols that provide safety to all
    b. To review the responses and outcomes to provide insight in effective practices
    c. To ensure that work operations return to business as usual as quickly as possible
    d. To focus on any and all activities that occur during a disaster

43. Match the emergency response plan responses to their key focus.
    a. Operational   1. Ensuring employees receive the information necessary
    b. Communications   2. Implementing protocols to first protect employees and then operations
    c. Management   3. Engaging and advising senior leadership regarding the emergency

44. Which of the following statements regarding internal investigations are TRUE? (Select all that apply.)
    a. It is a best practice to always escalate issues and complaints to a third-party investigation.
    b. Investigations should be conducted with good-faith efforts.
    c. Investigations should be conducted by professionals who have been properly and formally trained.
    d. It is best practice to interview only the individual making the complaint and the individual the complaint is against.

45. Which of the following resolutions could be initiated to resolve a complaint? (Select all that apply.)
    a. Changing policy
    b. Creating a training program
    c. Conflict resolution between employees
    d. Discipline

46. Why is it important for internal investigations to be independent and impartial?
    a. Allows for a fair and accurate investigation, conclusion, and recommendation
    b. Allows for a broad investigation, identifying new resources with information
    c. Avoids allegations or the perception of conflicts of interest
    d. Affects cultural change and promotes appropriate and respectful behavior

47. Match the term to its definition.
    a. Data security   1. Allowing unauthorized individuals access to private information
    b. Data privacy   2. Ensures only the sender and recipient of an email have access to information
    c. Encryption   3. Controlling the confidentiality, availability, and integrity of data
    d. Security breach   4. Appropriate use and control of data

48. Which of the following statements are TRUE regarding security breaches? (Select all that apply.)
    a. Security breaches can have a negative impact regarding publicity.
    b. Security breaches do not have an impact to customer loyalty and business, as they affect employees only.
    c. It is not necessary for employees to have a feeling of security regarding their personal information.
    d. It is crucial for organizations to manage privacy and security as a core competency of the business.

49. What actions should occur when a security breach happens? (Select all that apply.)
    a. Implement the emergency management action plan
    b. Report the incident immediately
    c. Inform leadership only when the issue has been resolved
    d. Communicate to employees the breach and any ramifications

50. Match the term to its definition.
    a. Collective bargaining   1. The duty of both parties to demonstrate sincere and honest intent
    b. Good faith bargaining   2. The process of voting to approve or deny proposed settlements
    c. Ground rules   3. The process of negation between management and unions
    d. Ratification   4. Items agreed upon by both parties to assist the process

51. Which of the following are objectives that collective bargaining seeks to achieve? (Select all that apply.)
    a. Resolve differences
    b. Agree to amicable terms
    c. Protect the organization's interests
    d. Maintain union and employee relationships
    e. Settle disputes or conflicts regarding wages, benefits, and other concerns

52. What are the five basic steps to the collective bargaining process?
    a. Stop, Think, Act, Review, Settlement (STARS Method)
    b. Prepare, Discuss, Propose, Bargain, Settlement
    c. Who, What, Where, When, Why (5 W's Method)
    d. Why, Why, Why, Why, Why (5 Why Method)

53. Which of the following are items that ground rules should address? (Select all that apply.)
    a. Where, when, and how long the parties will meet
    b. Ratification process
    c. Communications plan regarding media
    d. Cut-off date for new proposals
    e. Employee interests

54. Drop and drag the appropriate items to the correct performance management purpose.
    a. Align performance and actions with organizational goals   Strategic
    b. Identify strong performing and high producing employees
    c. Allow for better decision making regarding position changes and salary increases
    d. Tie individual actions into broader organizational strategy   Administrative

55. _____ is the strategic process that creates a work environment where employees are enabled
and engaged to perform to the best of their abilities and achieve their goals.
    a. Performance reviews
    b. Performance management
    c. Performance goals
    d. Performance evaluations

56. Match the performance management phase with the appropriate description.
    a. Define   1. Evaluate performance and maintain a feedback record
    b. Document   2. State what should be achieved and accomplished
    c. Discuss   3. Provide learning opportunities
    d. Develop   4. Schedule regular conversations

57. Drop and drag the separation reason with the termination type.
    a. Poor performance
    b. Failure of probation   Voluntary Termination
    c. Retirement
    d. Resignation to accept another job Involuntary Termination
    e. Discipline
    f. Resignation to relocate with spouse

58. Which of the following types of information should be provided to employees during their separation,
regardless of the type of termination? (Select all that apply.)
    a. Contact information
    b. Final paycheck details
    c. Employee handbook
    d. Leave balance payouts
    e. Unemployment insurance
    f. Job flyers for other open positions in the area

Answer Explanations

1. A, C, & D: The employee lifecycle encourages a strong employee experience throughout an entire career, is the roadmap used to create a collaborative and engaged workforce, and should be revitalized and updated as necessary when feedback is provided. While the lifecycle includes the recruitment and selection of employees, it also includes the attraction of candidates, onboarding, developing and managing employees, retaining employees, and transitioning employees out of the organization.

2. A, B, C, D, E, F: All stages of the employee lifecycle are vital to the overall employee experience. While some stages will last longer periods of time, each stage is necessary and dependent on the others.

3. B: The response rate shows how effective a survey was in receiving feedback from employees. Satisfaction rates calculate a specific metric for a specific question in the survey. Communication plans and action items are specific actions and proposed recommendations that occur before and after the survey has been established and completed.

4. C: Surveys are most effective and productive when the information gathered is used to affect change. Surveys that are initiated to gather information solely will not have the same level of support and participation. Surveys are a best practice that can be used to assess specific needs and concerns as well as overall satisfaction. Surveys also allow an organization to assess the effectiveness and utilization of new programs. Additionally, all communications regarding surveys should be clear, concise, and specific, with employees fully understanding how the survey results will be used.

5. A – 2, B – 4, C – 3, & D – 1: The clan culture focuses on collaboration with leaders and is built on a foundation of employee development and participation at all levels of the organization. The adhocracy culture focuses on creativity with leaders and is built on a foundation of innovation, vision, and new resources. The hierarchy culture focuses on control and process with leaders and is built on a foundation of control and efficiency through the use of stable and consistent processes. The market culture focuses on competition with leaders and is built on a foundation of aggressive competitiveness and customer focus.

6. D: Communication is key to any initiative and can determine the ultimate success or failure of a program. Transformational leadership can reshape and change a culture as a response to an initiative or program. Organizational culture refers to the shared beliefs, values, philosophies, and assumptions within an organization. Culture fit ensures that an individual's beliefs and work ethic align with the organizational culture.

7. A – 2, B – 1, & C – 3: Diversity and inclusion refers to leveraging differences within the workforce to achieve better results and higher levels of productivity and efficiency. Equal employment opportunity refers to the enforcement of statutes, laws, and regulations to prevent employment discrimination. Affirmative action refers to the effort to achieve equity and equality in the workforce through outreach to eliminate barriers in the recruitment process.

8. A, B, & D: Employee resource groups, or ERGs, are excellent ways to engage the community. ERGs foster diversity and inclusiveness, providing opportunities to discuss valuable viewpoints. ERGs also allow for a deeper understanding of the work being done by an organization and the employees. ERGs are groups of individuals, though—not organizations—who participate in programs and activities with individuals from similar backgrounds or interests. While organizations may participate in an ERG, the focus is on the individual level.

9. A, C, & D: The main objectives of a health and safety workplace program are to reinforce a culture of health and wellness, promote a healthy workplace environment, and prevent injuries and illnesses. While many actions could be implemented by employees within their own homes to create a healthy and safe environment, it is not an objective of a workplace program. Additionally, engaging leadership is not an objective of a health and safety workplace program; however, it is necessary for these programs to be effective.

10. A – 3, B – 4, C – 1, & D – 2: Policies are the standards or guides to the philosophy, mission, and values of an organization. Procedures are specific action plans to achieve goals. Employee handbooks are the manuals that communication employer expectations of employees. Standard operating procedures are documents that describe specific actions and instructions to accomplish a task.

11. A, B, & E: Employee handbooks are structured manuals that should ensure compliance with laws, provide employees with their rights and responsibilities, and define work schedules. Additionally, handbooks should strive to communicate expectations; introduce the culture, mission, values, and goals of the organization; and showcase the offered benefits. Forms and documents should be provided as separate paperwork during the onboarding process; introducing new employees to key senior leadership should be a part of the onboarding process as well, but not a component of the employee handbook.

12. B: Time and attendance procedures establish the requirements and expectations of employees regarding reliability as well as stipulate the consequences for not adhering to these requirements. FMLA is a type of medical leave that should be described and discussed within time and attendance procedures. Disciplinary actions may be warranted to address violations to time and attendance procedures and should be described and discussed within these procedures. Additionally, time and attendance procedures should be included in the employee handbook provided to new employees.

13. C: The ultimate goal of handling any complaint is to resolve the issue at the lowest level possible. While it is important to follow a structured process to resolve issues and inform leadership of the issues, effective resolution of the issue with the lowest amount of intervention is the goal. Resolving complaints does require being respectful and responsive, as do all other issues and concerns brought forward and in day-to-day interactions with others, not just in handling a complaint. Please note that some complaints must proceed directly to a formal and escalated response due to the complaint.

14. A, B, D, & E: Conflict resolution identifies feelings, perceptions, and opinions regarding an issue, recommendations and actions to resolve the issue, problems that are causing thee issue, and potential impacts of the issue. While it is important to communicate the resolution with all parties as appropriate, communication techniques are not identified during a conflict resolution.

15. D: Open door policies encourage and nurture open communication between employees and managers, which can result in a healthier workplace. Open door policies are a best practice that can ensure strong and effective partnerships. Best practices also include incorporating multiple ways of communication, in addition to open door policies.

16. B: Employee and labor relations is the maintenance of effective working relationships with employees and the labor unions that represent them. Employee and labor relations is the responsibility of management, leadership, and Human Resources and requires frequent communication and attention for maximum success. Additionally, multiple best practices such as open door policies, joint committees, frequent meetings, and accurate information exchanges are all cornerstones of positive employee and labor relations.

17. A: The performance management process begins with planning and concludes with employee recognition. The standard performance management process includes the following steps: planning, coaching, evaluating, and rewarding.

18. A, B, & D: Communication in both an upward and downward direction is important because this can increase the success of a process, help to ensure achievements are met, and allow for maximum engagement. It is the responsibility of all employees, managers, supervisors, and leadership to engage in open communication.

19. D: Job duties and organizational need should be the core basis in selecting a position for job elimination. Under no circumstances should employee information, performance, or disciplinary history be considered when making decisions regarding which positions to eliminate.

20. B: Severance packages can assist employees with their transition out of an organization and can include compensation, extension of benefits, transition services, and other services. Employee assistance programs can be—and usually are—included in a severance package. Reductions in force are actions that occur when downsizing is necessary and severance packages are a response to these actions. Performance management is the process by which an organization plans, coaches, evaluates, and rewards an employee.

21. A – 2, B – 5, C – 3, D – 1, E – 4, & F – 6: Employee relations is the study of the rules, policies, procedures, and agreements that employees are managed against. Employee Involvement is creating an environment that values employees and seeks out input directly from every individual. Employee communication refers to the messaging that occurs within an organization, both vertical and horizontal. Employee counseling is the process used to address a performance problem when training or coaching methods do not resolve the issue. Employee discipline refers to the tools used by management to improve poor performance and enforce appropriate behavior. Employee rights are the privileges that all employees are afforded, which include fair and equitable treatment.

22. Vertical – A, B, D, & H; Horizontal – C, E, F, G, & I: Vertical communications include suggestion boxes, face-to-face communications, department meetings, and are formal by nature. Horizontal communications include coordination, problem solving, learning, peer-to-peer, and are informal by nature.

23. A & D: Engaged employees and increased productivity are benefits that an organization will realize when practicing and maintaining strong employee relations. Indirect benefits may also include increased budgets and enhanced employee rights; however, there are many other factors in addition to employee relations that will affect the benefits being realized.

24. B: Good faith bargaining refers to the honest attempt made by both an employer and union to reach an agreement. Mandatory subjects of bargaining include the specific items that must be negotiated, such as benefits and wages. Collective bargaining is the entire process by which negotiations take place. Labor relations is the management of relationships between the organization, employees, and the union representatives.

25. A – 3, B – 2, C – 4, & D – 1: The Norris-LaGuardia Act endorses collective bargaining as public policy. The National Labor Relations Act governs relations between unions and employees, allowing the right to organize and bargain. The Taft-Hartley Act provides employers with the additional rights and protections. The Landrum-Griffin Act increased reporting requirements, regulated union affairs, and protected union members from inappropriate practices.

26. A, C, & D: Human relations focuses on how individuals interact and cooperate with each other. Human relations recognizes and respects each individual and also focuses on the hierarchy of needs. Human relations is the process by which an organization understands the needs of the individual employee, not the customer.

27. E, C, A, B, D: Maslow's hierarch of needs considers the levels needed for an individual to achieve maximum motivation and achievement. Physiological, Safety, Social, Esteem, and Self-actualization build upon each other and the first must be met before the second can be met, continuing on to the top of the pyramid.

28. A, B, C, & D: When conducting a survey to assess employee satisfaction, it is important to communicate before, during, and after with employees. Additionally, communicating the action plans and the specific things that will be done to address the survey and results is important.

29. D: Survey data should be shared consistently with all levels of the organization. Committed leadership is essential for an effective survey. Surveys should always ensure confidentiality and anonymity for employees. Organizations should not commit to surveying employee for a minimum of eighteen to twenty-four months.

30. A & C: Diversity and inclusion foster an inclusive environment in which differences are valued and respected. Diversity is the mixture and inclusion is making the mixture work. Diversity and inclusion strategies have an impact not only in the workplace, but also with the workforce, in the marketplace, and within the community. The effects of a strong diversity and inclusion strategy are seen within the organization and have a far reaching external impact, including social commitment and responsibility.

31. A – 4, B – 1, C – 3, & D – 2: Awareness is the pillar that raises the understanding of diversity initiatives. Mobilization is the pillar that sets up the policies and procedures that allow for accountability. Action is the pillar that implements strategies through specific actions and plans. Alignment is the pillar that analyzes, reviews, and revises policies and procedures.

32. A, B, C, D, & E: Increased innovation, stronger performance, expansion in market share, enhanced engagement, and greater motivation are all benefits that an organization may gain from establishing a commitment to diversity and inclusion.

33. C: Personnel files are one of the most important and fundamental recordkeeping functions within Human Resources. New hire documents and offer letters are components of the personnel file and timecards are generally retained within Payroll.

34. B & C: Records should be kept in a manner that ensures privacy and confidentiality, and each type of record should have a policy and retention schedule. It is important that recordkeeping meet the internal needs of the organization and applicable documents. Training records are absolutely necessary to maintain and retain for the required timeframe as applicable.

35. A & C: Expensive fines and loss of data are liabilities that could occur if an organization does not maintain compliance regarding recordkeeping. While records could be unorganized and information hard to find, this is more a nuisance and concern than a liability.

36. D: Personal protective equipment (PPE) is the required gear provided to employees to perform their jobs safely and effectively. Work boots, uniforms, and tool belts are all forms of PPE, and each job has its own required PPE that must be supplied by the organization.

37. B: Safety is the responsibility of everyone, not just leadership and management. The 5 W method is a technique that can be used to understand why injuries and illness occur. Safety programs require the organization to implement frequent training and analyze the workplace, employees, and operations.

38. A: The STAR technique refers to Stop, Think, Act, Review. The STAR technique can be implemented to address safety and security through action, avoidance, training, and assessing prevention.

39. B, C, & D: Evaluating, reducing, and controlling risks are required responsibilities by employers regarding workplace security. Additionally, employers need to work together with employees and inform supervisors about any potential safety matters. It is necessary for employers to identify hazards and remove these risks, not create workarounds; therefore, Choice *A* is incorrect. It is also necessary for employers to document and record any and all issues identified, along with the specific actions taken to address these issues; thus, Choice *E* is incorrect.

40. D: Ergonomics is defined as fitting an employee's workplace conditions to the job demands and specific individual needs. Workplace security is the management of all personnel, equipment, and facilities, including ergonomics. The STAR technique can be used to assess a situation, including one for which ergonomics could be applied and solutions discovered. Safety is the responsibility of all employees and is an overarching theory in which ergonomics falls under.

41. A – 3, B – 2, C – 1, D – 4: Preparedness activities include drafting plans and actions items, initiating evacuation drills, training employees, and providing opportunities to assess the plan effectiveness. Response activities include issuing public warnings, engaging emergency operations and centers of operations, evacuating facilities, and communication. Recovery activities include establishing temporary workspaces, initiating and processing injury reports and claims, providing counseling services, and approving time off. Mitigation activities include reviewing the response and corresponding outcomes, updating zoning and building codes, providing additional training and education, or scheduling additional evacuation drills.

42. A: The goal of any disaster management plan is to ensure that employees are prepared for emergencies and have the knowledge to follow appropriate protocols that provide safety to all. Reviewing the responses and outcomes to provide insight in effective practices is the focus of the mitigation step within an emergency management plan. Ensuring that work operations return to business as usual as quickly as possible is the focus of the recovery step within an emergency management plan. Focusing on any and all activities that occur during a disaster is the focus of the preparedness step within an emergency management plan.

43. A – 2, B – 1, C – 3: Operation responses focus on implementing protocols and procedures when responding to an emergency to protect employees first and the business second. Communications responses focus on ensuring that all employees, regardless of level or location, have all information necessary to react safely and quickly in the event of an emergency. Management responses focus on engaging and advising senior leadership regarding the emergency, actions taken, and any necessary action plans.

44. B & C: Investigations should be conducted with good-faith efforts and by professionals who have been properly and formally trained. While an investigation may need to be escalated to a third-party investigation, it is a best practice to attempt to resolve the issue at the lowest level possible. Additionally, as many witnesses as possible should be interviewed to fully gain understanding of the situation and provide support to any proposed recommendation.

45. A, B, C, & D: Potential resolutions that could be initiated to resolve a complaint include changing policy, creating a training program, conflict resolution between employees, discipline, and/or various combinations of these four resolutions. Each concern should have a resolution(s) that is appropriate and supported based on the evidence and conclusions from the investigation.

46. A & C: It is important for internal investigations to be independent and impartial because this allows for a fair and accurate investigation, conclusion, and recommendation, and avoids allegations or the perception of conflicts of interest. Being proactive allows for a broad investigation, identifying new resources with information. Aligning recommendations with policies and procedures as well as making updates to these items based on investigation results affects cultural change and promotes appropriate and respectful behavior.

47. A – 3, B – 4, C – 2, D – 1: Data security is defined as the security relating to controlling the confidentiality, availability, and integrity of data. Data privacy is defined as the appropriate use and control of data. Encryption is a best practice that ensures only the sender and recipients of an email have access to the information contained within the email. A security breach occurs when unauthorized individuals gain access to private and sensitive information.

48. A & D: Security breaches can have a negative impact regarding publicity, and it is crucial for organizations to manage privacy and security as a core competency of the business. Security breaches can absolutely have an impact to customer loyalty and business, as they affect both employees and customers. Additionally, it is absolutely necessary for employees to have a feeling of security regarding their personal information.

49. A, B, & D: When a security breach occurs, it is vital that organizations implement the emergency management action plan, report the incident immediately, and communicate to employees the breach and any ramifications. It is also important to inform leadership when the issue occurs and throughout the action plan, not only when the issue has been resolved.

50. A – 3, B – 1, C – 4, D – 2: Collective bargaining refers to the process of negotiation between management and union representatives. Good faith bargaining refers to the duty of both parties to demonstrate a sincere and honest intent to reach agreement. Ground rules refers to a set of items agreed upon by both parties to assist the negotiations process. Ratification refers to the process in which represented employees vote to approve or deny a proposed settlement.

51. A, B, E: Collective bargaining seeks to resolve differences, agree to amicable terms, and settle disputes or conflicts regarding wages, benefits, and other concerns. Collective bargaining seeks to protect the employees' interests while maintaining the employee and employer relationship.

52. B: The five basic steps to the collective bargaining process are: prepare, discuss, propose, bargain, and settlement. The STARS method is used to evaluate different situations and respond accordingly, such as in emergency situations. The 5 W's method is used to determine the full assessment of a situation before responding to address the concerns. The 5 Why method is used to determine the root cause of an issue before working to address the issue. The STARS, 5 W's, and 5 Why methods could be used to assess certain issues within the bargaining process during the preparation and discussion steps.

53. A, C, & D: Ground rules should address where, when, and how long the parties will meet, a communications plan regarding media, and cutoff date for new proposals. The ratification process and employee interests are components within the collective bargaining process, but not included in the ground rules.

54. Strategic – A & D; Administrative – B & C: The strategic purpose of performance management is to align employee performance and actions with overarching organizational goals. Additionally, it allows for employees to understand how their individual actions tie into the broader organizational strategy. The administrative purpose of performance management is to identify strong performing and high producing employees. Additionally, it allows for better decision making regarding administrative decisions such as position changes and salary increases.

55. B: Performance management is the strategic process that creates a work environment where employees are enabled and engaged to perform to the best of their abilities and achieve their goals. Performance reviews, performance goals, and performance evaluations all play an important role with the performance management process.

56. A – 2, B – 1, C – 4, D – 3: The define phase refers to the step in which managers define what should be achieved and accomplished throughout the review period. The document phase refers to the step in which managers evaluate performance and maintain a record of the feedback provided. The discuss phase refers to the step in which managers have a regularly scheduled conversation with employees to discuss performance. The develop phase refers to the step that provides learning opportunities to employees based on the specific performance.

57. Voluntary Termination – C, D, & F; Involuntary Termination – A, B, & E: Examples of a voluntary termination are retirement and resignation to accept another job or relocate to another location. Examples of an involuntary termination are poor performance, failure of probation, and disciplinary actions. Involuntary terminations are based on inappropriate actions by the employees or failure to perform at the appropriate standard, causing the employer to end the employment relationship.

58. A, B, D, & E: When an employee is separated from an organization, regardless of the reason, contact information, final paycheck details, leave balance payouts, and unemployment insurance information should be made available. An employee handbook is not necessary to be provided as this is usually provided when an employee begins employment, not ends employment. Additionally, providing job flyers for open positions within the area may be a nice gesture, but is not an accepted practice during the exiting process of an employee.

Greetings!

First, we would like to give a huge "thank you" for choosing us and this study guide for your PHR exam. We hope that it will lead you to success on this exam and for your years to come.

Our team has tried to make your preparations as thorough as possible by covering all of the topics you should be expected to know. In addition, our writers attempted to create practice questions identical to what you will see on the day of your actual test. We have also included many test-taking strategies to help you learn the material, maintain the knowledge, and take the test with confidence.

We strive for excellence in our products, and if you have any comments or concerns over the quality of something in this study guide, please send us an email so that we may improve.

As you continue forward in life, we would like to remain alongside you with other books and study guides in our library. We are continually producing and updating study guides in several different subjects. If you are looking for something in particular, all of our products are available on Amazon. You may also send us an email!

Sincerely,
APEX Test Prep
info@apexprep.com

FREE

Free Study Tips DVD

In addition to the tips and content in this guide, we have created a FREE DVD with helpful study tips to further assist your exam preparation. **This FREE Study Tips DVD provides you with top-notch tips to conquer your exam and reach your goals.**

Our simple request in exchange for the strategy-packed DVD is that you email us your feedback about our study guide. We would love to hear what you thought about the guide, and we welcome any and all feedback—positive, negative, or neutral. It is our #1 goal to provide you with top quality products and customer service.

To receive your **FREE Study Tips DVD**, email freedvd@apexprep.com. Please put "FREE DVD" in the subject line and put the following in the email:

a. The name of the study guide you purchased.

b. Your rating of the study guide on a scale of 1-5, with 5 being the highest score.

c. Any thoughts or feedback about your study guide.

d. Your first and last name and your mailing address, so we know where to send your free DVD!

Thank you!

DEC 2019

CPSIA information can be obtained
at www.ICGtesting.com
Printed in the USA
LVHW021605181219
640939LV00011B/488/P